Faulkner and Warren

Edited by
Christopher Rieger
&
Robert W. Hamblin

Faulkner and Warren

Edited by

Christopher Rieger
&
Robert W. Hamblin

Southeast
Missouri State University

Published for the Center for Faulkner Studies
by Southeast Missouri State University Press • 2015

Faulkner and Warren
Edited by Christopher Rieger and Robert W. Hamblin
Copyright: 2015 by Southeast Missouri State University Press

Published for the Center for Faulkner Studies by
Southeast Missouri State University Press
One University Plaza, MS 2650
Cape Girardeau, MO 63701
www6.semo.edu/universitypress

ISBN: 978-0-99035530-9-6

Cover design: Alex Hughes

Cover photograph of Warren is public domain, courtesy of the Warren
family

Library of Congress Cataloging-in-Publication Data

Faulkner and Warren / edited by Christopher Rieger & Robert W.
Hamblin.
      pages cm
  Includes bibliographical references.
  ISBN 978-0-9903530-9-6 (pbk.)
1. Faulkner, William, 1897-1962--Criticism and interpretation. 2. War-
ren, Robert Penn, 1905-1989--Criticism and interpretation. I. Rieger,
Christopher, editor. II. Hamblin, Robert W., editor.
  PS3511.A86Z783211168 2015
  813'.52--dc23
                        2015007940

Dedicated to the memory of Louis Daniel Brodsky (1941–2014)

Acknowledgments

The editors are extremely grateful to Southeast Missouri State University's Office of the Provost, College of Liberal Arts, Department of English, Kent Library, and University Center for their support of the Faulkner and Warren Conference that produced the essays printed in this volume.

We also extend our sincere thanks to David Becker, Mark Poor, Matthew Sissom, and Clare Paniccia, research assistants in the Center for Faulkner Studies, for their assistance in corresponding with contributors and editing essays, as well as helping plan and run the conference.

We thank Susan Swartwout, director of the Southeast Missouri State University Press, for her encouragement, guidance, and support, not only for this book but also for the series of which it is a part.

We owe a huge debt to L.D. Brodsky, without whom the Center for Faulkner Studies would not exist. L.D. passed away as we were working on this book, and we dedicate it to him as a token of appreciation for his amazing life's work as a collector, scholar, and artist.

Contents

Notes on the Conference

On October 25–27, 2012, Southeast Missouri State University's Center for Faulkner Studies hosted "Faulkner and Warren," a conference devoted to the writings of William Faulkner and Robert Penn Warren. The conference featured presentations by forty-one scholars representing sixteen different American states and five foreign countries (Australia, France, Nigeria, Japan, and Taiwan).

The conference featured an opening banquet and keynote address on Thursday evening, October 25. Dr. Ronald Rosati, the University Provost, welcomed the participants. Dr. Carol Scates, Chairperson of the English Department, introduced the keynote speaker, Patricia Bradley, Professor of English at Middle Tennessee State University and former president of the Robert Penn Warren Circle. Following the keynote address, Dr. Robert W. Hamblin, the Director of the Center for Faulkner Studies, and Mrs. Hamblin hosted a reception at their home in honor of Professor Bradley.

Panels and presentations were offered Thursday through Saturday, October 25–27. The papers examined Faulkner's and Warren's treatments of such topics as race, gender, class, slavery, religion, war, and nature.

On Friday evening, October 27, conference participants were treated to "William Faulkner and Robert Penn Warren: Storytellers," a readers' theater program based on the writings of the featured authors, scripted and directed by Dr. Roseanna Whitlow, a published playwright who is an instructor of Communication Studies at Southeast Missouri State University.

Throughout the conference, Faulkner and Warren books, manuscripts, and other memorabilia were exhibited in Kent Library. The exhibit, which included Warren materials from Joseph Millichap and Patricia Bradley and Faulkner materials from the Louis Daniel Brodsky Collection, was arranged by Dr. Lisa Speer, Southeast Missouri State University's Archivist and head of the University's Special Collections. Dr. Speer and Dr. Hamblin hosted a special showing of the exhibit on Friday, October 27.

Also on display throughout the conference was art created by students and professors from the Art Department at Southeast Missouri

State University. The Faulkner-themed art exhibit included work from students in the classes of Professor Louise Bodenheimer and Professor Chris Wubbena, as well as from the professors.

The conference concluded on Saturday afternoon, October 27, with a historical tour of downtown Cape Girardeau and the Mississippi River riverfront, guided by Dr. Hamblin.

Introduction

Like the other volumes in this series, this book brings together William Faulkner and another great writer—in this case, Robert Penn Warren, an outstanding poet, novelist, critic, and the only author to have been awarded a Pulitzer Prize in both fiction and poetry. The guiding principle of this series, as of the conferences that generate the books, is that examining the lives and works of authors "intertextually," that is, through comparison and contrast, creates fresh insights and a broader understanding of the achievements of each writer, as well as the contexts in which they lived and wrote.

Both Faulkner and Warren, of course, are important in their own right. Faulkner, one of the world's great novelists, was awarded the 1949 Nobel Prize for Literature, while Warren, one of the finest among modern poets, was named the first poet laureate of the United States. There have been many separate studies of these two authors, but viewing their lives and works intertextually has been only occasionally or marginally attempted. Joseph Millichap's informative essay, "Warren's Faulkner," in the Spring 2007 issue of the *Mississippi Quarterly* demonstrates the value of pairing the two authors, but few critics have followed his lead.

Roughly contemporaries, Faulkner and Warren are generally considered "Southern" writers, although Warren, as an academic professionally schooled in both modernist and traditional literature, is more firmly grounded than Faulkner in the larger literary history from which Southern literature developed and grew. Indeed, Warren rendered Faulkner a great service in arguing, in his influential review of Malcolm Cowley's *The Portable Faulkner*, that Faulkner's characters and themes should be viewed in relation to human, even universal, concerns rather than merely Southern ones. Faulkner often made the same point about his novels and stories, but Warren's academic background and credentials lent greater authority to the claim. In any event, considering to what degree, and in what manner, both Faulkner and Warren are "Southern" writers is one question that an intertextual approach addresses.

As the essays in this volume attest, Faulkner and Warren share many interests in common: for example, race, socio-economic class, gender issues, nature and the environment, politics, religion, history, and narrative technique. By comparing and contrasting the two authors' treatments of these and other topics, readers may arrive at a new understanding of one or both of the focal authors, as well as sharpen and clarify their own views on the subjects.

The opening essay in this volume, Patricia L. Bradley's "Angelic Acrobats and Fallen Southern Women: William Faulkner and Robert Penn Warren Go to the Circus," examines both actual and metaphorical circus elements in both authors' fiction. Expanding on her analysis in her book, *Robert Penn Warren's Circus Aesthetic and the Southern Renaissance*, Bradley analyzes Warren's use of the ringmaster, clown, and acrobat as character types who recur throughout Warren's oeuvre. In particular, Bradley argues that the "New Woman" figure who appears in both writers' works is indebted to and connected with female circus performers of the early twentieth century. Bradley specifically cites the celebrity circus marriage of Alfredo Codona and Lillian Leitzel as a source of inspiration for Warren in particular and argues that their famous "double passing trick" can be read as a metaphor for the interpersonal relationships in *All the King's Men*.

Noting Faulkner's admiration for the Cass Mastern subplot in *All the King's Men*, Robert W. Hamblin, in "'The world is like an enormous spider web': The Contrasting Legacies of Thomas Sutpen and Cass Mastern," suggests that Faulkner may have recognized in the Cass Mastern story parallels with the Thomas Sutpen story in *Absalom, Absalom!*. Both Mastern and Sutpen are white, Mississippi plantation owners whose lives are tragically affected by slavery and the Civil War. Moreover, their stories have a significant influence on the lives and attitudes of two young men in the next century: Sutpen's on Quentin Compson and Mastern's on Jack Burden. However, Hamblin argues, the Mastern/Burden story contains an element of hope missing in the Sutpen/Compson narrative. The former, like the epigraph for *All the King's Men* that Warren borrowed from Dante's *Divine Comedy*, reflects the theological concept of redemption, while Faulkner's story seems to offer no future hope. Hamblin concludes: "Unlike *All the King's Men*, *Absalom, Absalom!* contains no Purgatory, and certainly no thought of Paradise. The characters Faulkner gives us in *Absalom, Absalom!* all live in Hell."

Ted Atkinson's "Class Fantasies, Hollywood Liberalism, and the

Bush Doctrine in Film Adaptations of 'Two Soldiers' and *All the King's Men*" analyzes Aaron Schneider's 2003 short film *Two Soldiers* and Steve Zaillian's 2006 version of *All the King's Men* in light of the Iraq War and subsequent terrorism policies. Atkinson argues that *Two Soldiers* is far more effective at raising issues of class division, political power, and nationalism than the heavy-handed and disappointing big-budget version of Warren's novel.

In "Civil War Evasions: Race in Faulkner's 'Mountain Victory' and Warren's *Wilderness*," Andrew Leiter argues that Faulkner's short story "Mountain Victory" (1932) and Warren's novel *Wilderness* (1961) complicate simplistic assumptions about racism in America through their unconventional protagonists. However, Leiter contends that both works are problematic in their depictions of race, particularly in the ways that they divorce slavery from the Civil War. Although each of these works is not necessarily representative of the author's complete views on the subject, they both offer apologies of slavery and are important pieces to consider in assessing the overall views of Faulkner and Warren on the subject of race.

Shinya Matsuoka, in "Unsustainable Freedom: The Civil War Narratives of Warren and Faulkner," uses the examples of *Wilderness* and *Absalom, Absalom!* to illustrate how both authors demonstrate that freedom is unsustainable when based on the exploitation of others. Relating Sutpen's project to American imperialism in the Caribbean, Matsuoka suggests the parallels of Sutpen's paternalistic attitude towards his slaves and the paternalistic foreign policy of the United States. The protagonist of Warren's *Wilderness*, Adam Rosenzweig, temporarily obtains his freedom by refusing to take the kind of measures that Sutpen took in exploiting the freedom of others.

In his essay "Naples Re-Visited: A New Perspective on Same-Sex Desire in 'Divorce in Naples,'" Pip Gordon begins with Joseph Blotner's brief reading of this story in his biography of Faulkner and argues for a different interpretation, particularly of the story's ending. As arguably Faulkner's only story with overtly homosexual characters, "Divorce in Naples" is important for understanding Faulkner's views on sexuality, Gordon claims. He uses a biographical approach to suggest that Faulkner may well have based elements of this story on his own experiences with his friend and gay roommate William Spratling.

"From the Circle of Time and Memory to the Circus of Fiction:

Bolton Lovehart and a Few Faulknerian Puppets" by Françoise Buisson links circus and circles both etymologically and conceptually in an intertextual reading that argues that the authors' characters are "often ensnared in repetitive patterns which deprive them of their freedom and turn them into puppets." Buisson shows how numerous Faulkner characters, as well as Warren's Bolton Lovehart, are trapped by family, time, and memory. She also finds parallels in the ways that these characters engage in largely failed attempts to become artists and to write their own histories.

Rebekah Taylor applies an ecocritical approach in "Modernist Ecologies: Faulkner's Wilderness and Warren's Wasteland" and analyzes how Warren, as both critic and novelist, responds to Faulkner's portrayal of the natural environment. She reveals Faulkner's environmental anxieties and suggests that Warren goes further in terms of envisioning a post-pastoral relationship of humans and nature. Analyzing numerous examples of Warren's work, Taylor demonstrates how he anticipates many of the concerns of contemporary ecocriticism.

"'There Ought to Be a Law': Prohibition in Faulkner and Warren" examines how Faulkner and Warren represent the Volstead-era South in their fiction. Conor Picken argues that both authors use bootlegging and alcohol to depict a South averse to progress and change. He shows how Faulkner in *Sanctuary* reveals stark class differences in characters' relationships to alcohol, the wealthy flaunting the law while the poor are punished by it. Warren, in *All the King's Men*, demonstrates the link between blatant disregard of Prohibition and the political corruption that is the more obvious focus of the novel.

Jason Zerbe examines the role of college football in Faulkner's work in his essay "'The only way a young man could earn money in school': 'Wild Palms,' The National Sporting Press, and the Professionalization of College Football." Zerbe's essay situates Faulkner's portrayal of college football (and its players) within the context of the debate being carried out in the national press over the professionalization of the supposedly amateur college game. He argues that although critics have paid attention to all sorts of references to popular culture in *The Wild Palms*, they have almost completely overlooked Faulkner's engagement with the national press's discussions and representations of college football. This essay suggests that in *The Hamlet* and *The Wild Palms,* football and sports are much more than curious additions or window dressing and are, in fact, important instances of Faulkner's engagement with topics of debate in the national popular culture.

Daniel Anderson's essay, "'Long Years Ago, in Minneapolis. . .': The Late Resurfacing of Robert Penn Warren's Minnesota Years," uses archival research to reassess Warren's time in Minnesota. He argues that this period is more influential on Warren's later work than previous critics have granted. Specifically, Anderson links Warren's work from the late 1970s and early 1980s, including a 1981 introduction to *All the King's Men*, to his experiences in Minnesota from 1942 to 1950, suggesting Warren reused material from that important time in his life throughout his career.

In "Approaching the Other Through Aesthetics: Faulkner, Warren, Native Americans, and Modernism," Benjamin Wilson examines the portrayal of Native Americans in terms of modernist aesthetics, rather than the anthropological, historical, and ethnographic studies of other critics. In Faulkner's work, he argues, "Native Americans are typically evoked, as opposed to presented outright, to underpin the mythological nature of Faulkner's fictional landscape" in works such as "A Justice" and *Go Down, Moses*. In his long-form narrative poem, *Chief Joseph of the Nez Perce*, Warren romanticizes Chief Joseph to some degree but also gestures toward the postmodern as he complicates the understanding of "history," both within the poem and through literary technique.

"William Faulkner's Dilsey, Robert Penn Warren's Manty, and Race Politics" by Dennis Negron suggests that considering the two authors' portrayals of black characters with a comparative approach can help us to view each author in new ways. Negron examines public statements and nonfiction works by each author on the subjects of race and integration in order to better understand their literary representations of race and blackness. He specifically analyzes Faulkner's Dilsey from *The Sound and the Fury* and Warren's Amantha "Manty" Starr from *Band of Angels* to offer a nuanced reading of how each author's characterization of these African-American women reveals something of their personal politics and themselves.

Fadia Mereani illustrates in "The Inadequacy of Language in William Faulkner's *As I Lay Dying* and Robert Penn Warren's *Brother to Dragons*" how both authors reveal the problematic nature of language and human communication in general. She claims that nature is able to communicate more effectively than humans in *As I Lay Dying*, while both the form and content of *Brother to Dragons* reflect Warren's similar sense that language fails to communicate ideas more than it succeeds.

Patricia L. Bradley

Angelic Acrobats and Fallen Southern Women:
William Faulkner and Robert Penn Warren Go to the Circus

Even for us jaded inhabitants of the twenty-first century, the circus is an alluring, exciting, potentially transgressive topic; it is, as we used to say back in the nineties, SEXY. Certainly, William Faulkner and Robert Penn Warren found it so, and no surprise. Both authors have baffled their critics, and not just their feminist critics, with their vexed portrayals of women. Just as importantly, these two writers also came of age when the circus was at the zenith of its allure among the American public. Since during the second decade of the twentieth century Warren was verging upon adolescence and Faulkner, slightly older, was well into young manhood, I find it extremely significant that this was the period of circus history when female circus aerialists had edged out their male counterparts in popularity, a trend that would eventually reverse itself by the 1950s (Tait 2–3). Even so, audience appreciation for women's circus performances, similar to the general cultural response to the advent of the New Woman, was ambivalent at best. According to Janet Davis's cultural history of the circus, "the mobile circus [of the early twentieth century] was a staging ground in which multiple shifting American attitudes about gender, race, and the female body were negotiated and contested" (Davis 141); with the cultural influence of the popular entertainment form in mind, Faulkner's and Warren's novelistic deployments of circus tropes prove neither casual nor isolated.

Faulkner's 1935 novel *Pylon*, for example, demonstrates an extended use of the cultural phenomenon, the enigmatic Laverne perfectly characterized as the "aerial body" of the female that Helen Stoddart asserts as a general signifier for the circus (7). A wing-walker and parachutist, Laverne's act is reminiscent of some of the earliest circus aerialist acts for women, the butterfly and angel acts of the early century. Laverne's billowing parachutes, like wings, create the effect of lightness, even weightlessness. Hers is a body literally suspended in mid-air, and all the more dramatically so because it is a female body. In her study *Circus Bodies: Cultural Identity in Aerial Performance*, Peta

Tait establishes that the female aerial body captures the attention of the circus audience more effectively than the male body because "observers . . . conflate the dangers of physical risk-taking with those of a seductive sexual identity considered socially dangerous. The female aerialist performed an idea of heightened danger" (21). Indeed, the scene of Laverne's first parachute jump is the most highly sexualized of the novel: to work herself into a frame of mind to make the leap from the wing, she first seduces the pilot, Roger Schumann, as he flies the plane (perhaps literature's first incidence of "joining the mile high club"). Furthermore, when she does execute the successful jump, landing semi-nude in a rural cornfield, the men and boys gathered to watch are so inflamed by her appearance that she and Schumann barely escape the mob with their lives. This episode from the novel perfectly illustrates Tait's summation of the cultural impressions women circus artists made upon the audience of the period: such women were "exposed to sexual inference and . . . men's perceptions . . . that they were not only sexually available but were also temptresses" (21).

Or consider Sue Murdoch in Warren's 1942 novel *At Heaven's Gate*. She is one of several of his characters for whom circus imagery—and in her case, hallucinations of her own "aerial body"—confirms her questionable social status and foreshadows her violent death. Sue has escaped the machinations of her duplicitous father, Bogan Murdoch, the Bernie Madoff of his day, to pursue a bohemian lifestyle, taking several lovers along the way. In a series of striking dreams brought on by the fevered after-effects of an abortion, she imagines she is a circus aerialist, performing daring feats high over her audience. As she lies in the midst of one such dream, she is strangled to death by Slim Sarratt, a lover whom she has spurned.

Faulkner's and Warren's best known works, however, *The Sound and the Fury* (1929) and *All the King's Men* (1946) respectively, perfectly reveal the varying levels of desire for and anxiety about the female body that Davis outlines in her study of how the early twentieth-century circus directed and reflected American culture. In both works, Jason Compson's niece Quentin and Jack Burden's childhood friend Anne Stanton enact circus identities that reveal their potentials—and those of their sisters—for social and sexual agency.

One temporal layer of *The Sound and the Fury* is its setting during the Easter weekend of 1928, but just as meaningful to that present action of the novel is its conjunction with the arrival of "the show" that sets its tent up just outside of Jefferson in "Beard's lot" (206). Although obviously a much smaller traveling circus than Ringling Bros. and Barnum & Bailey's, its presence further irritates the already splenetic Jason Compson, whose response to the circus is typical of most small town merchants of the period (Davis 29). Although the arrival of circuses brought great numbers of people into the towns selected for the shows, businessmen knew they would see little profit from such occasions; indeed, Jason takes the presence of the show as a personal financial affront, noting that it will "pick up Saturday night and carry off at least a thousand dollars out of the country" (248). This irritation proves minor, however, compared to the financial loss Jason will incur when his niece Quentin runs away with the circus, taking the seven thousand dollars he has stolen over a number of years from three generations of Compson women: Quentin, Caddy, and Caroline.

Furthermore, Jason's power struggle with his niece Quentin, whom he vainly seeks to define and contain, is played out in overt references to stock circus figures. Jason hopes to relegate Quentin to clown status, focusing hatefully on her ungainliness and her inexpert application of cosmetics; "her face [was] painted up like a dam clown's" he notes, and "her nose look[ed] like a porcelain insulator" (145, 161). Yet his condemnations of her appearance not only echo those leveled at the revealing clothing worn by the New Women of the 1920s and '30s but exemplify the very cultural resistance to women's freedoms that the example of early century women aerialists in the circus helped overcome. Jason rails at (although we suspect he is pervertedly titillated by) Quentin's near nakedness beneath her morning kimono and by her dressing, in his words, in no more "than [will] cover her legs and behind" (249). To demonstrate her will to be financially free of him, Quentin later threatens to tear her dress off as she stands at the end of the Compsons' drive, attracting an avid audience as well as Jason's angry threat of a public whipping. This episode is especially reminiscent of Janet Davis's descriptions of classic circus "disrobing acts on the trapeze and high wire: female aerialists wore layers of clothing which they speedily abandoned until they [were] dressed [only] in fleshlings [meant to simulate nudity] and leotard" (Davis 109). The suggestion of Quentin's disrobing will have even more meaningful circus applications when she makes her dramatic escape from Jason later that night.

Of course, Jason's worst fear is realized when Quentin runs away with the circus man with the red tie, claiming her money, her status as what grandmother Caroline calls a "fallen woman" (237), and her acrobat identity by climbing the rain spout to break into Jason's room and then escaping in the night down the very pear tree the youthful Caddy had herself ascended and descended to discover the intertwined secrets of mortality and sexuality. This episode of the novel also rings with circus significance as it is the moment of Quentin's "transformation by inversion," a term semiotician Paul Bouissac uses to describe a suspenseful twist to a basic acrobatic performance (25–26). The twist comes as an upstart member of the clown troupe foolishly claims he is also capable of doing the stunts that the acrobats have performed. As I describe the act in my book *Robert Penn Warren's Circus Aesthetic and the Southern Renaissance*, "miraculously, after a series of near-disasters, which the clown seems to survive by mere chance, he flings aside his clownish garb, reveals acrobatic tights, and steals the show by successfully performing the most difficult stunts of all" (Bradley 79). The act Bouissac cites, by the way, is a version of the equestrian act Mark Twain includes in *Adventures of Huckleberry Finn* (1885). Huck watches this performance, initially with great discomfort, feeling sorry for a sad drunken interloper who asserts himself into the unforgiving hierarchy of the circus. As with Faulkner's readers of Quentin's situation, however, Huck's embarrassment for the foolish braggart turns to pleased surprise and admiration. Quentin's reversal of fortune is just as dramatic, even to the details of her carelessly discarded clothing, discovered by her shocked family as the only remaining sign of her temporary habitation with them.

While *All the King's Men*'s Jack Burden freely grants Anne Stanton a literally exalted aerialist status in his romantic memories of their youthful summer love, the circus parallels he imagines in connection with her are just as fraught with anxiety as Jason's regarding Quentin. Again, Davis's study analyzes how women acrobats and aerialists were portrayed in circus lore, advertising posters, and newspaper and magazine articles and how those images reflected the changing roles of women in the early twentieth century; her analysis stresses three cultural trends in young women's behaviors that also reveal Anne's somewhat conflicted New Woman status and inform our understanding of her circus aerialist identity: first is the increasing numbers of women pursuing higher education and public activism, next the growing popularity of women's athleticism as a result of the physical-culture movement, and the last is the resulting changes in women's attire made in part to accommodate the first two trends (Davis 89–91).

Throughout the novel, Anne's sexual nature, hinted at by her daring leaps from the diving tower with a bemused and aroused Jack as audience, maintains a delicate balance with the purity he also associates with her. She, of course, attends an expensive finishing school and later a "refined female college in Virginia" (450), not to prepare her for a career necessarily but because her father Governor Stanton can afford to send her. Still, as she approaches her thirties, her role as an unmarried woman, mitigated only by her elevated class status, is cause for some cultural alarm. Certainly her work with orphaned children serves a double purpose in the conservative thirties as an appropriate substitute for having a husband and family of her own, and clearly it is the kind of socially responsible activism Anne herself envisions as appropriate to her gender and economic status. Significantly, it also brings her to the attention of Willie Stark, the target of her ladylike lobbying efforts on the orphans' behalf.

Thus, Anne's social demeanor is the very model adopted by many successful women performers in the early twentieth-century circus. Press releases regarding the social status of performing women in the circus frequently asserted their having been "born into respectability," often into aristocratic households (Davis 95). To most effectively publicize these women circus performers, who commanded large audiences and equally large salaries, their roles as New Women, career women, and emancipated women often had to be downplayed, and magazine and newspaper features about them "revealed" their secret yearnings for stable lives of maternity and domesticity. In essence, audiences were asked to simultaneously accept (as Jack initially attempts to do with Anne) what to them were alternating and contradictory views of womanhood.

In her cultural examination of the circus, Davis also notes the intersection of growing athleticism among women at the turn of the twentieth century with the popularity of female circus performance, although public opinions of women's entry into the "physical-culture movement" were guarded, with some voices decrying the resulting loss of femininity and others welcoming challenges to nineteenth-century stereotypes of "neurasthenic, asexual women" (Davis 90). Anne Stanton's athleticism during her girlhood first establishes her as a playmate and comrade for her brother Adam and their mutual friend Jack, but it also defines her relationship with Jack when, as a teenager, he begins to see Anne as an object of desire. Whether beating the lackadaisical Jack on the tennis court, swimming boldly out into the storm-troubled sea, or executing spectacular dives from tall platforms, Anne, the youngest of the three, is the daring one, taking risks and drawing her more cautious comrades along in her wake.

As with Laverne's body in Faulkner's *Pylon*, Anne's is another example of the aerial body, which is a signifier of the circus, a connection confirmed through Jack's description of one of the most climactic of her dives: jumping from the board, she "seem[ed] to hang there an instant . . . just an instant before the heady swoop and the clean swishing rip into the water as though she had dived through a great circus hoop covered with black silk spangled with silver" (Warren 433). The adolescent Jack is fascinated with Anne's experiments with jumping from such great heights, but he is drowsily disinclined to participate in them himself; indeed, his habit of observing safely from the edge of the pool foreshadows his later failure to consummate his relationship with Anne, a moment in the novel also detailed in a way that reflects her daring dives of the summer and Jack's passive observations of them. Only once is he emboldened to join her in her dive, but only from the ground level, never from her daring height. Significantly, when he does dive in from the side of the pool, their slow, breathless rise from the depths of the water as they are locked together in a passionate kiss mirrors Jack's breathless anticipation of the crowd's roars of support as Willie Stark travels throughout the state to deliver the speech designed to defeat the politicians howling for his impeachment. For Jack, this tensely awaited moment is also "like a deep dive," and when the crowd's roar of approval comes, "you pop out of the water . . . and the air bursts out of your lungs and everything reels in the light" (219).

Jack's tendency toward passivity, even paralysis, at a pivotal moment in his relationship with Anne, later reconfigured to illustrate the lure Willie Stark holds for him, should recall a scene from an earlier part of the novel that includes similarly pointed circus references. Examining it reveals not only the centrality of circus imagery to the themes of *All the King's Men* but also the degree to which the author was influenced, perhaps more than readers would consider any New Critic to have been, by the popular culture of the pre-World War II era.

The scene, of course, occurs in chapter five as Jack locates his putative father, Ellis Burden, in his mission at a third floor walkup over a Mexican restaurant. There Ellis attends to George, one of his mission unfortunates, just as he once had attended to the needs of his small son. Jack is only vaguely aware of his jealousy of George, who in his distress is comforted by the Scholarly Attorney; furthermore, he is completely unaware that George's temporary physical paralysis replicates Jack's own emotional paralysis in the face of devastating loss. George has witnessed the tragic death of his wife, who in the performance of her angel act for the circus "fell down a long way with white wings which fluttered as though she were flying" (297). In a related fashion, Jack similarly struggles with the possible loss of his ideal of Anne Stanton, not to mention his suspicions of his mother's serial promiscuity. George, who can no longer perform his circus act, commemorates his wife's death by fashioning masticated bread angels, partially as a gesture of communion with his lost love and partially to seek transcendence through the grief he experiences at her loss.

How integral, then, is the circus to Warren's greatest novel, and indeed to his several other works in which circus imagery appears? I strongly suspect that the celebrity circus marriage of Alfredo Codona and Lillian Leitzel is the popular culture source from which Warren draws his brief but thematically meaningful portrayal of George and his dead wife, in whose memory George creates gaudy bread dough angels to support himself. Codona, a member of the famed Mexican aerialist family, became Leitzel's third husband in 1927 (Davis 116), when she, a wildly popular aerialist in her own right, was at the pinnacle of her career. Leitzel was a headliner who performed her one-woman act not on a trapeze but on several vertical ropes referred to in circus parlance as "webs" (Tait 5), a word that provides a significant image in Warren's novel. The woman who would later become Codona's wife debuted with the Ringling Bros. Circus in 1915 (Davis 95), and it is entirely possible the circus-struck Warren would have seen her perform when he was a child or teenager.

Alfredo Codona was his wife's equal in talent and daring. By 1920, he had mastered the triple—that is, the triple somersault executed as he leapt from his trapeze to the grasp of his catcher. His athletic prowess and reputation made him a natural choice as Johnny Weismuller's stunt double in some of the early Tarzan films. In contrast, Leitzel's *tour de force* was her ability to execute anywhere from one hundred to over two hundred swingovers a performance. Hanging one-handed above her audience from a loop of rope that was itself fastened to a metal swivel ring, she would throw "her entire body head over heels with her shoulder socket as a fulcrum" (Bradley xiv). As she performed, her husband Alfredo would post himself below her, confident that, should she ever fall, he would be able to catch her. Her fatal accident, however, occurred when they were touring separately in Europe during the offseason of their American circus commitments. Leitzel met her death as the result of a fall in Copenhagen in 1931 ("Lillian Leitzel"), not, as Jack speculates of George's wife's death, because "the rope broke" but because, as Ellis Burden corrects him, "Something went wrong with the apparatus" (Warren 297). In Leitzel's case, the metal swivel ring to her apparatus crystallized and snapped, a circumstance not uncommon among rings subjected to "sudden extremes of heat and cold," and a fact affirmed by the superintendant of properties for the Ringling Bros. and Barnum & Bailey Circus in an interview with the *New York Times* ("Circus Rings Kept Safe" 52). This detail probably explains one of Warren's many arcane passages on fate in the novel as Jack characteristically and philosophically muses, "How life is strange and changeful, and *the crystal is in the steel at the point of fracture*, and the toad bears a jewel in its forehead, and the meaning of moments passes like the breeze that scarcely ruffles the leaf of the willow" (Warren 26, my emphasis). Leitzel's death was front page news from the East to the West Coast. After her ashes arrived in San Diego a few months later aboard the Panama Pacific liner *Pennsylvania*, they were hand delivered to Alfredo Codona in Long Beach, California ("Leitzel's Ashes" 18). Warren, who as his biographer Joseph Blotner confirms, was vacationing in California that very spring with his wife Cinina and his widowed father-in-law (115), may from that newspaper detail have decided that Long Beach was a fit destination to which bereaved young men retreated to mourn the loss of an ideal, and so Long Beach, California, is of course where Jack also heads when he discovers Anne's fall from grace, her affair with Willie Stark.

As with Ellis Burden's poor unfortunate protégé George, Codona lapsed into a self-imposed retirement after Leitzel's death, but he finally returned to the Flying Codonas after a three-month hiatus, performing with his brother Lalo and another trapeze aerialist, Vera Bruce, who eventually became Alfredo's third wife. The Flying Codonas' act bears interesting similarities to the triangulated character dynamic Warren establishes in *All the King's Men* with Jack, Anne, and Willie. Ruth Manning-Sanders describes the Codonas' performance of their specialty, the double passing trick:

> Lalo hangs from his trapeze, swinging Vera by the ankles. Alfredo swings from his trapeze by the hands. The two trapezes swing towards each other; Lalo releases Vera's ankles and flings her forward; at the same moment Alfredo shoots over the top of his trapeze, and passes above Vera in mid-air. The next moment, Vera has caught the trapeze that Alfredo has just left, and Alfredo's wrists are gripped by Lalo's strong hands. (qtd. in Tait 98)

Then, the cast and catch is repeated in reverse, Alfredo and Vera always passing each other, never connecting with each other, and dependent upon Lalo to keep them in motion during the act. In her gender study of circus aerial performance, Peta Tait is quick to point out that the strength and skill required to perform such an act lies not so much in the abilities of the fliers—Alfredo and Vera Bruce—but in the "strength and skill" exhibited by Lalo, who is both caster and catcher (27)—the facilitator who either makes flight a possibility for the other two or who with his failure orchestrates their falls. Nevertheless, given the public persona attributed to the tragically bereaved Alfredo, his loss shapes the central narrative of the act, which Tait interprets in this reading:

> This story [told through this series of leaps and catches] suggests ideal love thwarted by death. Emotional pain dominates the Alfredo narrative when the aerialist and the aerial act converge into loss that merges melancholy about an unattainable love and mourning for a dead lover. (Tait 98)

As I point out in my study of Warren's circus aesthetic, however, Jack's repeatedly crossing paths with Anne but never connecting with her is not the only loss he suffers; when, as with Alfredo and Lalo, Jack makes intermittent contact with Willie, only to be cast from him and replaced by Anne, he and Willie and Anne are also perpetually enacting Girardian triangular desire, in which the male to male relationship is just as significant, if not more so, as the male to female relationship. To fully accommodate this reading, we might consider Noel Polk's restored text of Warren's novel, which replaces the name "Stark" with "Talos," the author's original choice for Willie's surname; the latter is much more aurally analogous to "Lalo" and could provide another piece to the influence puzzle taking shape before us. In further support of this idea, I might add that the Talos of Greek myth is also occasionally portrayed as a winged figure.

The final act of Alfredo Codona's personal tragedy took place on July 30, 1937. Once again, as Blotner details, Warren and his wife Cinina were visiting in San Francisco and Oakland, California (163), and thus had a ringside seat for the melodramatic events that provided newspapers statewide with front-page news for several days. Codona had left the circus in 1933 after a shoulder injury ended his career. Permanently "grounded" from his flying act, he retired once more to Long Beach to take a job as a gas station attendant in a local garage. I must confess that in my nerdy academic imagination, I like to picture Codona gassing up Jack Burden's car before Jack begins his long cross-country return home to witness the unraveling of both Willie's career and Adam Stanton's sanity. At any rate, Codona's relationship with Vera Bruce, which had suffered considerably from his many changes in fate that culminated in their divorce, ended abruptly with a dramatic murder/suicide as Codona shot her and then himself to death in her lawyer's office ("Codona Kills Self" 30). That this event would have resonated with Warren, whose own stormy marriage with Cinina was proving more and more strained, seems obvious. With her, he came to California ill and overworked, having just put the final touches on his poem "Bearded Oaks," in which he poignantly reveals the paradoxical aftermath of passion: two lovers lying side by side in adjoining graves. Blotner reads the poem as indicative of "the inevitable victory of death over love" (161–63).

Circus legends hold that Codona had never recovered from Lillian Leitzel's death, and they are certainly partially correct. He joined

Leitzel in death at the foot of a massive seventeen-foot monument he had commissioned for her grave in the Inglewood Park Cemetery in Inglewood, California. Sources attribute different titles to the monument: one calls it "Reunion" and another "The Spirit of Flight." Either way, the face of the winged angel who seems to be carrying his fallen lover's figure heavenward—or who could even be perceived as catching her before she falls to earth—bears a striking resemblance to Codona himself. Only Robert Penn Warren knows if it is also the face of Jack Burden, reunited with Anne Stanton at last, but possibly not forever. For the year is 1939, and Jack envisions their return to Burden's Landing, should it ever transpire, as a ghostly one when they will "move among trees as soundlessly as smoke" (661).

Peta Tait maintains "the importance of the circus as a social idea, especially since aerialists became synonymous with circus, and subsequently with notions of desire and longing" (Tait 6). The circus then is a natural subject for writers like William Faulkner and Robert Penn Warren as they interweave their characters' cultural awareness of the popular entertainment form with their individual desires and longings—no isolated practice for either author since in *Pylon* we see the reporter's fascination with the "romantic" lives of the barnstormers, and especially with the wing-walker and parachutist Laverne (another Girardian display of triangular desire in a fictionalized Louisiana setting) and in *At Heaven's Gate* we witness Sue Murdoch's similarly circus-imaged quest for and failure to achieve social and sexual autonomy. These are lesser examples, however, both in the two authors' canons as well as in the extents to which those novels adopt the image of the circus. In *The Sound and the Fury* and *All the King's Men*, overarching themes and characterizations depend even more heavily upon the circus structures on which they are founded. As these two major works and the title of this present study suggest, Faulkner and Warren shared the social ambivalences experienced by many of the circusgoers of their youths. Observing how the changing roles of American women mirrored the precarious freedoms and dangers enacted in the performances of women circus acrobats, both writers acknowledged in these their greatest novels the death of the "angel in the household"—a concept that had once dominated nineteenth-century thinking about gender roles—and announced the emergence of the transgressive circus angels who, with every public appearance, showed their willingness to leap unhindered into the cultural unknown.

Works Cited

Blotner, Joseph. *Robert Penn Warren: A Biography*. New York: Random House, 1997. Print.

Bouissac, Paul. *Circus and Culture: A Semiotic Approach*. Bloomington: Indiana UP, 1976.

Bradley, Patricia L. *Robert Penn Warren's Circus Aesthetic and the Southern Renaissance*. Knoxville: U of Tennessee P, 2004. Print.

"Circus Rings Kept Safe for 37 Years." *New York Times* 23 April 1950: 52. ProQuest. Web. 15 Aug. 2012.

"Codona Kills Self, Shooting Ex-Wife." *New York Times* 31 July 1937: 30. ProQuest. Web. 15 Aug. 2012.

Davis, Janet M. *The Circus Age: Culture & Society under the American Big Top*. Chapel Hill: U of North Carolina P, 2002. Print.

Faulkner, William. *Pylon*. New York: Signet, 1957. Print.

———. *The Sound and the Fury*. Ed. David Minter. 2nd ed. Norton Critical Edition. New York: W.W. Norton, 1994. Print.

"Lillian Leitzel." *Ringling Bros. and Barnum & Bailey Circus*. www.ringling.com. Web. 15 Aug. 2012.

Stoddart, Helen. *Rings of Desire: Circus History and Representation*. Manchester: Manchester UP, 2000. Print.

Tait, Peta. *Circus Bodies: Cultural Identity in Aerial Performance*. New York: Routledge, 2005. Print.

Warren, Robert Penn. *At Heaven's Gate*. New York: New Directions, 1985. Print.

———. *All the King's Men*. New York: Mariner, 2001. Print.

Robert W. Hamblin

"The world is like an enormous spider web": The Contrasting Legacies of Thomas Sutpen and Cass Mastern

The lives and works of William Faulkner and Robert Penn Warren intersect in a number of interesting and significant ways. Contemporaries, although Warren was nearly a decade younger, both were native Southerners, although Faulkner came from the Deep South and Warren from the Upper. Both wrote, in varying degrees, poetry, short stories, novels, criticism, and social commentary; both were fascinated by the history of their region, particularly as that history had been shaped by slavery, the Civil War, Reconstruction, and Jim Crow. Both men's views on race evolved considerably over their lifetimes, though both remained ambivalent about many of the changes they saw coming. Warren lived to see major changes brought by the Civil Rights Movement; Faulkner did not.

While in many ways they share similar experiences and write about similar subjects, not only race but also nature, socio-economic issues, politics, and religion, they held highly contrasting views of each other's work. Warren was a great admirer of Faulkner; he wrote a number of influential Faulkner reviews and essays, and even edited a book of Faulkner criticism.[1] Invited to speak at the University of Mississippi during the turmoil of the university's integration crisis, Warren chose Faulkner as the focus of his remarks on race, conflict, and reconciliation.[2] Faulkner, on the other hand, paid very little public notice to Warren. When their mutual friend Albert Erskine brought the two men together in 1952 for dinner and conversation, Faulkner evidenced some knowledge of Warren's novel *At Heaven's Gate* and at least one Warren short story; but perhaps more telling is the fact that in the transcriptions of Faulkner's interviews, lectures, and class conferences at the University of Virginia in 1957–58, in which Faulkner alludes to dozens of authors, there is not a single mention of Warren or any of his writings.[3]

The only extended commentary by Faulkner on Warren is to be found in a letter Faulkner mailed to Lambert Davis, a Harcourt, Brace editor who had sent Faulkner an advance review copy of Warren's *All the King's Men*, hopeful that Faulkner might supply a promotional blurb. What Davis received back was a mixed but largely unfavorable view of Warren's novel. "The Cass Mastern story is a beautiful and moving piece," Faulkner wrote. "That was his novel. The rest I would throw away." Faulkner continued: "The Starke [*sic*] thing is good solid sound writing but for my money Starke and the rest of them are second rate. . . . I didn't mind neither loving him nor hating him, but I did object to not being moved by pity. . . . He was neither big enough nor bad enough. But maybe the Cass story made the rest of it look thinner than it is. . . ." (*Letters* 239).

In this paper I propose that one of the reasons for Faulkner's admiration of the Cass Mastern subplot in *All the King's Men* may perhaps have been his recognition of the parallels between Warren's Cass Mastern story and Faulkner's treatment of Thomas Sutpen, whose tragic story provides the centerpiece of *Absalom, Absalom!*. In reading the narratives of these two characters intertextually, we see some of the common concerns of Faulkner and Warren, but also some important differences.

Both Thomas Sutpen and Cass Mastern are white plantation owners in Mississippi whose lives and relationships are radically affected by their interracial attitudes and actions. Those actions for both are closely entwined with slavery and the Civil War. The two men's behaviors not only wreak havoc upon their contemporaries but also strongly affect two young men in the following century, Quentin Compson and Jack Burden. But the ultimate effects of the two stories, both in their immediate climaxes and their consequences, are quite opposite in nature.

Thomas Sutpen's story belongs with the rags-to-riches narratives that have been so conspicuous in American history and literature—from Benjamin Franklin's Poor Richard, to Horatio Alger's Ragged Dick, to William Dean Howells's Silas Lapham, to F. Scott Fitzgerald's Jay Gatsby. Son of poor mountaineer parents in western Virginia, Sutpen as a young boy moves with his family to Tidewater Virginia, where he first views the huge plantations dependent upon slave laborers; then, as a young man, on to Haiti, where his education in plantation economics and personal relationships is furthered; and finally on to Jefferson, Mississippi, where he carves out his own plantation, called "Sutpen's Hundred," and becomes one of the leading landowners in antebellum Yoknapatawpha. None of the several narrators who present Sutpen's story—the communal narrator, Rosa Coldfield, General Compson, Mr. Compson, Quentin, Shreve—ever questions Sutpen's courage, ambition, confidence, industriousness, or perseverance. In these regards he possesses exactly the pragmatic character traits needed to tame a wilderness, build a mansion, and establish a dynasty. But what is missing in Sutpen is a moral or ethical center: as the narrator states, "They did not think of love in connection with Sutpen. They thought of ruthlessness rather than justice and of fear rather than respect, but not of pity or love" (43). In short, Sutpen is a crass materialist, an obsessive, manipulative egomaniac possessing "valor and strength but without pity or honor" (20).

Sutpen's self-serving ruthlessness is dramatized in many ways throughout the novel, most notably in his abandonment of his Haitian wife when he discovers she is part-black; in his cruel and inhumane treatment of his Negro slaves and the French architect; in his arranged marriage with Ellen Coldfield to further his "grand design"; in his callous proposal to Rosa Coldfield that she produce him a male heir as a pre-condition to their being wed; in his savage rejection of the teenaged Milly Jones when the child she gives him is a female; and, most importantly, in his rejection of and conspiracy against his son Charles Bon because he is part-black.

I have argued elsewhere that Sutpen's Negrophobia, the dominant trait in his characterization, may be traced back to his childhood, when his first encounters with blacks left him psychologically bruised, emasculated, angry, and vengeful.[4] The first black man he ever sees, as his family migrates from the mountains to the Tidewater, manhandles and ridicules the boy's father: "a huge bull of a nigger . . . who emerged [from the tavern] with the old man over his shoulder like a sack of meal and his—the nigger's—mouth loud with laughing and full of teeth like tombstones" (182). Later, in the Tidewater, he and his sister are nearly run over by a carriage driven by a "nigger coachman in a plug hat"; and on another occasion he listens as his father excitedly and proudly recounts the beating of a black man by a group of night riders. Then, when Thomas is about thirteen or fourteen years of age, he is turned away from the front of a "big house" and ordered to go to the back door by a "monkey-dressed nigger butler" (187). Such frightening and dehumanizing experiences involving blacks, I contend, lay the basis for Sutpen's racism that is only extended and heightened by the horrors of the racial insurrection in Haiti. It seems predictable, even inevitable, that these childhood and youthful experiences will have continued consequences for the older Sutpen after he arrives in Mississippi. And, of course, they do. Given the horrors of his previous experience with blackness, Sutpen must resort to all means and measures to prevent Judith's marriage to the biracial Bon. As I stated in my previous discussion of this matter, "The logic of the racist may appear to others to be confused and irrational, but to the racist it has the precision and inevitability of a mathematical equation" (281).[5]

I stress the deterministic nature of Sutpen's fate to emphasize how bleak and pessimistic his story is. That pessimism is underscored and heightened by the end of the man and his dream: his death at the hand of Wash Jones, the eventual destruction of his mansion, the ironic survival of his blood lineage in the "idiot Negro" (301) Jim Bond—and the reader's foreknowledge that the chief inheritor and preserver of Sutpen's narrative, Quentin Compson, will all too soon commit suicide by drowning himself. No better description of the deterministic nature of Sutpen's tragedy can be found than the words used by Jack Burden to describe Cass Mastern's dark night of the soul:

> He learned that the world is like an enormous spider web and if you touch it, however lightly, at any point, the vibration ripples to the remotest perimeter and the drowsy spider feels the tingle and is drowsy no more but springs out to fling the gossamer coils about you who have touched the web and then inject the black, numbing poison under your hide. It does not matter whether or not you meant to brush the web of things. Your happy foot or your gay wing may have brushed it ever so slightly, but what happens always happens and there is the spider, bearded black and with his great faceted eyes glittering like mirrors in the sun, or like God's eye, and the fangs dripping. (188–89)

This passage is one of the best descriptions in American literature of the deterministic theory that lies at the heart of literary naturalism, and one can readily imagine its being written by Stephen Crane, Frank Norris, or Theodore Dreiser. However, as I shall argue later,

Cass Mastern and Jack Burden manage finally to escape the spider's web, and its deterministic implications, but the characters of *Absalom, Absalom!* do not.

Cass Mastern's story begins much like that of Thomas Sutpen's. He was born, as he notes in his journal, "in a log cabin in north Georgia, in circumstances of poverty" (161). Like Sutpen, he eventually becomes a plantation owner in Mississippi. And, like Sutpen in Haiti, he experiences a time of "darkness and trouble" (162) that irrevocably alters his life. Cass's fall into awareness of evil and personal culpability occurs in Lexington, Kentucky, where he is enrolled in Transylvania College; and, like Sutpen's initiatory experience in Haiti, Cass's too involves a woman and an issue of race. While in Lexington, Cass engages in an affair with Annabelle Trice, the wife of his best friend; and when the friend, Duncan Trice, discovers the affair, he commits suicide. Realizing that her personal slave Phebe knows about the affair, and fearing that she might make it known to others, Annabelle sells Phebe to a slave dealer who will ship her "down the river" to New Orleans, thus separating her from her husband and likely condemning her to a life of sexual servitude. When Cass questions this mistreatment of Phebe, Annabelle turns her rage upon him: "[O]h, I see, you are concerned for the honor of a black coachman . . . why did you not show some such delicate concern for the honor of your friend?" (162) The cumulative effect of this series of actions is described by Cass in his journal:

> [A]ll of these things—the death of my friend, the betrayal of Phebe, the suffering and rage and great change of the woman I loved—all had come from my single act of sin and perfidy, as the boughs from the bole and the leaves from the bough. Or to figure the matter differently, it was as though the vibration set up in the whole fabric of the world by my act had spread infinitely and with ever increasing power and no man could know the end. (178)

Cass's conscience-driven grief, as well as his recognition and regret that his actions have had serious, unexpected social consequences, contrasts sharply with the attitudes and behavior of Thomas Sutpen. Significantly, Cass's journal entries are laced with the biblical language of temptation, sin, guilt, damnation, shame, repentance, penance, and hope of grace and forgiveness. "I write this down," Cass notes, "with what truthfulness a sinner may attain unto, that if ever pride is in me, of flesh or spirit, I can peruse these pages and know with shame what evil has been in me, or may be in me. . . " (161). In another entry he writes that "hopeless of Grace I yet clung to the hope of Grace" (182), and in yet another he voices a prayer to "O God and my Redeemer" (166). The narrator notes that Cass Mastern's schooling has included "a great deal of Presbyterian theology" (163), and his journal reads like a casebook in Calvinism.

A major component of Calvinism, indeed all Christianity, is a belief in repentance, penance, and salvation. Cass's guilt over his adultery and his betrayal of a friend drives him to seek to atone for his sinful acts. He ends the affair with Annabelle and engages in a futile quest to locate Phebe with the intention of buying her and then setting her free. Back home in Mississippi, he resumes operation of his plantation, spends time in prayer and Bible study, and then, to the consternation of his brother Gilbert, frees his slaves. When the Civil War breaks out, Cass feels obligated to join the Confederacy, but with the rank of private rather than that of a major or colonel, as Gilbert had advised, and with a secret promise to himself that he will never take the life of another human being: "How can I who have taken the life of my friend, take the life of an enemy, for I have used up my right to blood" (186). After participating in numerous battles, including those at Shiloh and Chickamauga, he is mortally wounded in a battle outside Atlanta and dies with other soldiers in a military hospital, feeling at the end that he has come to know "the common guilt of man" and accepting of "the Justice of God, that others have suffered for my sin, for it may be that only by the suffering of the innocent does God affirm that men are brothers, and brothers in His Holy Name" (187). The last words of Cass's journal are "Blessed be his Name" (188).

How different is the language used by and about Thomas Sutpen. Unlike Cass Mastern, who learns humility and gentleness through his personal ordeal, and who views his experience in the context of a universal struggle between good and evil, Sutpen resorts to violence and cruelty to effect a selfish goal in a world that he perceives to be amoral. Although to Rosa Coldfield, Sutpen is an "ogre" or "demon" (13), "fiend blackguard and devil" (15)—words that appear to identify

Sutpen as immoral—Sutpen is more often associated in the text with the amoral world of "brutehood" (261). As a result of his boyhood experience at "the big house," he comes to view himself and his family "as cattle, creatures heavy and without grace, brutely evacuated into a world without hope or purpose for them, who would in turn spawn with brutish and vicious prolixity" (235). Immediately following his being turned away from the front door by the "monkey nigger" (232), he retreats to the woods, where, animal-like, "he crawled back into the cave and sat with his back against the uptorn roots" (233). Shortly thereafter, overcome by hunger, he returns home, where he observes

> his sister pumping rhythmic up and down above a
> washtub in the yard, . . . broad in the beam as a cow,
> the very labor she was doing brutish and stupidly out
> of proportion to its reward: the very primary essence of
> labor, toil, reduced to its crude absolute which only a
> beast could and would endure. (236)

In Haiti, Sutpen is thrown into an atavistic world described as "the halfway point between what we call the jungle and what we call civilization," "a theater for violence and injustice and bloodshed and all the satanic lusts of human greed and cruelty" (250). Arriving in Jefferson, he brings with him a wagonload of slaves "smelling like a wolfden" (35) and a French architect who is the only one of the group "resembling a human creature" (37). Soon the community learns that Sutpen regularly engages in hand-to-hand fights with his Negro slaves, "both naked to the waist and gouging at one another's eyes as if they should not only have been the same color, but should have been covered in fur too" (29). "Horse or mare?" Sutpen asks the Negro midwife who delivers his child by Milly Jones. Then, hearing the disappointing news, he says to Milly, "Too bad you're not a mare too. Then I could give you a decent stall in the stable" (286).

All such animal imagery suggests that Sutpen's story belongs not in the context of Calvinistic (and Augustian) Christianity, as Cass Mastern's does, but rather in the context of literary naturalism and social Darwinism, which were highly prevalent emphases in American literature during the early years of Faulkner's career. One of the chief proponents of a naturalistic and Darwinian interpretation of life was

Theodore Dreiser, a writer Faulkner greatly admired.[6] "On the tiger no responsibility rests," Dreiser writes in *Sister Carrie* (90); and his Frank Cowperwood, a railway tycoon who as a young boy is persuaded that he has discovered the organizing principle of life—and business—when he observes a lobster devouring a squid (*The Financier*, 21–23), is one of the principal literary forebears of Thomas Sutpen. Like Cowperwood and other robber barons, real and fictional, Sutpen intends to let nothing stand in the way of his desire and design for material success.

The contrasts herein noted between Thomas Sutpen and Cass Mastern—and their respective worlds—also play out in the stories of the narrators who, in the next century, recount the older stories, Quentin Compson and Jack Burden.[7] Quentin Compson, as readers know from *The Sound and the Fury*, is a young idealist who is disillusioned by a world given over to pragmatic and material values. In narrating the Sutpen story in *Absalom, Absalom!*, Quentin expresses sympathy for Charles Bon, the son rejected by his father. Quentin identifies with Bon in part because he too, in a sense, has been rejected by his father. Yes, Quentin possesses incestuous desires toward his sister Caddy, just as Charles Bon pursues an incestuous relationship with his half-sister Judith Sutpen, but it can be argued in both cases that it is principally the father-son relationship that pushes each story to its fateful climax.

"Father said" is a constant refrain that runs throughout the Quentin section of *The Sound and the Fury*, from the first page until the last. And everything that Mr. Compson tells Quentin is grounded in the father's alcoholic, nihilistic condition: "[N]o battle is ever won he said. They are not even fought. The field only reveals to man his own folly and despair, and victory is an illusion of philosophers and fools" (93). Thus, according to Mr. Compson, nothing matters—neither honor ("people cannot do anything that dreadful, they cannot do anything dreadful at all" [98]), nor morality ("Purity is a negative state and therefore contrary to nature" [143]), nor virginity ("Because it means less to women" [96]), nor time ("the reducto absurdum of all human experience" [93]), nor even life itself ("stalemate of dust and desire" [153]). "But to believe that it doesn't matter," Quentin objects, only to have his father respond, "nothing is even worth the changing of it" (96).

Just as Bon desires recognition from his father, and possibly pursues the marriage with Judith partly (or even only) as revenge for his father's rejection (as Sutpen's life has been a revenge against his being turned away from a door), so too is Quentin's suicide related to Mr. Compson's indifference to Caddy's pregnancy and loveless marriage. Both fathers turn their sons away in a moment of personal crisis and thus are complicit in the sons' deaths. In this regard, Quentin's story parallels and repeats the tragic pattern of the Sutpen narrative. On the last day of his life Quentin recalls the times when

> I seemed to be lying neither asleep nor awake looking down a long corridor of grey halflight where all stable things had become shadowy paradoxical all I had done shadows all I had felt suffered taking visible form antic and perverse mocking without relevance inherent themselves with the denial of the significance they should have affirmed. (211)

This is Quentin's version of the Humpty Dumpty experience that his world has become, and in his case, truly, "all the king's horses and all the king's men / couldn't put Humpty Dumpty together again." The phrase "all stable things had become shadowy paradoxical" links to all those passages in *Absalom, Absalom!* that describe the Sutpen narrative as a clouded mystery, indecipherable and incomprehensible. And Quentin's ultimately futile role as a detective trying to unravel that mystery and make sense of it can be read as an analogue to his failure to order and control his own life. The end result of both stories, for Quentin, is "Nevermore of peace. Nevermore of peace. Nevermore Nevermore Nevermore" (373).

Jack Burden likewise has a vicarious involvement in the story he tells about Cass Mastern. Like Mastern, Jack has a personal history marked by irresponsibility, infidelity, betrayal, and guilt. A history student and journalist, Burden becomes the "dirty tricks" man for Governor Willie Stark, using his research skills to supply the corrupt and amoral governor with information that Stark then uses to bully or blackmail his political enemies into submission. Unwittingly, however, in one crucial instance, in what he calls "The Case of the Upright Judge," Jack uncovers information that leads to startling revelations that, when exposed, cause a series of tragic events for himself, his family, and his best friends. Ordered to find some type of scandalous behavior by Judge Irwin, close friend to the Burdens when Jack was a boy, Jack succeeds in discovering that the Judge, as attorney general under Governor Stanton, the father of Jack's best friends Anne and Adam, had accepted a lucrative bribe from a utilities company and that Governor Stanton had assisted him in covering up the crime. Now threatened with the public exposure of his actions, Judge Irwin commits suicide. Additionally, the disillusionment Anne Stanton feels over her father's cover-up of Irwin's crime makes it easier for her to become Willie Stark's mistress; and when Anne's brother Adam learns of Stark's affair with his sister, he assassinates Stark. Burden experiences still another shock amid these catastrophes when his mother informs him that Judge Irwin, the next door neighbor who was her lover, is Jack's actual father. Like Cass Mastern, Burden recognizes that an action of his has had far-reaching, unexpected, and tragic consequences. He has touched the edge of the spider's web, and the entire web has been shaken. And like Mastern, and Quentin Compson as well, Burden "felt that the world outside of me was shifting and the substance of things, and that the process had only begun of a general disintegration of which I was the center" (177).

For a time Burden seeks to deny any personal responsibility for this string of events, finding comfort and escape in the philosophy that he calls the Great Twitch. He gets the idea from observing an old man with an uncontrollable twitch in his face.

> [Y]ou would suddenly see a twitch in the left cheek, up toward the pale-blue eye. You would think he was going to wink, but he wasn't going to wink. The twitch was simply an independent phenomenon, unrelated to the face or to what was behind the face or to anything in the whole tissue of phenomena which is the world we are lost in. (313)

A wink, of course, would be an act of will, chosen behavior; whereas a twitch is involuntary, the effect of a natural cause over which one has no control. A twitch, therefore, is a useful symbol for the theory of determinism, and Burden, for a while, finds that philosophy to be very comforting, since if there is no free will, there can be no responsibility, and thus no consequent guilt, for one's actions. "But later," Jack observes, "much later, he woke up one morning to discover that he did not believe in the Great Twitch any more" (436). He has seen "too many people live and die," he says; and he has heard Willie Stark say at the end of his life, "It might have been all different, Jack. You got to believe that" (436).

In his rejection of the Great Twitch and his acceptance of personal responsibility, Burden has moved from a deterministic philosophy of human behavior to an existential one that insists on human freedom. "History is blind," Hugh Miller tells Jack, "but man is not" (436). In other words, even in a world that is confusing and unpredictable and even absurd, and one in which the consequences of individuals' actions can never be assured or even foretold, one still must make choices and assume responsibility for those choices. This is the lesson that Cass Mastern learned, and it is the one that Jack Burden likewise learns. And just as the Thomas Sutpen story serves as an analogue for the tragic experience of Quentin Compson, so does the Cass Mastern story stand as an analogue for the redemptive experience of Jack Burden.

I have sought to demonstrate that there are a number of intertextual connections between *Absalom, Absalom!* and *All the King's Men*, but I want to conclude by noting what I perceive to be the principal difference in the two novels. The key to that difference is found in the epigraph that Warren appends to his story: "*Mentre che la speranza ha fior del verde*" ("while hope has speck of green"), from Canto III of the Purgatory section of Dante's *Divine Comedy*. The full quotation from which Warren takes these words reads: "one is not so lost that the Eternal Love cannot return, while hope has speck of green." This concept is echoed on the next-to-last page of the novel, in the words of the tract that the Scholarly Attorney is writing—words that Jack Burden confesses that, in his own way, he possibly too believes:

> Separateness is identity and the only way for God to
> create, truly create, man was to make him separate
> from God Himself, and to be separate from God is
> to be sinful. The creation of evil is therefore the index
> of God's glory and His power. That had to be so that
> the creation of good might be the index of man's glory
> and power. But by God's help. By His help and in His
> wisdom. (437)

All the King's Men is a novel about things gone wrong, about human mistakes and sins and their consequences. But it is also a novel about redemption, about *felix culpa*, the good that can be made to come out of evil. The novel is a tragedy, but it ends in hope. Like Dante's "Purgatory," or Milton's *Paradise Lost* (which is perhaps alluded to in the last paragraph of the novel), or Shakespeare's *The Tempest*, Warren offers the possibility of a future that can be better than the mistaken past. That depends, of course, on individuals' making better choices than they have done previously.

Absalom, Absalom! is an altogether different type of book. It is unquestionably one of the greatest tragedies ever written, belonging in the company of such classic works as *Oedipus Rex*, *King Lear*, and *Moby Dick*. But even these dark tragedies contain a greater degree of hope than is to be found in Faulkner's greatest novel. Simply put, *Absalom, Absalom!*, like the biblical story of David and Absalom upon which it is based, is not a work that posits hope for the future. Its principal character, Sutpen, is an individual who not only cannot escape his past but also is fated to repeat it; and the principal narrator, Quentin Compson, is a young man who likewise has no future—in fact, is already dead when he narrates the story.[8] The Sutpen story ends in holocaust and ruin:

> it was all finished now, there was nothing left now,
> nothing out there now but that idiot boy to lurk around
> those ashes and those four gutted chimneys and howl
> until someone came and drove him away. They couldn't
> catch him and nobody ever seemed to make him go
> very far away, he just stopped howling for a little while.
> Then after a while they would begin to hear him again.
> (376)

The "idiot boy" is Jim Bond, "the scion, the last of his race" (376), the one remaining Sutpen. His howl is the only aspect of the Sutpen story to last into the future, and it is projected "to conquer the western hemisphere" (378). Unlike *All the King's Men*, *Absalom, Absalom!* contains no Purgatory, and certainly no thought of Paradise. The characters Faulkner gives us in *Absalom, Absalom!* all live in Hell. And that Hell encompasses the entire universe: "the single profound suspiration of the parched earth's agony rising toward the imponderable and aloof stars" (362).

Notes

1. Warren's review of Malcolm Cowley's *The Portable Faulkner* helped launch the academic interest in Faulkner's work. See also Robert Penn Warren, ed., *Faulkner: A Collection of Critical Essays* (Englewood Cliffs, NJ: Prentice-Hall, 1966), which includes Warren's essay, "Faulkner, the Negro, the South, and Time." For a detailed and enlightening survey of Warren's ongoing dialogue with Faulkner's texts, see Joseph Millichap, "Warren's Faulkner," *Mississippi Quarterly* 60.2 (2007): 351-67.

2. See Robert W. Hamblin, "The 1965 Southern Literary Festival: A Microcosm of the Civil Rights Movement," *Journal of Mississippi History* 53 (May 1991): 83-114.

3. Joseph Blotner, *Faulkner: A Biography* (New York: Random House, 1974), 1426; Frederick L. Gwynn and Joseph Blotner, eds., *Faulkner in the University: Class Conferences at the University of Virginia, 1957–58* (Charlottesville: University of Virginia Press, 1959). Millichap (p. 353) speculates that the Warren story Faulkner had read may have been "Prime Leaf," since both it and Faulkner's story, "Ad Astra," appeared in the same issue of *The American Caravan* in 1931.

4. See Robert W. Hamblin, "'Longer Than Anything': Faulkner's 'Grand Design' in *Absalom, Absalom!*," in *Faulkner and the Artist: Faulkner and Yoknapatawpha 1993*, eds. Donald M. Kartiganer and Ann J. Abadie (Jackson: UP of Mississippi, 1996), 269-93.

5. Cleanth Brooks has argued that Sutpen's acceptance and treatment of Clytie, his other biracial child, evidences that he is not particularly concerned with race (*William Faulkner: The Yoknapatawpha Country* [New Haven, CT: Yale University Press, 1963], 298-99). But, as Brooks acknowledges, Clytie is no threat to Sutpen's design, whereas Bon is. In my view, Sutpen's design, like the antebellum, pro-slavery South it mirrors, is at heart racist. Sutpen is tolerant of Clytie because she accepts her role as a domestic servant and never makes any demands to be treated as an equal or a member of the Sutpen family.

6. See, for example, *Lion in the Garden*, 167, 250.

7. For an interesting comparison of Quentin Compson's and Jack Burden's respective searches into the past, see Mary Ann Wilson, "Search for an Eternal Present: *Absalom, Absalom!* and *All the King's Men*," *Connecticut Review* 8.1 (1974): 95-100.

8. I mean by this statement that Faulkner, and readers who have previously read *The Sound and the Fury*, already know that Quentin committed suicide in that novel. Interestingly, in the original "Chronology" that Faulkner appended to *Absalom, Absalom!* (altered in the "Corrected Edition" of the novel), Quentin and Rosa Coldfield make their trip to Sutpen's Hundred in September, 1910, although Quentin in the earlier novel committed suicide on June 2, 1910. Thus, according to Faulkner's original chronology, Quentin was already dead when he narrated the Sutpen story!

Works Cited

Blotner, Joseph. *Faulkner: A Biography*. New York: Random House, 1974. Print.

———, ed. *Selected Letters of William Faulkner*. New York: Random House, 1977. Print.

Dante, Alighieri. *The Divine Comedy*. Trans. Charles Eliot Norton. Chicago: Encyclopedia Britannica, Inc., 1952. Print.

Dreiser, Theodore. *The Financier*. 1912. New York: Dell Publishing Co., 1961. Print.

———. *Sister Carrie*. 1900. New York: Dell Publishing Co., 1960. Print.

Faulkner, William. *Absalom, Absalom!* 1936. New York: Vintage, 1972. Print.

———. *The Sound and the Fury*. 1929. New York: Vintage, 1954. Print.

Gwynn, Frederick L., and Joseph Blotner, eds. *Faulkner in the University: Class Conferences at the University of Virginia, 1957–58*. Charlottesville: U of Virginia P, 1959. Print.

Hamblin, Robert W. "'Longer Than Anything': Faulkner's 'Grand Design' in *Absalom, Absalom!*" *Faulkner and the Artist: Faulkner and Yoknapatawpha, 1993.* Eds. Donald M. Kartiganer and Ann J. Abadie. Jackson: UP of Mississippi, 1996. 269-93. Print.

Meriwether, James B., and Michael Millgate, eds. *Lion in the Garden: Interviews with William Faulkner, 1926–1962.* New York: Random House, 1968. Print.

Warren, Robert Penn. *All the King's Men.* 1946. New York: Bantam Books, 1973. Print.

———, ed. *Faulkner: A Collection of Critical Essays.* Englewood Cliffs, NJ: Prentice-Hall, 1966. Print.

Ted Atkinson

Class Fantasies, Hollywood Liberalism, and the Bush Doctrine in Film Adaptations of "Two Soldiers" and *All the King's Men*

Two months after the attacks on New York and Washington on September 11, 2001, over forty influential members of the Hollywood film industry gathered for a meeting with Karl Rove, the top advisor to President George W. Bush, in an event that came to be known as the Beverly Hills Summit.[1] The organizers were Sherry Lansing of Paramount Pictures and Jonathan Dolgren of Viacom, whom Marc Cooper calls "two stalwarts of Liberal Hollywood" (14); the purpose of the event was to consider how the film industry might aid the Bush Administration in the fight against terrorism.[2] The goodwill and shared sense of purpose on display at that meeting had completely dissipated by the time the U.S. launched an invasion of Iraq in 2003. The invasion launched under the aegis of the controversial Bush Doctrine—a set of post-9/11 policies and strategies including the option of waging preemptive war as an essential component. The war in Iraq elicited responses from Hollywood in the form of opposition expressed by outspoken actors and directors and critiques staged most pointedly in documentaries and films produced in the vein of *cinema vérité* (Kellner 199–219). This highly charged cultural politics also influenced the production and initial reception of fictional films not ostensibly *about* the war in Iraq generally or the "war on terror" specifically. Two such films were based on works by William Faulkner and Robert Penn Warren—namely, *Two Soldiers*, a 2003 short film adapted from a Faulkner short story, and *All the King's Men*, a 2006 adaptation of Warren's celebrated novel of political intrigue and corruption.

A low-budget indie featuring a cast of unknowns, *Two Soldiers* unfolds quietly and sweetly to hit sentimental notes in a show of fidelity to the tone of Faulkner's story, which first appeared in *The Saturday Evening Post* in the immediate aftermath of the Japanese attack on Pearl Harbor in 1941. *All the King's Men* boasted a big budget and an impressive cast of luminaries, projecting a cinematic style that reviewers described as overwrought.[3] *Two Soldiers* received an Oscar without even seeming to try; *All the King's Men* failed to do so while appearing to try way too hard. For all that sets these films apart, though, they do share a reliance on familiar tropes associated with southern poor whites that serve as focal points of historical reflection and regional sites for exploring how the state makes claims on individual subjects as citizens. This common feature, viewed in the context of the Bush Administration's reassessment and revision of core values and policies elemental to U.S. democracy and nationalism, lends an element of timeliness to these cinematic works of historical fiction. Emphasizing familial bonds and blood ties as determinants of class and character, these films explore how the state works to reconcile the balkanizing elements of ethnic nationalism with the broader unifying aims of civic nationalism by promoting what Jacqueline Rose calls "states of fantasy." Drawing on psychoanalytic theory, Rose posits a definition of fantasy not as mere fiction to be exposed as such but as a means of directing individual desires along the lines of unification and affective investment necessary for coherent discourses of nationalism and viable nation-states. This desire for nationhood is consistent with the comprehensive Lacanian model of fantasy as a function of ideology described by Slavoj Žižek when he argues that fantasy not only projects an ideological illusion affording escape from social reality but also structures that reality by animating and organizing desires (7–8).

The pronounced class consciousness emerges in the opening sequence of *Two Soldiers*, which centers on a relationship between brothers—the tandem referenced in the title. An establishing shot focuses on Pete Grier and his young brother, Willie, having a conversation as they move along a riverbank. When the two brothers happen upon a shikepoke's nest, Willie delivers an impromptu lecture, explaining the "special" quality of the bird because it returns to the same nest each year as a matter of "instinct." Willie misses the intended point and instead makes one of his own, remarking that the bird "sounds lazy as Pap." Willie's observation and the tattered overalls that he and Pete both wear signal that these characters fit the conventional mold of the southern poor white. For viewers well versed in Faulkner, Pap's alleged laziness calls to mind Anse Bundren from *As I Lay Dying* or one of the myriad Snopeses sorely lacking the vaunted Protestant work ethic.

The comparison gains further credence later in the film when Pete informs his parents that he plans to enlist in the Army after hearing news of the attack on Pearl Harbor. As it happens, Pete and Willie actually overheard the news while poaching a broadcast of *The Lone Ranger* as they hid on the front porch of a house owned by neighbors who, unlike the Griers, can afford electricity and a radio. Instead of bestowing his blessing on Pete, the father takes issue with his son's determination to serve his country, declaring that his own conscription in World War I fulfilled the Griers' obligation and that Pete's absence will put the father's farm work behind. "You been behind as long as I can remember," Pete responds, echoing Darl Bundren's assessment of Anse's deficient work ethic in *As I Lay Dying*. In contrast, the mother responds by appealing to a kind of ethnic nationalism rooted in familial and local identity. "You ain't rich," she says to Pete. "The rest of the world outside Frenchman's Bend never heard of you, but your blood is decent. And your heart is as rich as any man's anywhere. Don't you forget it." In this case, the national trauma exacted by Pearl Harbor enables a fantasy of reconciled class antagonism. The mother repurposes ethnic nationalism—essentialist rendering of "decent" blood and a "rich" heart—to assert equality in keeping with the ideals of civic nationalism. In the mother's estimation, her son's willingness to answer the national call to arms elevates him from the humble origins of Frenchman's Bend to a rightful place in the broader public sphere of national service in world war.

Throughout the film, this fantasy of poor white ascendancy on the strength of commitment to the national cause finds expression through deeply felt emotional ties that bind the nation and the family through definition of the nation *as* a family. "Them soldiers that died could be Ma or Pa or even you," Pete says to Willie as he explains why he must enlist. "I sure as hell ain't gonna put up with it." Such familial attachment to the nation and the citizenry channels Pete's desire such that his answer to the call to arms becomes unequivocal. "I'm going. I got to go," he tells his family. The other soldier in the story, young Willie Grier, feels strongly that he has "got to go" as well. The centerpiece of the film becomes Willie's journey to reunite with his brother in Memphis, so that he can help out with the war effort by hauling wood and buckets of water just as he does on the farm. Willie's determination to play the same role in the national war effort as he does on the farm derives from his need to remain close to his brother, his surrogate father. For Willie, the pain of separation feels much too heavy to bear. "It hurts my heart," he says to Pete, describing the feeling of imminent and perhaps permanent sibling loss. Like Pete, then, Willie understands the national cause through familial relations and the affective investments that they entail.

The brothers' momentary reunion takes place in a colonel's office at the Army recruiting station where Pete awaits departure on an airplane that he likens to a "gray bird," thus establishing a symbolic variation on the shikepoke that leaves but instinctively returns home. The scene unfolds as a national family drama or, better yet, family romance. In the foreground, the two brothers confront the reality of separation while visual references to iconic American figures—a bust of Abraham Lincoln on the colonel's bookshelf, portraits of George Washington and Theodore Roosevelt on his walls—appear in the background or through cut-away shots. Literally in the sequence, and figuratively in terms of what it appears designed to convey, Pete and Willie, two poor whites from Frenchman's Bend, Mississippi, serve as the focal point of a national cause that would make two soldiers of citizens. Pete responds to Willie's request that he not forget the way home by insisting, "I could never forget; it's instinct," leaving the younger brother, carrier of the prized shikepoke egg, to make the return to Frenchman's Bend while the "gray bird" ascends with Pete in tow. Willie understands by now that Pete's pledge never to forget the way home does not mean that he will come back. Like Faulkner's story, the film ends with overwhelming affect: a close-up of Willie in tears as a soldier drives him back to Mississippi.

In the bonus features included on the *Two Soldiers* DVD, the director, Aaron Schneider, describes how 9/11 loomed over the film's production to the point that it became a concerted response to the national tragedy. Along these lines, *Two Soldiers* might read as a retro homage to the films produced during World War II to boost national morale and to reaffirm the ideals of civic nationalism that Hollywood championed in contributing to the war effort. But the film's release came after the Bush Doctrine had emerged and had been implemented through controversial military campaigns in Iraq and Afghanistan. Thus the reception of *Two Soldiers* derived major influence not from the unifying emotional effects of post-9/11 national trauma but from the fractious debates over the ethics of preemptive war. In this context, the Academy Awards ceremony has been a lively staging ground for Hollywood's cultural intervention, ranging from conspicuous antiwar protest to benign appeals to "support our troops." Schneider opted for the latter approach when *Two Soldiers* garnered an Oscar for Best Short Film (Live Action), arguably because the majority of Academy members had read the film's reference to Pearl Harbor as a point of historical contrast able to illustrate what a just cause for war looks like. "Like a sibling's love," Schneider said in his acceptance speech, "a soldier's devotion is selfless and unconditional and need not concern itself with the politics of war" (Schneider). Schneider's statement seems curious—stunningly so when considering that the film in question conveys such a poignant reminder that the politics of war penetrate and take hold precisely at the point where family ties bind. Moreover, Schneider's reference to "selfless and unconditional" sacrifice seems inconsistent with how forcefully his film's acute class consciousness resonates given the wide socio-ecnomic gap between civilians and soldiers, the military increasingly constituted from the lower ranks to the point that every military campaign now unfolds as a poor man's and woman's fight by definition. In the context of the Academy Awards, such yellow-ribbon rhetoric as Schneider's projects a class fantasy of easily resolved social antagonism that links the labors of the Hollywood film industry to those of the selves whose participation in the national cause as defined by the Bush Doctrine was hardly unconditional and unconcerned with the politics of war.

Schneider's moment in the Oscar spotlight indicates a clear reluctance to ignite a highly charged political moment energized by the change in contextual circumstances from the moment of his film's production to that of its reception. For certain principals involved in *All the King's Men*, by contrast, such wariness was not the case. While *Two Soldiers* evolved into its encounter with the cultural politics of Hollywood and the Bush Doctrine, *All the King's Men* arrived fully formed as a conspicuous vehicle of high-minded Hollywood political commentary. Sean Penn, who plays Willie Stark, and Mark Ruffalo, who plays Adam Stanton, transformed press conferences designed to promote the film into forums for charging the Bush Administration with malfeasance. When *All the King's Men* earned a coveted premier spot at the Toronto Film Festival, long considered a pathway to Oscar contention, Penn took advantage of the spotlight to liken George W. Bush to Beelzebub ("Sean Penn"). The Iraq war motivated Penn's protest, but he was also enraged by the Bush Administration's response to Hurricane Katrina, including the imposition of martial law in a manner that relocated highly militarized Bush Doctrine foreign policy to the domestic front. This perspective suggests a reading of *All the King's Men* quite literally as political theater devised to achieve crafty and meaningful adaptation of its source material—Warren's trenchant exploration of mass manipulation and abuse of the public trust to fulfill an overarching design on power.

All the King's Men has an aura laden with class consciousness, indicating that the filmmakers remixed this one hue among many in Warren's novel to serve as the film's bold primary color. Whereas *Two Soldiers* deploys a remarkable combination of brevity and emotional depth to explore how the state of fantasy compels the poor man's fight, *All the King's Men* approaches the issue through the opposite extremes of broad sweep and stylized surfacing. Through a visual and narrative lexicon of class coding, the film moves on a register from deep melancholy to high anxiety in tracking what Donald Pease, drawing on Giorgio Agamben, defines as an American "State of Exception," a development coinciding with the onset of the Cold War "when the National Security State declared itself as an exception to the rules of the legally constituted national order to protect and defend" against external threats to the American way of life (30). Such a concern would offer an explanation as to why the film muddies the water of the setting through a mash-up of the Great Depression and the Cold War that yields ambiguous temporality. Transported by automobiles from the late 1940s and 1950s, Willie Stark delivers barnstorming speeches of Depression populism in which this self-proclaimed "redneck hick" rouses the rabble to "declare war on the rich," as Jack Burden, played by Jude Law, intones in a voice-over.

Montage sequences are the filmmakers' preferred technique for depicting momentum emanating from the ranks of the working class as a kind of alternative energy source that Willie exploits to fuel his class ascendancy in mounting a challenge to the powers that be. Cut-away shots from Willie to integrated audiences made up of "common folk" looking as though they have just posed for Walker Evans stage a class fantasy that uses mise-en-scène to reconcile historically entrenched racial divisions. Darker hues emerge (literally black and white ones!) to convey Willie's turn from ego-driven populism toward id-driven fascism, the montages now projecting sharp and extreme angles recycled from aesthetic staples of Third Reich propaganda films and antifascist allegories such as *Citizen Kane* that appropriated their visual effects for critique. Through this class-conscious representational scheme, the film places in the thematic foreground the ordering imperative of state fantasies that can work a kind of magic, as Pease explains, by making the legislative mandate appear to be "an enactment of the will of the national subject rather than an imposition of the state" (6). Pease describes how state fantasies "regulate the symbolic order," organizing citizens' desires such that they experience "inherent rifts and contradictions as if they were sources of personal enjoyment rather than pain or resentment" (6). Precisely along these lines, Willie mobilizes the masses to counter the impeachment endorsed by the Honorable (or not so much, as it happens) Judge Irwin and driven by the corporate interests tired of Willie sharing their wealth. "My crooks, unlike theirs, are all a-tremble to be too crooked," he tells a throng gathered outside the State Capitol. "They itty-bitty compared to their crooks." The rhetorical strategy here—the class fantasy—projects Willie as an agent of ideological enjoyment whose fiery populism organizes desire for symbolic, material, and emotional investment in the state such that its subjects imagine themselves benefitting from rather than beaten down by the status quo. The fantasy promotes Willie's state of exception that seeks to validate his brand of corruption as a means to invalidate that of the aristocratic-industrial class opposed to his grand schemes.

While *Two Soldiers* projects class ascendancy as a fantasy that redirects the bloodlines of ethnic nationalism through arteries coursing toward the broader reaches of civic nationalism, *All the King's Men* envisions an altogether different path that brings descent (in every sense of the word) into the frame. True to the form of Warren's novel, the point of view belongs not to Willie Stark but to Jack Burden. Allegorically speaking, in keeping with critical consensus on the novel, Willie's stark transformation to embrace the very political corruption that he originally decries becomes Jack's burden. The film conveys this fall from innocence to experience through gauzy flashbacks that evoke idyllic scenes of yesteryear in Burden's Landing when Jack spent his youth with the Stanton siblings, Adam and Anne, who might as well have the name "Eve," as several critics have noted. Like *Two Soldiers*, *All the King's Men* views engagement with the state in the context of family romance—in this case, Adam's and Anne's implication with

Willie as a matter of tainted aristocratic honor and Jack's as one of misbegotten longing for paternal connection that exposes the full measure of his involvement in a hopelessly tangled Oedipal weave. Through an overdetermined aesthetic, the film aims to achieve the proportions that Warren's biblical and classical literary allusions merely evoke. Such aesthetic excess reaches a crescendo by film's end as the assassination scene features yet another cut to black and white cinematography and a downshift in gears to slow motion for heightened dramatic effect. The culmination of this sequence is an overhead shot of Adam and Willie fatally wounded and splayed out across the seal of the State of Louisiana emblazoned on the floor of the State Capitol, their arms outstretched as if reaching for one another. A close-up shot reveals lines of Stark and Stanton blood coursing across a stone relief of the state and eventually commingling, further projecting the film's pronounced and heavy-handed class coding as the preferred mode of tracing out political corruption. Along these lines, the tragic consequences of Willie's rise and fall and Adam's fall transform the floor of the Louisiana State Capitol into a variation on the ceiling of the Sistine Chapel—an effect made all the more pronounced by the shift back to color at film's end. Willie's frequent invocation of divine sanction as a rhetorical strategy to validate his political cause suggests a god complex that this final shot confirms. The Adam lying next to this would-be god reaches out defiant and defiled as a consequence of investment in a state of exception, holding that the inherently corrupted and corrupting temptation of political power makes citizenship an invariably compromised enterprise.

The issue of legitimacy in assuming and exercising power would be at the heart of this adaptation of *All the King's Men*—if it had one. The detached, paralyzing cynicism delivered in a highly stylized form undermines the emotional claims that the film struggles to make, the affective reach far exceeding the aesthetic grasp. Legitimacy forms the ground on which the principals of the film tried to offer it up as a work of meaningful historical reflection and political commentary responsive to the sense of urgency fueled by the imperatives of the Bush Doctrine. But *All the King's Men* fails to rise to the occasion of compelling political theater, in large part because it falls prey to a self-righteous form of Hollywood liberalism that mistakenly figures conspicuous handwringing in despair as a grand and effective political gesture. Limited by an overdetermined frame that views politics in abstract terms as blood sport waged through class contamination, *All the King's Men* lacks the deep impact and resonance of *Two Soldiers*. With unapologetic sentiment yet timely affect, *Two Soldiers* cuts through the state fantasies it invokes, compelling viewers to think about and to feel the consequences of knowing that blood spilled owing to the politics of war comes straight from the hearts of those whose losses will surely exceed what deeply felt emotional investment in any national cause could ever return.

Notes

1. The meeting took place at the Beverly Peninsula Hotel and included all the heads of the major film and television studios in addition to actors and directors serving as union representatives. See Cooper; Stockwell; and Brady (111–12) for further details of the summit and analysis of its implications in terms of cultural politics.

2. According to Cooper, Rove stressed the following points: terrorism, not Islam, was the target of the fight against terrorism; promoting support for U.S. troops was critical to the mission; the fight was global in scope; the enemy was evil; American children needed comfort and reassurance; the war required an honest and accurate narrative framework rather than propaganda to garner support (14).

3. A.O. Scott calls the film "overwrought and tedious." David Denby brands it "grandiose," adding that it "indulges in passages of languorous funk and ornate literary reflection." Peter Travers writes, "Overthought, overwrought and thuddingly underwhelming, this high-profile misfire makes a congealed gumbo out of Robert Penn Warren's Pulitzer Prize-winning 1946 novel and the Oscar-winning 1949 movie that followed it, sinking a classy cast in the goo."

Works Cited

All the King's Men. Dir. Steve Zaillian. Perf. Sean Penn, Jude Law, Kate Winslet, Anthony Hopkins, and Mark Ruffalo. Sony, 2006. DVD.

Brady, Sara. *Performance, Politics, and the War on Terror: "Whatever it Takes."* New York: Palgrave MacMillan, 2012.

Cooper, Marc. "Lights! Cameras! Attack!: Hollywood Enlists." *The Nation* 10 Dec. 2001: 13–16. *Discovery.* Web. 10 Mar. 2014.

Denby, David. "Power Players." *The New Yorker* 2 Oct. 2006. Web. 10 Mar. 2014.

Kellner, Douglas M. *Cinema Wars: Hollywood Film and Politics in the Bush-Cheney Era*. Malden, MA: Wiley-Blackwell, 2010. Print.

Pease, Donald. *The New American Exceptionalism*. Minneapolis: U of Minnesota P, 2009. Print.

Rose, Jacqueline. *States of Fantasy*. New York: Oxford UP, 1998. Print.

Schneider, Aaron. 76th Annual Academy Awards. Kodak Theatre. Los Angeles, CA. 29 Feb. 2004. Acceptance Speeches. The Academy of Motion Picture Arts and Sciences. Web. 21 Oct. 2012.

Scott, A.O. "Southern Fried Demagogue and His Lurid Downfall." *New York Times* 22 Sept. 2006. Web. 10 Mar. 2014.

"Sean Penn Plugs Festival Film, Rails Against Bush Administration." *TO411 Daily*. Mediasaurus, 10 Sept. 2006. Web. 21 Oct. 2012.

Stockwell, Stephen. "The Manufacture of World Order: The Security Services and the Movie Industry." *M/C Journal* 7.6 (2005). Web. 11 March 2014.

Travers, Peter. "All the King's Men." *Rolling Stone* 21 September 2006. Web. 10 March 2014.

Two Soldiers. Dir. Aaron Schneider. Perf. David Andrews, Ron Perlman, and Deacon Dawson. Westlake, 2007. DVD.

Žižek, Slavoj. *The Plague of Fantasies*. London: Verso, 1997. Print.

Andrew B. Leiter

Civil War Evasions: Race in Faulkner's "Mountain Victory" and Warren's *Wilderness*[1]

In Robert Penn Warren's essay *The Legacy of the Civil War*, commissioned by *Life* magazine for the centennial of the war in 1961, Warren considered the relationship between his contemporary, post-*Brown v. Board* South and the Civil War era and wondered if the Southerner ever felt himself trapped in the regional history of slavery and racism: "Does he ever, for a moment, feel the desperation of being caught in some great Time-machine, like a treadmill, and doomed to an eternal effort without progress? Or feel, like Sisyphus, the doom of pushing a great stone up a hill only to have the weight, like guilt, roll back over him, over and over again?" (56–7). Such notions of racial guilt and regional entrapment were not uncommon among white intellects and authors of the twentieth-century South and contributed to what Fred Hobson has termed "the white southern racial conversion narrative," a prevalent southern autobiographical impulse relative to this racial guilt. A similar sense of white guilt permeates the fiction of Warren, Lillian Smith, William Styron and, of course, William Faulkner, among many others. Numerous Faulkner characters espouse some version of C. Vann Woodward's much used but still apropos "burden of southern history"; however, none express the sense of guilty entrapment with as succinctly powerful of a metaphor as Joanna Burden in *Light in August* (1932). In response to her father's explanation that the murder of her grandfather and brother during Reconstruction was part of "the curse which God put on a whole race" (252), Joanna envisions a tortured relationship between whites and the "black shadow":

> And I seemed to see the black shadow in the shape of a cross. And it seemed like the white babies were struggling, even before they drew breath, to escape from the shadow that was not only upon them but beneath them too, flung out like their arms were flung out, as if they were nailed to the cross. I saw all the little babies that would ever be in the world, the ones not yet ever born—a long line of them with their arms spread, on the black crosses. (252–3)

Considered within the full context of their respective works, the analogies to Sisyphus and to the crucifixion suggest ongoing white punishment and suffering that originated from the sin of slavery—a sin that was only partially expiated in the bloodletting of the Civil War and its aftermath and still troubles the twentieth-century white Southerner in the form of the continued black presence.

Although neither Warren nor Faulkner are writing about themselves explicitly in these instances, the sentiments of individual guilt for the Southerner caught in the cycle of racial history recur throughout their respective oeuvres in a manner that suggests very personal investments in such concerns and contributed to some of their most celebrated characters, fiction, and poetry, such as Quentin Compson of *Absalom, Absalom!* (1936), Isaac McCaslin of *Go Down, Moses* (1942), Jack Burden and Cass Mastern of *All the King's Men* (1946), and Warren's poetic persona considering the Lilburn Lewis atrocity in *Brother to Dragons* (1953). These prescient, segregation-era considerations of history and racial guilt represent one aspect of what were, for both authors, multifaceted, inconsistent, evolving, and at times troubling approaches to racial problems in the South. This essay addresses Faulkner's short story "Mountain Victory" (1932) and Warren's *Wilderness* (1961) for their problematic treatment of the "black burden" during the Civil War. These works complicate simplistic assumptions about racism in America through unconventional protagonists who bear the black cross as it were—a Confederate Choctaw plantation owner in "Mountain Victory" and a Bavarian Jewish would-be freedom fighter in *Wilderness*—but in this process of complication, apologist defenses of slavery emerge. We have a vast array of astute criticism on both Faulkner and Warren relative to their career-long treatments of race, and I do not intend my essay as a summative assessment of their perspectives on race or slavery. These two works do, however, offer insight to the manner Faulkner and Warren could, at times, displace the historical relevancy of slavery and, in particular, divorce slavery from the War Between the States.

I. Faulkner, Slavery, and the Displaced Burden of Patriarchy

Faulkner's life and work exhibited an extensive engagement of southern race relations that is rife with contradictory impulses. Various characters from his fiction reflect offensive stereotypes, yet he also makes efforts to create more fully realized African-American characters, even while cognizant of the limitations of white perspectives on African-American life. In some of his best fiction, he is as perceptive about race in terms of its shaping presence in white minds as any author of the segregation era. In his life, he treasured relationships with Caroline Barr, or Mammie, as well as Ned Barnett, and others. These relationships, however, reflected the racial hierarchical patterns extending out of slavery and continuing through the racially defined economic dependencies of segregation. During the Civil Rights era, Faulkner cogently defended African Americans' right to equality while undermining such assertions with a gradualist approach to desegregation and, at his worst, made the infamously retrograde comment to Russell Warren Howe of the London *Sunday Times* that "if it came to fighting I'd fight for Mississippi against the United States even if it meant going out into the street and shooting Negroes. . . . I will go on saying that the Southerners are wrong and that their position is untenable, but if I have to make the same choice Robert E. Lee made then I'll make it" (Blotner, *Faulkner* 1591). In his essay "Man in the Middle," Noel Polk has written of such Faulknerian contradictions and argued convincingly that Faulkner was a moderate, which is to say liberal by southern white standards, but still a product of southern conservatism. Grace Elizabeth Hale and Robert Jackson have suggested that Faulkner's contradictions can be best understood in terms of the shifting political climate around him. They situate Faulkner and his best work on race in terms of 1930s liberalism, when he could write liberally about race and white moral conscience without having to address an actual integrated space. This "middle ground" evaporated under him in the wake of *Brown v. Board* when he espoused an increasingly untenable gradualist approach. Hale and Jackson present convincing arguments in terms of the changing racial environment relative to Faulkner's considerations of race in *Light in August* and *Absalom, Absalom!*; however, Faulkner's writing in the 1930s still evinced at times a conservative, even reactionary, approach to race and southern history. Whereas Faulkner's comment in 1956 on emulating Robert E. Lee at least acknowledged a continuum of violent racial oppression from slavery to segregation, his depiction of the Civil War-era in "Mountain Victory" suggests the burdensome nature of benign slavery.

"Mountain Victory," first published in *The Saturday Evening Post* in 1932,[2] relates the story of a one-armed Confederate soldier, Saucier Weddel, and his faithful slave, Jubal, who have a fatal encounter with a Unionist mountain family in Eastern Tennessee in the immediate wake of the Civil War. Vatch, the eldest son of the family, is a vitriolic Union veteran who wants to shoot Weddel as soon as he sees his Confederate coat approaching the family cabin. Vatch appears to suffer from some sort of Post-Traumatic Stress Disorder and has nightmares of Confederates with "unloaded guns, yelling . . . like scarecrows across a cornpatch, running" (767). Weddel's simple hope for an evening's lodging on his way home from the war is further complicated when the mountain family's daughter develops an almost instantaneous desire to run away with Weddel, and Jubal passes out from the family's corn liquor. Vatch and his father eventually murder Weddel and Jubal while also accidentally killing Hule, the younger son of the family, who tries to help Weddel escape down the mountain. Although Vatch's lingering wartime antagonism toward Weddel provides the primary motivating factor for the murders, the nuances of the conflict interrogate the collapse of traditional southern patriarchy in terms of gender, class, and especially race.

The focus of the story is not on the aftereffects of patriarchal collapse—the emergence of the New Woman, the rise of the Snopeses, or the racial violence in the Segregation era—that Faulkner addresses in so much of his work. Rather, the patriarchal collapse is played out as brutal denouement to the Civil War violence that brought about such transitions on a grand scale or at least fears of such. In "Mountain Victory," the southern triad of those subordinate to traditional notions of southern patriarchy—African Americans, women, and poor whites—all contribute to Weddel's death in a manner that suggests the burdens of traditional southern patriarchy. Their various contributions to Weddel's demise emanate from their shared desires to find a role for themselves in his life as comfortable dependents. Although I concentrate primarily on the racial aspects in this essay, the gender and class pressures on the genteel southern patriarchy are also prominent. The unnamed mountain girl is barefoot, contained in the kitchen, and beaten by her father when she intrudes into the men's conversation. As Bradley A. Johnson has argued, she serves as a catalyst for the violence by forcing patriarchal attempts to control her sexuality. Her attraction to Weddel and even her invitation to him via Hule to sneak into her room, however, do not reflect the stereotypes of white "trash" hypersexuality popularized in the work of Faulkner's bestselling contemporary Erskine Caldwell. Rather, the girl's interest lies in a more comfortable life as evident in her repeated questioning of Jubal: "Do the girls down there at Countymaison wear shoes?" (757). Likewise, her brother's effort to help her elope extends from his desire to escape poverty and reach Weddel's plantation, which he imagines as a realm of ease: "Do you hunt all day, and all night too if you want, with a horse to ride and nigras to wait on you, to shine your boots and saddle the horse, and you setting on the gallery, eating, until time to go hunting again?" (768–9). Hule's solicitation of Weddel's patronage, however, is defined by a violent resentment manifested in his hands on Weddel's throat and the threat of murder if Weddel refuses to incorporate the mountain siblings into the plantation order.

To an extent, we might read this story as unmasking some of the concerns inherent to antebellum social structure that the plantation tradition masked with its depictions of a happily ordered society, and as I discuss below, Faulkner does invoke aspects of the plantation tradition. The degree to which he critiques patriarchal power structures, merely explores their collapse during the Civil War, or sympathizes with the southern aristocratic "burden" of power is ambiguous. Faulkner further complicates this ambiguity by removing the southern white aristocrat from the equation and replacing him with Choctaw gentry. The combination of a racist Unionist family and a Choctaw slave owner in "Mountain Victory" has been described as ironic racial interplay by early critics of the story and more recently by Lindsey Smith as a complication of the traditional simplistic binaries of black and white in American literature (Smith 51). Vatch even mistakes Weddel for "a damn nigra" (751) based on his half-Choctaw features, which has led various critics to assert that miscegenation fears contribute to Weddel's death.[3] Faulkner clearly intends to challenge any easy assumptions about racism and slavery, and it is worth noting that "Mountain Victory" was published in the same year as *Light in August*, in which Faulkner explores the socially constructed binaries of black and white through the racially indeterminate Joe Christmas. The displacement of the white slave holder in "Mountain Victory," however, does more than complicate racial dynamics; it includes a tacit exculpation and, when this is read in conjunction with the projected stereotypes of gender, class, and especially race, it suggests a reluctance to accept the white male Southerner at the center of the historical problem even while portraying him as victim.

Saucier Weddel bears all the aristocratic trappings of a southern gentleman. He rides a thoroughbred horse with "silvermounted" bridle (745) and, though now much worn from the war, his ruffled shirt and dancing slippers were once the clothes of a fine gentleman. Reading "Mountain Victory" in the context of Faulkner's other Indian stories, Robert Woods Sayre suggests that Weddel's fancy shoes allude to Faulkner's short story "Red Leaves" (1930) and Mokketubbe's ill-fitting slippers in a manner that indicates Weddel's complete acculturation to the plantation South. He has been accompanied to war and back by his faithful body servant, and Contalmaison, the extensive Weddel plantation, cannot be traversed in a single day by a rider on muleback according to Jubal. Most significantly for my argument, Weddel also exhibits a pronounced sense of *noblesse oblige* that is highlighted by the burden of caring for his slave. A hallmark of plantation fiction, the purportedly benign relationship between a caring, indulgent master and a foolish, faithful slave who cares not for freedom appears from the antebellum era through the segregation era in works such as William Gilmore Simm's "The Lazy Crow" (1845), Thomas Nelson Page's "Marse Chan" (1891), and Margaret Mitchell's *Gone with the Wind* (1936). Irving Howe has written that Jubal's relationship to "the 'ole massuh' school is vivid enough to be faintly annoying" (264). I think it fair to take this assessment a step further and characterize Jubal as a gross stereotype who, at best, can only be distinguished from the most facile indulgences of the minstrel tradition by his role as a symbolic factor in the destruction of southern patriarchy.

As Jubal and Weddel initially approach the mountain cabin, Jubal does not appear human from the family's perspective but rather as a "shapeless something larger than a child" (745), and he is subsequently referred to as "it" multiple times before the mountaineers perceive that he is a black man. Described as "a creature a little larger than a large monkey" (746) and possessing "a pompous, parrot-like voice" (746), Jubal's subhuman stature is established throughout the text and emphasized in the last line of the story as he stares down the barrel of Vatch's gun: "Crouching, the Negro's eyes rushed wild and steady and red, like those of a cornered animal" (777). Similarly, Jubal speaks in a heavy dialect that is sprinkled with eye dialect for good measure and suggests at times a comic imitation of humanity. He fully identifies with his owners and their wealth, refuses to believe that his mistress died of the pneumonia she contracted while burying the family silver, and exudes a "swaggering arrogance" toward the mountain family, "which he had assumed as soon as he saw the woman's bare feet and the meagre, barren interior of the cabin" (748). He proudly boasts of the size of Contalmaison and of the importance of "Marse Soshay" and the Weddel family.

Jubal's loyalty to the Weddel family extends from his conception of himself as an essential component to the wellbeing of the family as Weddel's caretaker. He threatens to tell Weddel's mother whenever Weddel's behavior appears unbecoming of the family name in Jubal's view, and he succinctly defines his role in the war in one of his remonstrations to Weddel: "When here I done been fo years trying to take care of you en git you back home like whut Mistis tole me to do" (752). Despite such claims, Jubal is a clear burden for Weddel whose sense of *noblesse oblige* requires that he continue to care for his dependent despite emancipation. Weddel's solicitous behavior on behalf of Jubal's comfort is evident from the opening scene as Jubal rides one of the two horses while Weddel walks to spare both horse and slave. Similarly, he has cut out the sable lining of his cloak to make footwear for Jubal. This act resonates with Christ bathing the feet of his disciples and bears great significance for the barefoot mountain girl who would like to share in Weddel's providence. Weddel also secures Jubal a drink that will prove a precipitating factor in their deaths after Jubal later helps himself to the mountain corn liquor and passes out. The hope of any graceful exit from the impending conflict with Vatch disappears with Jubal in a stupor, and it is at this point as well that the burdensome nature of caring for the slave becomes pointedly established. Despite the father's warning to leave him behind since "he is nothing but a nigra," Weddel will not abandon Jubal: "I am sorry. Not after four years. . . . I've worried with him this far; I reckon I will get him on home" (765). Rather, the one-armed gentleman literally takes the black burden on his shoulders, as he helps Jubal into the barn loft.

Weddel's sense of obligation to care for his slave, even though it will cost him his life, inverts—in most uncomfortable apologist fashion—the realities of slavery while also invoking the notion of slavery as the South's destructive burden, and this inversion has a counterpart in the manner the text inverts notions of freedom. When Vatch mistakenly calls Weddel "a damn nigra" based on his Choctaw features, Weddel responds, "And you fought four years to free us, I understand" (751). Obviously, when a Union soldier makes such comments, it complicates any simplistic notions about racism relative to the Civil War and why it was fought, but when Vatch's racism is coupled with both Weddel's sacrifice on behalf of Jubal and Jubal's death at Vatch's hands, we have a clear reversal of the notion that Union soldiers sacrificed themselves on behalf of slaves during the Civil War.[4] Weddel's sardonic response to Vatch's racism mockingly questions the same assumptions, but it also offers an ironic presage of Weddel's later assertion that the slave owns the master: "He believes that I still belong to him; he will not believe that I have been freed. He wont even let me tell him so. He does not need to bother about truth, you see" (769).

We need not accept Weddel's words as Faulkner's beliefs about slavery; however, the story offers nothing to contradict Weddel's perspective that the Union had no moral intent in waging the war or that the slave is a burden to his master. Faulkner, of course, would go on to produce far more penetrating considerations of slavery, southern history, and patriarchy. Weddel's comment reversing freedom and slavery is itself a precursor to Faulkner's later treatment of freedom in *The Unvanquished* (1938) and, especially, *Go Down, Moses* (1942), where the texts not only conflate and confuse notions of freedom from the human bondage of American slavery with more abstract notions of the human struggle for meaning but also investigate the troubling relationship between these notions in the American South. Even in this early story that I read as one of his most retrograde in terms of race, however, I find in Faulkner's choice of an aristocratic Choctaw planter as protagonist an indication that Faulkner might have felt some unease over whitewashing slavery. Weddel's ethnicity relative to his identity as a slaveholding Confederate is not historically inaccurate. As Lewis Dabney has shown, Native Americans in antebellum Mississippi did own slaves and fight with the Confederacy (8).[5] The choice of a Choctaw veteran, however, is in large part superfluous to the development of the plot. With the exception of Vatch's comment on Weddel's features and a section in which Weddel relates his family history, the text offers nothing to distinguish Weddel from "white" plantation culture.

Faulkner's separation of "Mountain Victory" from his other Indian stories in *Collected Stories* suggests he did not consider it to be in the same vein as his more Indian-focused pieces. Rather, as I have indicated, Weddel's ethnicity serves primarily to complicate notions of race in the Civil War era.

I agree with those critics who contend that Faulkner is being highly ironic in undermining standard associations of region, race, slavery, and prejudice, but he also engages in a strategic displacement in terms of the culpability for slavery. Scholars such as Annette Trefzer, Peter Mallios, and Robert Dale Parker have discussed displacement regarding slavery in Faulkner's more pervasively "Indian" stories as Faulkner's means of critiquing various aspects of American and southern culture, but the displacement in "Mountain Victory" serves an apologist function as opposed to a critical function.[6] Although Indian conversations in "Red Leaves" comically suggest that slavery is a burdensome practice for the Indian community, "Mountain Victory" is far more invested thematically in the implications of such a burden for the patriarchal white South in defeat, despite the story's ostensibly Choctaw protagonist. Even for the popular readership of *The Saturday Evening Post* in the 1930s, the presentation of a faithful slave and loving Confederate master who are murdered by a racist Union veteran would appear excessively defensive of southern history. By shifting the traditional racial parameters of slavery in America away from white and black, "Mountain Victory" mitigates the objectionableness of such a defense by removing southern whiteness from the equation. Looking back from a segregation-era perspective to the Civil War as the precipitating moment for the long southern patriarchal crisis, Faulkner rejects any moral association of the war with slavery while embodying the pressures on white patriarchy in the figure of the black male even as the text disingenuously suggests through Weddel's character that it is not about southern "whiteness" at all. Three decades later during the Civil Rights era and on the centennial of the start of the Civil War, Robert Penn Warren would follow a similar pattern in *Wilderness*, a novel that attacks Northern self-righteousness with a portrait of the war that largely ignores southern whites and slavery.

II. Idealism and Black Burdens in Warren's Civil War

Warren's public engagement with race did not begin propitiously from a post-Civil-Rights-era perspective, since Warren contributed the pro-segregationist essay "The Briar Patch" to the Agrarian manifesto *I'll Take My Stand* in 1930. Despite his assessment (thirty-one years later) of "The Briar Patch" as a "cogent and humane defense of segregation," he admitted that he wrote it with a "self-consciousness indicat[ing] an awareness that in the real world I was trying to write about, there existed a segregation that was not humane" (*Who Speaks* 11).[7] Warren's intellectual approach to segregation and his artistic treatment of America's racial history, however, would evolve over the remainder of his career. Increasingly, his creative work placed slavery and its legacy in the foreground of his examinations of evil, human nature, and human identity. In particular, this evolution is evident in three of Warren's major works from the ten-year span of 1946–55. *All the King's Men* (1946), *Brother to Dragons* (1953), and *Band of Angels* (1955) present a clear shift in emphasis from a silenced African-American background presence that Warren employs to universalize human nature, to a voiced African-American presence that dominates Warren's patented exploration of human identity relative to history. And as the Civil Rights movement gathered momentum in the South, Warren became involved in a manner that disavowed the segregationist sentiments of "The Briar Patch." In 1956, he researched and wrote an article on desegregation for *Life* and subsequently published an expanded version with Random House as *Segregation*. He would remain engaged with the Civil Rights movement, and in 1965 he published *Who Speaks for the Negro?*, a collection of edited and interpreted interviews that he conducted with various African-American leaders.

We have a substantial body of criticism at this point evaluating Warren's career relative to the racial issues that defined twentieth-century America. Ralph Ellison was one of the first to notice or at least to verbalize Warren's expanding interest in racial issues. In a 1957 interview with Warren, Ellison describes an "exciting spiral from *I'll Take My Stand* through the novels to *Segregation*," in which Warren's work "has become more intense and has taken on an element of personal confession" (Warren, *Warren on the Art of Fiction* 34–5). Not all of the critics have been as generous as Ellison. Some have highlighted paternalistic tendencies in *Who Speaks for the Negro?*, and Michael Kreyling argues that "Warren's career . . . is propelled by the psychological imperative to 'speak for the Negro' . . . when the moral imperative is to let the Negro speak for himself" (52). Others have reproached Warren for his tendency to subordinate issues of race and slavery to the thematic consideration of individual identity. Forrest G. Robinson, for example, argues that Warren fails to pay sufficient *critical* attention to slavery and its legacy because "he could neither fully deny nor fully accept the burden of his own Southern past" (528).[8] Whether critics consider Warren's approach to racial issues as problematic or praiseworthy, most have noted, like Ellison, an increased willingness on Warren's part later in his career to engage the complexities of race. Fred Hobson has described Warren's later attention to racial issues as a means of "restitution" for his defense of segregation in "The Briar Patch" (81), and others have contended in various manners that, if that early essay necessitated a redemptive effort, Warren had successfully redeemed himself during the Civil Rights era.[9]

Warren's efforts on behalf of social justice notwithstanding, his writings during the Civil Rights era—particularly *Wilderness* and *The Legacy of the Civil War*—still exhibited a degree of evasiveness when it came to southern history and racism. He had no embarrassing public reactionary moments on par with Faulkner's association of himself with Robert E. Lee, but Warren, too, viewed the Civil Rights movement through the historical lens of the Civil War. *Segregation*, for example, begins with Warren's reverie on his grandfathers who fought at Shiloh, and as Christopher Metress has noted, this personal reflection "establishes the controlling metaphor of his book: the South is once again a battleground, and Warren is among the soldiers, both black and white, listening to their stories" (168). More problematically, in *The Legacy of the Civil War*, Warren postulates segregationist violence as a continuum with the Civil War, although in this case as an "obscene parody":

> Does he [the white Southerner] ever realize that the
> events of Tuscaloosa, Little Rock, and New Orleans
> are nothing more than an obscene parody of the mean-
> ing of his history? It is a debasement of his history,
> with all that was noble, courageous, and justifying
> bleached out, drained away. Does the man who, in
> the relative safety of mob anonymity, stands howling
> vituperation at a little Negro girl being conducted into
> a school building, feel himself at one with those gaunt,

barefoot, whiskery scarecrows who fought it out, breast
to breast, to the death, at the Bloody Angle at Spotsyl-
vania, in May, 1864? Can the man howling in the mob
imagine General R. E. Lee, CSA shaking hands with
Orval Faubus, Governor of Arkansas? (57)

According to Warren, such twisted association—between demagogue and Confederate demi-God, between mob members and heroic
soldiers—extends from what he terms the Great Alibi, or that Southern sense of defensiveness and exculpation about all things Southern,
including the worst aspects of poverty and racism that developed from
being on the losing end of the Civil War. The passage is an acerbic
indictment of rabid segregationists to be sure; however, as David Blight
contends, Warren here "retreat[s] into personal nostalgia" (67). Slavery,
the obvious historic parallel to segregation, is noticeably absent from
Warren's equations for "obscene parody." Furthermore, the description
of the Civil War as "noble, courageous, and justifying" clearly points to
Warren's reluctance to associate slavery with the war. Instead, Warren turns to the counterpart of the South's Great Alibi. The Northern
Treasury of Virtue, he argues, amounts to a blanket pardon for all the
historical racism in the North that is whitewashed away for the victors
of the war.[10]

Wilderness was published in the same year as *Legacy of the Civil
War*, and as various critics have observed, it represents an obvious
fictional companion piece (Blight 59, Casper 51, Justus 250). With its
trenchant assault on the Northern Treasury of Virtue that highlights
Union racism and questions conventional assumptions of the North
occupying the moral high ground during the Civil War, *Wilderness*
also bears distinct similarities to "Mountain Victory." Warren, of
course, was keenly interested in Faulkner's work, which he declared
in his essay titled "William Faulkner" to be "without equal in our
time and country" (197), and he edited a collection of critical essays
on Faulkner's work. In his essay on *All the King's Men* and *Absalom,
Absalom!* included in this collection, Bob Hamblin contends that strong
arguments can be made for valid and valuable intertextual readings
of Faulkner and Warren's work, and such is the case with "Mountain
Victory" and *Wilderness*. Faulkner's short story was published in three
different venues—*The Saturday Evening Post* (1932), *Doctor Martino and*

Other Stories (1934), and *Collected Stories* (1950)—and various aspects of *Wilderness* suggest that Warren was familiar with and invoking "Mountain Victory." Such indicative evidence includes one-armed veterans, characters who solicit whiskey for their Negroes, and fatal or nearly fatal run-ins with poor white families in which a sympathetic family member tries to help the protagonist choose the right path and avoid being murdered. More significantly, Warren follows a similar method of defensive displacement relative to race and the Civil War. As with Faulkner's "Mountain Victory," *Wilderness* engages a series of ironic reversals of the popularly held beliefs about region and racism in America while likewise positioning a black man as the protagonist's albatross.

In this exploration, Warren does not evince the same interest that Faulkner has in the patriarchal tradition of the South, nor is Warren interested here in the plantation tradition and its obliviousness to the evils of slavery. Rather, Warren's protagonist, Adam Rosenzweig, is a naïf whose obliviousness moves in the opposite direction. He exhibits a blind attachment to a notion of freedom that is focalized in his intent to fight against the Confederate States but is divorced from any realistic concepts of human nature or racial dynamics in America. Adam is a Bavarian Jew with a clubfoot who embodies the romantic European notions of liberty inculcated from his father who fought in the German insurrections of 1848, but who, on his deathbed, renounced his faith in man as a betrayal of his Jewish identity. Determined to validate his father's belief in man and freedom, Adam determines to disguise his clubfoot with a corrective boot and travel to America to fight for freedom. A highly symbolic character whose name invokes universal man, Adam and his experiences, as various critics have contended, suggest Everyman and Bunyan's Christian (Justus 252, Moore 150, Shepherd 17). Adam's journey takes him from an immigrant conscript ship (where the accidental revelation of his clubfoot ruins his chance to join the Union army) through the New York City draft riots of 1863 and southward in the employ of a sutler. His adventures culminate with his semi-accidental participation in the Battle of the Wilderness when he kills a Confederate soldier in a skirmish. L. Hugh Moore Jr. has correctly argued that the Wilderness battleground—infamous for its bewildering terrain that complicated the fighting—served Warren as "an excellent image of his philosophy of history and nature—man struggling with the confused blankness and horror that everywhere confront him in the wasteland of history and nature" (159). With an epiphany centered on a newly conceived sense of identity similar to various other Warren protagonists, Adam emerges from the violence cured of his blind idealism by his acceptance of individual responsibility and recognition of human nature.

Reading this conclusion in light of the novel's focus on freedom, Randy J. Hendricks summarizes Warren's emphasis in Adam's transition, "Freedom, particularly, would not be an abstraction to be gained for others in a gleaming moment of identity, but an ongoing existential problem" (131). This assessment accurately reflects Warren's intent as Adam's new knowledge subsumes his emancipatory ambitions; however, this prioritization of individual identity as a concern more significant than the institution of slavery—as problematic as this is in its own right—extends from Adam's initiation into the innate racism within himself as well as the realities of American racism, both of which Warren presents as a corrective to the popular historical legacy of race and the war. In doing so, Warren offers an evasive, albeit not historically inaccurate, portrait of racism in antebellum America that deflects attention away from slavery while positioning blackness as a moral and psychological burden for Adam.

Adam expresses his idealism (and, Warren suggests, his ignorance) about the war succinctly to his uncle before leaving Germany, "Would you have a man stand aside and wait? In America now—this minute—men are fighting for freedom" (13), but his indoctrination into the complexities of racism in America and within himself begins immediately upon arrival as he stumbles into the draft riots. The first human being Adam encounters in his new country is a mutilated black man hanging from a lamppost. This is also the first black man that Adam has ever seen and, when he realizes the lynching victim's race, Adam recognizes the first suggestion of his own innate racism: "With a gush of shame, even of desperation, he thought that as soon as he recognized the man as black, the deepest, instinctive blood-sympathy had begun to ebb. *Can I be that vile?* he demanded of himself. *Oh, can I be?*" (45). Considering the symbolically blank slate that Adam represents in terms of his psychological relationship to black Americans, Warren would have his readers understand from Adam's diluted sympathy that racism is presumably both universal and a natural or "instinctive" reaction to a different skin color. Adam's momentary, disturbing realization establishes the novel's primary tension, as Adam's idealistic faith in freedom is challenged by his interaction with blacks in America.

Adam's engagement with the race he intends to free becomes concrete and prolonged when Mose Talbutt, a former slave, saves Adam's life during the riot and then attaches himself to Adam for protection. Aaron Blaustein, a family friend and would-be patron of Adam, summarizes Mose's claims of dependency and its implications for Adam. After referring to Mose as "your Negro," Aaron reverses the role of ownership or obligation: "the one who says he saved your life. Or maybe that makes you his, and not him yours" (58–9). This quip echoes the assertions of defenders of slavery who contended, like Saucier Weddel, that it is really the slave who owns the master, and Mose and Adam's relationship becomes the defining relationship of the novel, with Mose playing a similar role to that of Jubal as the embodiment of the racial burden during the war. Rather than a genial master, Adam tries to establish a fraternal equality with Mose that would validate his idealism. This effort includes Adam's refusal to assert any racial privilege, his attempts to teach Mose to read, his willingness to room with Mose at the Union winter camp, and his placid endurance of accusations of "nigger loving."

Despite such well-intended gestures toward equality, Adam finds it increasingly difficult to deal with Mose, who takes liberties with Adam that he does not take with other white men. He cruelly names Adam "slew-foot," mockingly sexualizes Adam's relationship to a soon-to-be war widow by referring to her repeatedly as "sawf and juicy" (119), and so forth. The give and take between Adam and Mose in terms of racial etiquette is uncomfortably reminiscent of the racist nineteenth-century aphorism familiar to readers of *Narrative of the Life of Frederick Douglass* or *Adventures of Huckleberry Finn*, "If you give a nigger an inch, he will take an ell." Warren, of course, resisted idealized characters of any race throughout his career, and my interest here is not so much that Mose is imperfect or ungrateful for Adam's overtures of equality, but rather that in his relationship with Adam, Mose ultimately occupies the space of responsibility for Adam's disillusionment with fighting slavery. This becomes clear in Adam's moment of racial crisis on the eve of the Battle of the Wilderness, when it is revealed that Mose, now identified as Mose Crawford, is a deserter from the Union army. Despite Mose's desperate attempts to maintain some sense of self-esteem by explaining that he deserted only because the Union army wouldn't let him fight, Adam cannot forgive Mose and instead betrays his dedication to racial equality by calling Mose a "black son-of-a-bitch" (223). This worst of insults, according to Mose, brings their companionship to a close, leads Mose to murder and robbery, and subsequently contributes to Adam's epiphany on responsibility and human nature. Although Warren views the destruction of Adam's idealism as necessary to his growth, the subtext emerges as problematically defensive and didactic, particularly in light of Warren's Civil Rights-era audience. Adam's development through his "exposure" to Mose's blackness suggests that dedication to equality is easy until one actually has to deal with a black person, the corollary of which is to say that blacks bear a substantive degree of responsibility for white racism.

The separation of ideality from reality that Warren presents in Adam's development is explored prominently on the broader historical level of the Civil War as well. Warren's dismissal of Northern virtue begins with Adam's voyage to America and persists throughout the novel. When Adam accidentally reveals his clubfoot aboard the immigrant conscript ship *Elmyra*, he defends his presence by declaring that he "wants to fight for freedom"—a proclamation that draws uproariously derisive laughter from the rest of the immigrant recruits who do not share his noble sentiments about the war in America (24). The recruits' cynical perspectives prove to be the reality that Adam encounters repeatedly in his journey to join Union forces. The draft riots capture the most notorious wartime example of Northern racism and resentment of the conflict, and they serve to remind Warren's readers that the racist mob violence so thoroughly associated with the South was not exclusive to the region. The subsequent series of disillusioning events includes, among numerous other scenes, a Pennsylvania man's reluctance to drink after Mose on the grounds of Gettysburg; a recreation of Ellison's battle royal scene in a Civil War setting with a Union war hero who delights in torturing blacks by suffocating them in flour while they bob for dollars; and another Union soldier who resents Mose watching a white woman being whipped for prostitution. Such scenes effectively undermine any pretensions of a just war fought for moral purposes, and they amount in their various ways to Saucier Weddel's summary of the Union war effort relative to slavery when he sarcastically comments to Vatch, "And you fought four years to free us, I understand" (751).

The Gettysburg episode warrants specific attention as it both echoes aspects of "Mountain Victory" and represents Warren's most sardonic attack on the North's Treasury of Virtue. Adam and Mose are in the employ of the sutler Jedeen Hawksworth who intends to sell merchandise to Union troops in Virginia where Adam hopes to join the war. The three men stop at Gettysburg on their way South and visit the "slaughter pen," where they encounter three locals drinking whiskey (135). One of the men is a young veteran who, like Weddel, lost an arm in battle and wears his sleeve pinned to his shirt where it stirs in the breeze "like an idle flag" (151). Amputees were, of course, common during the war, but as the men discuss the battle, Adam—again reminiscent of Weddel—declines the whiskey proffered by Mordecai Sulgrave, a disgraced and drunken doctor. When Sulgrave appears reluctant to drink with a black man, Jedeen (as Weddel does for Jubal) solicits on Mose's behalf: "And I'm sure you want my nigger to have him a snort. Yeah, give the nigger a snort right here where they kicked the be-Jesus out of Ginnal Lee. Les have us a drink to kicking the be-Jesus out of Ginnal Lee. Hell, don't a nigger git just as thirsty as a white man?" (141). Replete as it is with racial epithets, Jed's comment invokes a certain fraternal spirit relative to the martial conflict that Sulgrave grudgingly honors by passing the jug to Mose but then immediately undermines with a reluctance to drink after him. Compared to some of the racial brutalities in *Wilderness*, a moment of racist germaphobia might be written off as a minor detail were it not for the geographical and temporal context of the Gettysburg battlefield, and it is within this context that we might also draw more substantial comparisons to "Mountain Victory."

The Gettysburg of *Wilderness* functions as a particularly fitting place for Warren to scrutinize the morally reductive conceptions of the Northern war effort since Gettysburg provides arguably the most familiar touchstone for those who, in Warren's words, mistake the war for "a consciously undertaken crusade . . . full of righteousness" (*Legacy* 64). Warren first links Gettysburg to Northern racial hypocrisy relative to the New York riots when Aaron Blaustein reveals that troops from Gettysburg are helping to quell the draft riots. The Union troops are killing Northern civilians who are killing blacks because they "do not want to be killed by Rebels" (69). Warren pursues a more subtle attempt to disabuse whitewashed notions of history at the Gettysburg site. Adam and his companions arrive at the battlefield over two months after the violence and a month or two before the historical Lincoln would have delivered the Gettysburg address on November 19, 1863, at the dedication of the Soldiers' National Cemetery. Sulgrave and his companions are disinterring the dead soldiers, purportedly to rearrange them for the cemetery, and Sulgrave regales the new arrivals with a mock grandiose account of the battle that parodies Lincoln's address. Union forces turned away the Rebel charge, according to Sulgrave, because "our covenant, it is with the hills. Jehovah reacheth out His hand" (143), and he goes on to explain that "the Governor of our state proposes a great cemetery on this hallowed spot, a shrine of patriotism" (146). The (pre)echoes of Lincoln are clear, but the character delivering the sentiments is such a debased human being that his words are not only bereft of any value, but the assertions of moral sanctification are rendered quite grotesque. Sulgrave reveals that he spent the battle hiding not only under his bed but behind his wife as well. His drunkenness is only one of his various moral failings that have driven him from a variety of professions, and the last the reader sees of him, he is passed out face down in the dirt with his companions trying to move him so they are not caught at the open graves. The implication is that Sulgrave has been despoiling the dead as opposed to contributing to the memorialization.

One could, perhaps, extrapolate from this scene that Sulgrave, as a drunkard and coward who dishonors the dead while espousing moralistic rhetoric, represents a savage indictment of Lincoln's address, but I think rather that Warren intends to criticize the position that the address holds as an iconic moment of American history contributing to the nation's collective amnesia. Such curative fiction can certainly be valuable to the extent that it resists the southern scapegoat by unveiling the national culpability for its reprehensible racial history, but in this effort Warren also exhibits his reluctance to associate the war with race. This is the same gap apparent when Warren distinguishes the Civil War soldiers from segregation mobs in *The Legacy of the Civil War*. The Gettysburg scene of *Wilderness* concludes with a poignantly painful reaffirmation of Warren's attachment to such separation. The surviving Union soldiers have provided what measure of dignity they can to their fallen comrades by covering their faces with any cloth available before their burial. Mose is in the act of removing one of those covers from a dead soldier in a reopened grave when Jed reprimands him for disturbing the dead: "Take your black son-of-a-bitching hands off that man" (155). On one level this is simply an angry demand meant to enforce some respect for the dead soldier; however, it also serves as a renunciation of Jed's earlier fraternal spirit regarding the whiskey—a renunciation that might be read as a metaphor for Warren's presentation of race relative to the Civil War: don't sully the graves or memories of the dead with fatuous assertions about race and the war— or more simply, keep blackness out of it.

As I have tried to suggest, the same might be said of "Mountain Victory" as of *Wilderness*, and the two works do not represent the authors at their best, as their attempts to complicate issues of race appear, not necessarily as justifications of southern history, but certainly as defensive displacements. Nothing in Faulkner's short story or in Warren's novel is historically inaccurate or beyond the realm of possibility in the scope of American racial history. The emphasis on Union racism, Jewish and Choctaw protagonists, and evading slavery, however, cumulatively indicates a shared interest in redirecting critical attention away from historical southern racism and, in this redirection, the authors reveal their own uneasy, twentieth-century efforts to cope with the black presence in the South. Presumably recognizing a kindred struggle permeating Faulkner's art, Warren once rebuked those critics who accused Faulkner of hating African Americans. Alluding to Joanna Burden's vision of the black cross, Warren contends that these critics mistake Faulkner's exploration of southern guilt for hatred of the Negro:

> It is slavery, not the Negro, which is defined quite flatly
> as the curse, and the Negro is the black cross in so far as
> he is the embodiment of the curse, the reminder of the
> guilt, the incarnation of the problem. The black cross
> is, then, the weight of the white man's guilt. . . . The
> curse is still operative, as the crime is still compounded.
> ("William Faulkner" 211)

Every bit as much as Warren defends Faulkner in this assessment, he also defends himself. Hatred is too strong a term for either Faulkner or Warren's view of African Americans. A more accurate assessment would be resentment toward the source of one's sense of guilt and, in "Mountain Victory" and *Wilderness* at least, that resentment surfaces to be embodied in black men and shrouded in historical defensiveness.

Notes

1. This essay was supported by a Lycoming College Sabbatical Leave.

2. Originally published as "A Mountain Victory," the story was republished in revised form as "Mountain Victory" in Dr. Martino and Other Stories (1934). For details on the story's publication history, see Skei or Meriwether.

3. In terms of racial irony, Duane Gage writes that "The story lends an ironic twist to the racial theme of Faulkner's Indians stories in that the mountaineers feel hostility toward Weddel because they suspect he is a Negro" (30), while M. E. Bradford contends that Faulkner plays with the ironies of a French slaveholding aristocrat and the "xenophobic" counties of the East Tennessee highlands (373). For discussions of the miscegenation fears, see Ho, Kinney, Peavy, Smith, and Towner and Carothers. There has been a tendency to overstate miscegenation fears as the leading factor in the murders, and I only agree with these critical assessments to the extent that they consider such fears within a more complex network of origins for the violence as do Towner and Carothers who write, "Racial stereotyping, including the fear of miscegenation, sexual tension, and class envy drive the story line of 'Mountain Victory,' with the victorious 'Yankees' expressing and acting violently upon the prejudices and taboos usually attributed to white southerners" (392).

4. For an insightful assessment of Faulkner's mountaineers' racism relative to the historical record in East Tennessee, see Inscoe.

5. It is worth noting, however, that Greenwood LeFlore, the historical Choctaw chief and model of sorts for Weddel's father who is featured in the short story "Lo!," was a Unionist through the war (Dabney 36).

6. Trefzer argues that Faulkner displaces the narration about slavery from whites to Indians to "estrange the familiar American logic of economic production and consumption" and "to signify on nineteenth-century discourses about 'savagery' and 'civilization' from the more unfamiliar perspective of the 'savage'" (73). Mallios writes, "Faulkner's 'Indians' perform and articulate themselves in a fashion that expresses numerous thinly-veiled aspects of white Southern cultural history, ideology, and narrative" (153), while Parker describes "Faulkner's portrayal of slave-holding Indians as an effort [at least in part] to disperse the blame for slavery" (82).

7. Critics have disagreed about the extent to which "The Briar Patch" should be considered a reactionary text when evaluated in the social context of 1930 and Warren's relationship with the other Agrarians. For some of the better discussions of this subject, see Blotner's, Robert Penn Warren (112–13), Butts, Davis, Ealy, Rubin (233), and Ruppersburg, *Robert Penn Warren and the American Imagination* (29–36).

8. Others view Warren's subordination of racial themes as less problematic. Hugh Ruppersburg, for example, views Warren's emphasis on human nature and identity to be a perspective that encompasses "his fundamental valuation of human beings as individuals with a variety of strengths and weaknesses and idiosyncrasies" (*Robert Penn Warren and the American Imagination* 160). On paternalist tendencies, see Karen Ramsay Johnson and Ruppersburg, "Robert Penn Warren and the 'Burden of our Time.'"

9. See also, Davis, Ealy, and Ruppersburg, "Robert Penn Warren and 'The Burden of Our Time.'"

10. For fuller discussions of the Great Alibi, the Treasury of Virtue, and The Legacy of the Civil War more generally, see Blight (59-79), Burt, Havard, and Ruppersburg, *Robert Penn Warren and the American Imagination* (161–78).

Works Cited

Blight, David W. *American Oracle: The Civil War in the Civil Rights Era.* Cambridge: Harvard UP, 2011. Print.

Blotner, Joseph. *Faulkner: A Biography.* Vol. 2. New York: Random House, 1974. Print.

———. *Robert Penn Warren: A Biography.* New York: Random House, 1997. Print.

Bradford, M.E. "A Late Encounter: Faulkner's 'Mountain Victory.'" *Mississippi Quarterly* 40.4 (1987): 372–82. Print.

Burt, John. "Robert Penn Warren's *The Legacy of the Civil War* and the Meaning of Pragmatism." *American Literary History* 19.4 (2007): 964–96. Print.

Butts, Leverett. "Raised in the Briar Patch: Misreading Warren's Essay on

Race." *rWp: An Annual of Robert Penn Warren Studies* 7 (2007): 63–74. Print.

Casper, Leonard. "Trial by Wilderness: Warren's Exemplum." *Wisconsin Studies in Contemporary Literature* 3.3 (1962): 45–53. Print.

Dabney, Lewis M. *The Indians of Yoknapatawpha: A Study in Literature and History*. Baton Rouge: Louisiana State UP, 1974. Print.

Davis, David A. "Climbing Out of 'The Briar Patch': Robert Penn Warren and the Divided Conscience of Segregation." *Southern Quarterly* 40.1 (2001): 109–20. Print.

Ealy, Steven D. "'An Exciting Spiral': Robert Penn Warren on Race and Community." *rWp: An Annual of Robert Penn Warren Studies* 2 (2002): 101–22. Print.

Faulkner, William. *Light in August*. 1932. New York: Vintage, 1985. Print.

———. "Mountain Victory." *Collected Stories*. 1950. New York: Vintage, 1977. 745–77. Print.

Gage, Duane. "William Faulkner's Indians." *American Indian Quarterly* 1.1 (1974): 27–33. Print.

Hale, Grace Elizabeth, and Robert Jackson. "'We're Trying Hard as Hell to Free Ourselves': Southern History and Race in the Making of William Faulkner's Literary Terrain." *A Companion to William Faulkner*. Ed. Richard C. Moreland. Malden: Blackwell, 2007. 28–45. Print.

Havard, William C. "The Burden of the Literary Mind: Some Meditations on Robert Penn Warren As Historian." *Robert Penn Warren: A Collection of Critical Essays*. Ed. Richard Gray. Englewood Cliffs, NJ: Prentice-Hall, 1980. 183–95. Print.

Hendricks, Randy J. "Warren's *Wilderness* and the Defining 'If.'" *Mississippi Quarterly* 48.1 (1994): 115–31. Print.

Ho, Wen-ching. "The Caste Taboo in William Faulkner's 'Elly' and 'Mountain Victory.'" *Euramerica* 25.3 (1995): 1–24. Print.

Hobson, Fred. *But Now I See: The White Southern Racial Conversion Narrative*. Baton Rouge: Louisiana State UP, 1999. Print.

Howe, Irving. *William Faulkner: A Critical Study*. 2nd ed. New York: Vintage, 1970. Print.

Inscoe, John C. "The Racial 'Innocence' of Appalachia: William Faulkner and the Mountain South." *Confronting Appalachian Stereotypes: Back Talk from an American Region*. Eds. Dwight B. Billings, Gurney Norman, and Katherine Ledford. Lexington: U Kentucky P, 1998. 85–97. Print.

Johnson, Bradley A. "Constructing the Female Gaze in Faulkner's 'Mountain Victory.'" *Faulkner Journal* 16.3 (2000): 65–80. Print.

Johnson, Karen Ramsay. "'Voices in My Own Blood': The Dialogic Impulse in Warren's Non-fiction Writings about Race." *Mississippi Quarterly* 52.1 (Winter 1998–99): 34–45. Print.

Justus, James H. *The Achievement of Robert Penn Warren*. Baton Rouge: Louisiana State UP, 1981. Print.

Kinney, Arthur F. "Faulkner's Other Others." *Faulkner at 100: Retrospect and Prospect: Faulkner and Yoknapatawpha, 1997*. Eds. Donald M. Kartiganer and Ann J. Abadie. Jackson: UP of Mississippi, 2000. 195–203. Print.

Kreyling, Michael. *The South That Wasn't There: Postsouthern Memory and History*. Baton Rouge: Louisiana State UP, 2010. Print.

Mallios, Peter Lancelot. "Faulkner's Indians; or, the Poetics of Cannibalism." *Faulkner Journal* 18.1–2 (2002): 143–78. Print.

Meriwether, James B. "An Unpublished Episode from 'A Mountain Victory.'" *Mississippi Quarterly* 32 (1979): 481–83. Print.

Metress, Christopher. "Fighting Battles One by One: Robert Penn Warren's *Segregation*." *Southern Review* 32.1 (1996): 166–71. Print.

Moore, L. Hugh, Jr. *Robert Penn Warren and History: "The Big Myth We Live."* The Hague: Mouton, 1970. Print.

Parker, Robert Dale. "Red Slippers and Cottonmouth Moccasins: White Anxieties in Faulkner's Indian Stories." *Faulkner Journal* 18.1–2 (2002): 81–99. Print.

Peavy, Charles D. *Go Slow Now: Faulkner and the Race Question*. Eugene: U of Oregon P, 1971. Print.

Polk, Noel. "Man in the Middle: Faulkner and the Southern White Moderate." *Children of the Dark House: Text and Context in Faulkner*. Jackson: UP of Mississippi, 1996. 219–41. Print.

Robinson, Forrest G. "A Combat with the Past: Robert Penn Warren on Race and Slavery." *American Literature* 67.3 (1995): 511–30. Print.

Rubin, Louis D. Jr. *The Wary Fugitives: Four Poets and the South*. Baton Rouge: Louisiana State UP, 1978. Print.

Ruppersburg, Hugh. *Robert Penn Warren and the American Imagination*. Athens: U of Georgia P, 1990. Print.

———. "Robert Penn Warren and the 'Burden of our Time': *Segregation* and *Who Speaks for the Negro?*" *Mississippi Quarterly* 42.2 (Spring 1989): 115–28. Print.

Sayre, Robert Woods. "Faulkner's Indians and Romantic Vision." *Faulkner Journal* 18.1–2 (2002): 33–49. Print.

Shepherd, Allen. "Robert Penn Warren as Allegorist: The Example of *Wilderness*." *Rendezvous* 6.1 (1971): 13–21. Print.

Skei, Hans H. *Reading Faulkner's Best Short Stories*. Columbia: U of South Carolina P, 1996. Print.

Smith, Lindsey Claire. *Indians, Environment, and Identity on the Borders of American Literature: From Faulkner and Morrison to Walker and Silko*. New York: Palgrave MacMillan, 2008. Print.

Towner, Theresa M., and James B. Carothers. *Reading Faulkner: Collected Stories*. Jackson: UP of Mississippi, 2006. Print.

Trefzer, Annette. "Postcolonial Displacements in Faulkner's Indian Stories of the 1930s." *Faulkner in the Twenty-First Century: Faulkner and Yoknapatawpha*. Eds. Robert W. Hamblin and Ann J. Abadie. Jackson: UP of Mississippi, 2003. 68–88. Print.

Warren, Robert Penn. *The Legacy of the Civil War*. 1961. Lincoln: U of Nebraska P, 1998. Print.

———. "Warren on the Art of Fiction." *Robert Penn Warren Talking: Interviews 1950–1978*. Eds. Floyd C. Watkins and John T. Hiers. New York: Random House, 1980: 27–53. Print.

———. *Who Speaks for the Negro?* New York: Random House, 1965. Print.

———. *Wilderness: A Tale of the Civil War*. New York: Random House, 1961. Print.

———. "William Faulkner." *New and Selected Essays*. New York: Random House, 1989. 197–215. Print.

Woodward, C. Vann. *The Burden of Southern History*. 3rd ed. Baton Rouge: Louisiana State UP, 1993. Print.

Shinya Matsuoka

Unsustainable Freedom: The Civil War Narratives of Warren and Faulkner

In *The Story of American Freedom*, Eric Foner demonstrates that freedom in America has been established and guaranteed by exploiting the freedom of "others" (79–94, 130–38).[1] If it is true that freedom can only be found in depriving others of the fruits of their labor and (natural) resources, we could also understand the ongoing issue of environmental crisis in terms of freedom derived from the exploitation of others. According to the principles of internationalized markets, wealth has been transferred from developing countries, which provide cheap labor forces and natural resources, to developed countries, which distribute the acquired wealth to their citizens through markets and assure them freedom as consumers. However, for the past few decades, production and consumption have drastically increased in the economies of developing countries, which are beginning to take measures to protect their own interests in negotiations at international meetings. Admitting that opportunities to accrue wealth, including obtaining the right to acquire natural resources and food, should be assured to developed and developing countries equally will lead to controversy over how one can maximize one's own rights to pursuing freedom and happiness without robbing others of those rights. The idea of "sustainable development" has become popular in environmental sciences lately because of this problem of the "unsustainability" of freedom.

In this paper, I will examine the relationship between freedom and slavery in the works of Robert Penn Warren and William Faulkner, framing the problems of freedom in terms of sustainability. The causes that led to the commencement of the American Civil War surely include the conflict between the Northern economy, based on free markets, and the Southern economy, based on a system of slavery that guaranteed the freedom of only the ruling-class whites. Warren and Faulkner, in their works situated in the Civil War era, depict poor whites and ethnic minorities, such as African Americans and Jews, as deprived of freedom at birth, struggling to achieve freedom, and then failing to attain or to maintain it. Herein, I will describe how these characters are able to attain freedom and how they inevitably lose it. In doing so, I will demonstrate how Warren's and Faulkner's stories of deprived individuals imply that freedom is unsustainable when based on the exploitation of others.

John N. Duvall points out in *Race and White Identity in Southern Fiction* that American Southern writers often create characters who are biologically white but whose behavior is delineated according to the patterns conventionally used for representing African Americans. Warren and Faulkner have created poor white male characters who, by becoming planters, struggle to rise within their societies' class hierarchies. Also, in Warren's *Wilderness: A Tale of the Civil War* (hereafter, *Wilderness*), a Jewish German man named Adam Rosenzweig wants to join the Northern army to fight for freedom. These stories compel us to see through the complicated layers of the characters' realities; class issues and racial discrimination among whites can be observed against the Civil War background alongside the well-known whiteness and blackness dichotomy, the simplified framework often used to discuss nineteenth-century slavery in the United States.

Cass Mastern in Warren's *All the King's Men* was born into and raised by a poor white family. He is asked to run a plantation in the South by his elder brother, Gilbert, who has already found notable success in managing a cotton business.[2] Cass feels guilty about the fact that his freedom comes from the wealth of a plantation to which slave labor is indispensable. He liberates the enslaved people who work for him and hires them as freed men to whom he pays wages (*All the King's Men* 258). This new arrangement fails after a year of struggle, and Cass realizes that running a plantation in the South requires endorsing slavery and is incompatible with the modern idea of wage contracts in the labor force. Freedom for the planter class cannot be maintained without exploiting an enslaved labor force, and it can barely persist if freedoms are shared with enslaved people.

In William Faulkner's *Absalom, Absalom!* (hereafter, *Absalom*), Thomas Sutpen is another poor white figure who comes from West Virginia and was born and raised in miserable circumstances described as animal-like. Sutpen becomes a member of the planter class, first in Haiti and then in Mississippi; he obtains his first opportunity to rise through the social hierarchy in Haiti, a place Faulkner describes as being between wilderness and civilization (*Absalom* 202).[3] When Sutpen follows the path to becoming a rich member of the ruling class in Haiti, he takes advantage of his whiteness; he could not use this trait to his advantage back in the United States because of his poverty-stricken family background. Further, the black people Sutpen presumably enslaves and brings back from the Caribbean region are the primary instruments with which he becomes a member of the Southern planter class when he arrives in Mississippi.

Foner, in his study *Free Soil, Free Labor, Free Men: The Ideology of the Republican Party Before the Civil War*, cites official pre–Civil War documents and news articles published in the North, in which Northern travelers to the South report their shock at witnessing the miserable lives poor whites lead. According to Foner, the poor whites seem to "retire to the outskirts of civilization, where they live a semi-savage life, sinking deeper and more hopelessly into barbarism" (47). Northerners, then, considered the Southern economy stagnant because of the system of slavery and the entrapment of their white brothers in poverty without any opportunities for self-improvement. As such, within its rigid hierarchy based on class, race, and gender, people in the antebellum South lacked social mobility. However, Thomas Sutpen rises through the ranks of this social hierarchy by manipulating his unique relationship to the people he has enslaved, one that began in a near fraternal manner. Faulkner writes of this relationship, "[T]heir skins should not only have been the same color but should have been covered with fur, too" (20), suggesting the racial differences temporarily disappear. Sutpen and the people he has enslaved work together, confirming the sense of a mutual bond among "semi-savage[s]" that have been relegated to the outskirts of civilization.

Let us review recent articles discussing the issue of Sutpen's relationship with the black workers he enslaves. Stanchich writes that Sutpen is driven by American imperialistic ideology when he travels to Haiti and becomes a member of the ruling class there. As a poor white man in the South, Sutpen grows up and lives in miserable circumstances that could be described as "semi-savage." Although biologically white, he lives in conditions of poverty equivalent to those in which other socially devalued peoples in the United States live. However, in Haiti, he can take advantage of his whiteness. He marries the daughter of a French sugar planter not only because of his achievements in his work but also because of the high status granted him as a white man from the United States. Additionally, when he successfully represses the rebellion of enslaved field workers, Sutpen is described as showing his white skin to the enslaved workers through his ripped shirt. Stanchich interprets this behavior symbolically, positing that Sutpen attempts to show his racial superiority because he expects this will prompt the angry enslaved workers to act in a more sober manner and refrain from rebelling further (606). To conclude, according to Stanchich, in Haiti, Sutpen embodies the ideology of American imperialism, in which the United States is the master of Caribbean nations that cannot conduct their own affairs independently and therefore need protection from others.

John T. Matthews insists that Sutpen's so-called "innocence" resembles America's paternalistic attitude toward the Caribbean islands during its period of imperialism in that region. Born and raised in the West Virginian mountains, Sutpen, as a young boy, does not understand the concept of private possession and racial hierarchy. He is thus traumatized when asked to go to the back door by a black servant at the planter's house, and he cherishes his "design" to become a man who orders others to go to the back door. To accomplish this, he uses people around him as instruments. Many critics say that Sutpen's personal experiences, including the suffering he experiences while imposing his ambition on others, result from his initial plan to become rich. They view the emergence of this desire as inseparable from the teenage Sutpen's innocence of the social realities he has entered into.[4] Matthews points out that Sutpen fails to see what he should have already known and, therefore, he should see the truth at the moment it becomes apparent (238). For example, Sutpen should have known that it is a reasonable assumption that the daughter of the French planter whom he marries has a mixed ethnic background. He should have observed that Haitian society has been creolized pervasively and thus inferred his wife may not be an exception. This mechanism of absent-mindedness, or the inability to see what is before one's eyes, is treated by Matthews as an imperialistic variation of innocence (239). Additionally, Matthews concludes that the workers that Sutpen has enslaved have been imported illegally from the Caribbean region (250–252). He argues against the hypothesis of the characters Quentin and Shreve that Sutpen obtains custody of his enslaved workers from a French sugar planter in exchange for the loss he suffers as a result of marrying that man's mixed-blood daughter.[5] Matthews observes that this hypothesis does not adequately explain the two-year gap between Sutpen's divorce and the time he brings the workers he has enslaved to Jefferson, Mississippi, offering instead his illegal-trade hypothesis.

Likewise, Gerend analyzes *Absalom* in light of imperialistic American paternalism. The paternalist attitude of the United States toward the Caribbean during the imperialistic period of the nineteenth through the early twentieth centuries can be understood through the metaphor of a triad relationship, with France as a father who abandons his children, Africa as a single mother, and the United States as a gentle uncle obligated to take care of "fatherless children in need in adult guidance," meaning the Caribbean nations (19). This metaphorical scheme reiterates itself in the relationship between Sutpen and his Haitian son, Charles Bon, whom he refuses to claim as his own. This may happen because Quentin and Shreve, who come up with their hypothesis about Sutpen and Bon's story in a dormitory at Harvard University in 1910, are affected by the contemporary ideological framework of paternalistic imperialism, which includes the aforementioned metaphorical triad relationship.

Eiko Owada's *Faulkner, Haiti, and Questions of Imperialism* offers further insight into the implications of Gerend's analysis. Owada begins her argument by asking why Sutpen faces a massive uprising of enslaved people in Haiti in the 1820s, when, historically, such an uprising had occurred and been mostly tamped out by the end of the previous century. Because Quentin and Shreve, as young narrators, are vividly influenced by the ongoing socio-political events on the international relations stage, in their creative reconstruction of the Sutpen story, they impose their contemporary contexts upon the material concerning Caribbean settings. Even though Sutpen merely mentions he had been on an island in the West Indies, Quentin defines this as Haiti, because Haiti became the center of sugar transactions under the guardianship of the United States during its Occupation period (1915–34). Owada states,

> [T]he West Indies Sutpen journeys to more closely
> resembles the socio-politico-economic relations
> between Haiti and the U. S. during the Occupation
> from 1915 to 1934 rather than those of the 1820s,

during which mainly negative images of Haiti were created in spite of the efforts by abolitionists. (123)

Owada goes on to cite popular publications around 1915 and illustrates how the Americans in this era dreamed of economic growth and prosperity on Haiti. People then believed the island offered inexhaustible natural resources and vast potential for development. Many Americans traveled to and lived in Haiti during this period. However, by the mid-1920s, they realized that the production and export of sugar, Haiti's major resource, had not increased as expected and began to believe Haiti's key industry no longer offered any successful prospects. As our survey of the literature has already indicated, many critics point out the quite powerful role that imperialistic ideology played, suggesting it implanted in people the analogical assumption that Haiti was an immature pre-nation in need of adult guidance and that the United States could provide the needed assistance. It is in this context that Gerend discusses the metaphor of the United States as the (surrogate) father and Haiti as its adopted son. In their narrative of Sutpen, Quentin and Shreve employ this basically imperialistic model of the U.S.-Caribbean relationship and sometimes try—though incompletely—to deconstruct it. Owada insists that Faulkner wrote *Absalom* immediately after the U.S. retreat from Haiti and that, therefore, it definitely reflects the author's understanding of the cultural atmosphere and discourse of the post-Occupation period.

Since most recent critics who direct their attention to the Haitian motifs in *Absalom* aim exclusively to elucidate the problem of the imperialistic relationship between the United States and Caribbean nations, it is worth mentioning that the transition that occurs in Sutpen's relationship to his enslaved workers during their voyage to Jefferson, Mississippi, and the later escape from his plantation, called Sutpen's Hundred, after the arrival of the Yankee (i.e., Northern) troops, has seemingly not been adequately discussed. Critics have attempted to demonstrate how Sutpen acted as an imperialist, making use of his sway over the inhabitants of the Caribbean to gain wealth in the form of Spanish coins, slave labor, and other such assets, to prepare for his future success in the Southern United States. This interpretation emphasizes the white master's paternalist relationship over the individuals whose slave labor he exploits and leads to the view of Sutpen as a prototype for the paternalist diplomatic policy of the United States toward the Caribbean nations during the imperialist era. Consequently, we are compelled to understand Sutpen as a typically patriarchal figure who imports Southern paternalist ideology to the Haitian soil, despite the fact that he was born, not in the South, but in the mountains of West Virginia as a poor white man. It is thus possible to avoid addressing Sutpen's alienation from Southern society and the fragility that characterizes his newly established "respectability" due to his background. Recent criticism tries to interpret *Absalom* in a broader cultural context, to shed light on issues of Southern culture in the context of global American imperialism. Such criticism, therefore, focuses less on the ways in which Sutpen's poverty and whiteness determine his life in rebellion against the Southern social hierarchy and more on Sutpen's becoming an American imperialist whose ideological background stems from patriarchal Southern paternalism. This paper aims to expand the "Sutpen as a rebel" interpretation, examining Sutpen's relationship to the individuals whose slave labor he exploits.

As the abovementioned quotation shows, Faulkner's novel describes both Sutpen and the black people he enslaves as wild creatures with skins covered with fur, making the differences in the color of their skin irrelevant. We should address this assertion carefully, because it was made by Miss Rosa, a character with a biased view of Sutpen. Her personal hatred of him is so intense that she may cherish any inappropriately depreciating judgments of him and the enslaved individuals who work for him, whose behaviors likely deviate from the norms deemed respectable by Southern society. However, this deviation from Southern cultural norms, described as forming a bond between wild men, indicates their affinity with the natural realm and helps them obtain the power they need to produce wealth from the wild swamps and virgin land of Jefferson, Mississippi. Sutpen and his enslaved workers toil together without rest and "carried plank by plank and brick by brick out of the swamp where the clay and timber waited" (28) the materials for Sutpen's mansion. The enslaved workers are called "wild" ones and also said to have "the power to actually conjure more cotton per acre from the soil than any tame ones had ever done" (57). The incredible productivity and industriousness of Sutpen and his enslaved workers stems from their affinity with nature, which gives them the mysterious ability to create wealth from nothing, an ability the established Southern planter class definitely lacks. As implied by the fact that Sutpen and his enslaved workers communicate with each other in a language assumed to be French Creole, they live according to entirely different cultural values. Additionally, the way they work collaboratively in the mud of the swamp and the fields exceeds the Southerners' comprehension.

Sutpen is able to find a niche in the established Southern society because of his affinity with nature. However, when the Civil War begins, his enslaved workers escape from his plantation, chasing after the Yankee troops that pass through Jefferson while Sutpen serves the Southern army on the battlefield (99). These workers reprise the actions Sutpen took when he departed to Haiti, dreaming of amassing wealth that he thought would ensure his freedom. Sutpen loses his enslaved workers, who constituted an important portion of his property and were the source of his success in the South, when they escape to pursue the freedom that supposedly exists in the North. After the end of the Civil War, Sutpen returns to Jefferson and begins working to reconstruct Sutpen's Hundred; however, he realizes that it is almost impossible to reconstruct the plantation as it used to be without exploiting the labor of the (formerly) enslaved black workers, who have long since escaped (136). The only course of action left to Sutpen is to leave all hope of reconstruction to the next generation. Because his only son, Henry, has disappeared, giving up the inheritance that was his birthright, Sutpen wants Milly, the granddaughter of his poor white manservant, Wash Jones, to beget a son for him. Sutpen insults Milly when he finds she has delivered a girl instead. This angers Wash Jones, who kills Sutpen with a scythe, a symbol of the sharecropper's labor (231).

In effect, Sutpen succeeds in climbing the social hierarchy and becoming the wealthiest planter in his region because he has an affinity with nature, which likely helps him work collaboratively with his enslaved field workers. However, this man who emerges from so-called animal-like origins, comes to treat poor white sharecroppers, whose origin exactly reflects his own, like his beasts of burden, tools for reconstructing his once-collapsed dream. This sends his life toward catastrophic collapse, as if embodying the themes of the story of Nemesis in Greek mythology. For Wash Jones, Sutpen embodies a harmonious relationship between the natural and human realms until he shatters that illusion by trying to exploit his poor white comrades. Sutpen loses his charisma, which had not even been destroyed by the defeat of the South in the Civil War, when he betrays his fellow poor whites in an effort to sustain his freedom.

As in the two stories I have discussed thus far, Warren's *Wilderness* (1961) describes the Civil War, this time from the viewpoint of a German Jewish man, Adam Rosenzweig, who believes in the North's cause for freedom, supports the liberation of enslaved people, and moves to the United States to volunteer as a soldier. His father had also wished to fight for freedom and revolution in his youth, but, as a Jew, was alienated from the communal bond established among other German revolutionaries and excluded from openly extolling the natural beauty found in the continuity of German mountains and rivers. When Adam's father praises these natural features in his poems, one of his comrades writes an editorial in the newspaper, countering, "Jew, you have no right to praise our mountains and our rivers, for they are ours. It is impertinent for you, Jew, to say you love them" (*Wilderness* 12). The beauty of nature guarantees German revolutionaries the ability and will to pursue freedom for others as free men themselves; however, Jewish Germans, such as Adam and his father, had been deprived even of the mere right to share their appreciation in a public way. This markedly contrasts Sutpen's case, in which his affinity with nature enables him to forcefully pull wealth and strength from nature itself; it also serves as the basis for the bond he establishes with other deprived ones, which leads to his rise in society and his attainment of freedom. The German Jews Warren describes are shunned, deprived of any aesthetic access to the land in which they are then living. Alienated like his father had been, Adam searches for an opportunity to join the noble war for freedom in America, a move that recalls the black enslaved workers' escape from Sutpen's Hundred to pursue the Yankee troops in hope of finding freedom. However, because his left leg is deformed, Adam is not allowed to become a soldier. Instead, he is introduced to a merchant, Jed Hawksworth, who accompanies the Northern army to Wilderness, Virginia, selling goods to soldiers. Adam has an illuminating realization at the end of the story when he kills a Southern solider. Regardless of which side the soldier has been fighting for, Adam believes he is obligated to rescue casualties. He chooses to carry out this obligation, embracing it as his mission, and he leaves the place where he killed the man. In tracing his path to this realization, we will see how Adam temporarily obtains his freedom by refusing to take the kind of measures that Sutpen took in exploiting the freedom of others.

In his effort to help liberate enslaved black people, Adam travels across the Atlantic Ocean and arrives in New York City. There, the first sight he sees is the corpse of a black man who had been lynched and hoisted into the air by a mob composed mostly of whites rioting against being drafted into a war to end slavery (43). Adam finds that his sympathy for black people, which has until then been an idealistic notion, has faded when he looks at the corpse of that man, the first black person he has even seen. Later, when Jed Hawksworth hires him along with Mose Talbot, an African-American man, Adam and Mose become colleagues who travel to the South together. Through Mose Talbot, Adam experiences his first authentic relationship with a black person, and he views Mose as a human being, not an idealized Other. In fact, displeased with Jed's discriminating remarks and treatment of Mose, Adam says to Mose at one point, "He didn't buy you. He is paying you wages." He then adds, "He is paying us the same wages" (90). In Adam's opinion, an employer and an employee are as equal as any two agents who make a deal regarding the selling and buying of labor; they are not master and slave. As previously shown, Cass Mastern in *All the King's Men* repudiates his right to enslave people as property, attempting instead to establish a legally guaranteed relationship with black people as employees. Similarly, Adam suggests equality between black and white employees should be insisted upon, because, theoretically, all of them sell their labor of their own will. Both Cass and Adam dream of a situation in which the individual subjects of every ethnic tribe receive civil rights as independent members of a workforce under the market principle in a capitalist economy. Adam and Mose contractually sell their labor at the same rate of pay. Indeed, because he sympathizes with his colleague, Adam spends time every night teaching Mose the letters of the alphabet, which supposedly could not be done overtly in the United States, not even in the North. As merchants selling products to soldiers, they head for Virginia, accompanying the Northern army. One day, Adam and Mose encounter a wounded white officer being treated by a doctor. The soldier is angry because his fellow black soldier has saved his life and then died. Witnessing this and then being verbally abused by this white officer, Mose almost loses his composure and begins talking about himself, unable to stop. He discloses his past as a slave in Georgia and tells Adam how he had been offended when he tried to enlist in the Army but was rejected, believing this happened because of his skin color. Exhausted from listening to Mose for an hour in the dark, Adam utters a racist epithet of the kind he had previously forbidden himself from uttering (223). He regrets this, but at the same time believes he has expressed what he truly feels, facing Mose directly for the first time. He becomes resolute, accepting the blame for what he had said and taking responsibility for whatever might happen as a result of his words. However, in a twist that Adam could not have expected, Mose directs his anger toward Jed instead; Mose kills Jed, steals his money belt, and then disappears.

Nothing of this sort happens in *Absalom*, a novel in which Sutpen is rewarded for his insults toward his manservant Wash and Wash's granddaughter Milly, when Wash kills him. In *Wilderness*, the unexpected sequence of events Adam experiences seem almost absurd, and Adam does not consciously realize, as he later will, that somebody else has died for him. Eventually, he will accept that one's life is based on the death of somebody else, and that one's life is already and always connected to the lives of others (230, 302). This realization that one person's existence almost always depends on another's loss of life and freedom, but that freedom is at the same time unsustainable when based on the exploitation of others, is one that Sutpen never does reach, or one he willingly ignores in his own effort to attain freedom. Adam faces this irresolvable problem on his trip to Wilderness.

Though now alone, Adam continues to move south with the Northern army, finally arriving in Wilderness, Virginia. While he rests, listening to the sounds of firearms ringing out in the neighborhood nearby, a group of Southern soldiers suddenly enter a forest clearing and begin to skirmish with Yankee soldiers who appear shortly thereafter. Adam becomes involved in this battle and accidentally kills a Southern soldier. Because his legs are of uneven lengths, Adam wears a special pair of boots tailored to hide his handicap and help him to walk straight. A Southern soldier, barefoot, possibly because he has lost or broken his boots, robs Adam, taking the boots hardly fit for men with sound legs and swiftly escaping. Lying on the ground, beaten and exhausted, Adam wonders if he should rob the Southern soldier whom he has just killed of his boots; unless he does this, he will not be able to escape from where he is, a place where danger remains imminent. When he carefully examines the boots the dead man wears, he notices that they are the type provided to Northern soldiers by their army. He realizes that this man is also wearing stolen boots. Again, he has an illuminating realization: he will walk "out of the forest wearing the boots that had, in the fullness of time and human effort, been passed from one dead man to another" (310). In other words, everything easily passes across borders set and defined by legislative or legal terms. Even the boots exclusively designed to compensate for Adam's handicap, which would be virtually useless to all others, had been stolen and passed on to someone else. This truth that Adam comes to grasp captures the fluidity of objects and the instability of states of affairs in this ephemeral world. For Adam, this realization might overlap with the observations he makes while travelling to the South: Mose steals the money Jed hoards and always wears in his money belt, then runs away from established social strictures, such as that of a field slave in Georgia and that of an employee or merchant. Almost everything, including Adam's special boots, passes from one to another regardless of the will of whoever possesses it. Here, in comparing *Wilderness* with *Absalom*, we can recognize this fluidity of human destiny as an aspect of life Sutpen could not discern. We tend to deprive others when we endeavor to obtain the kind of freedom firmly rooted in secured property. This inevitably leads to endless conflicts between others over the right to possess. If we admit to robbing others as a means of obtaining freedom, we must accept that we may be robbed in return at any time. The life of Sutpen, who becomes rich despite his poor background and is then killed in retribution for this social rise, exemplifies this.

According to Adam's realization, the fluidity of objects and human relationships seem to resemble the food chain metaphor for the natural world. In nature, substances and energies ceaselessly circulate in the interpenetrating network of animate and inanimate objects (302–304). Right before becoming involved in the skirmish, Adam meditatively observes a group of ants working amidst the sounds of gunfire and cannons. Absorbed in the activities of the tiny aspects of nature, he temporarily forgets to pay requisite attention to the human realm. Adam may have recalled his uncle's words, "[The Talmud] says, when two great forces collide, stand aside and wait for the Messiah" (13), which he had never previously been able to accept, when deciding to take a stand for neither the North nor the South and instead care for casualties from both sides equally. In this moment, he resolutely embraces the creed of standing outside two ideologies, and he begins to pursue freedom in his own way, giving up fighting for freedom in order to gain it. This, he comes to believe, is the only way to become a free agent.

One's life is founded on the sacrifices of others, and, often, trade-offs between one's freedom and the freedom of others become necessary. In most cases, this insight comes to bear on the situations confronted by the white cultural minorities that Warren and Faulkner delineate against the background of the Civil War. These characters, in their relationships with black people, confront the dilemma of how people may be robbed of their freedom in helping another person obtain freedom who expects to be kept from it but desperately hopes to attain it. As previously explained, Adam finds freedom when he decides not to further the cause of either the North or the South. He makes this resolution when he realizes that, to be able to stand up and walk away, he must rob a dead soldier of his boots: "[E]very man is, in the end, a sacrifice for every other man" is an enlightening insight that assures Adam he is right in making this specific decision and also in his greater resolution (302). However, if we consider Adam's newly found freedom in terms of its durability or sustainability, it should be noted that it can persist only as long as one continues to take a stand between the two parties, not aligning with either side. The basis for this freedom is transient and unsustainable; by definition, it cannot be positively asserted without reference to extrapolated signifiers. Sutpen, born and raised as a poor white person, establishes his wealth and social status; however, these elements collapse when his position as a master over other poor whites and over enslaved blacks becomes unilaterally (or overtly) exploitative. Adam finds his freedom when he decides to dissociate himself from the North's ideal of freedom and its mission to spread this ideal to the South. However, this sort of freedom must be constantly discovered somewhere between opposing ideals; therefore, it cannot continue to exist in one place in a stable form; it is transient and unsustainable, because it can only be attained when one decides to stand in a place undefined by conventional cultural norms. Thus, I conclude this paper by theorizing that the Civil War narratives of Warren and Faulkner may suggest that freedom is hardly sustainable, especially for those who struggle against the poverty and alienation they were born into as socio-economically disadvantaged whites. These individuals confront and fight for a type of freedom that is, by nature, unsustainable.

Acknowledgement:
This work was supported by the Japan Society for the Promotion of Science (JSPS) KAKENHI Grant Number 23720133, 25370322.

Notes

1. According to Foner, the word "slave" was rarely used in a metaphorical sense before the Civil War period, but later gradually became a term frequently used to refer to anyone who has been deprived of their civil rights as a United States citizen, including economic slaves (i.e., the working class), sexual slaves (almost always women), and ethnic minorities.

2. We do not know how Gilbert Mastern obtained the initial capital (i.e., money and enslaved workers) he needed to start his cotton business. However, it is suggested by Jack Burden, the narrator of Cass's episode in *All the King's Men*, that Gilbert might have committed something close to a criminal act ("How did Gilbert make his first dollar? . . . It is not recorded" [230]).

3. Haiti became the first independent black republic in 1804. American slaveholders in the South at the time were worried that, influenced by Haiti's independence, the individuals they had enslaved would also riot in an attempt to gain freedom. For many decades after it gained its independence, Haiti was "synonymous with revolution" (Godden 686) in the minds of Southern slaveholders.

4. Many critics have pointed out that Sutpen's "innocence" is the determining factor that triggers a series of tragic events in *Absalom*. According to Behrens, the factors that supposedly unwillingly lead Sutpen to his misdeeds against others are often referred to in terms of his "innocence," "hubris," the immanent evil of the South, or "the concept of dynasty." In his recent work, Weinstein gives this an ecological turn by attempting to explain Sutpen's discordance with Southern society by referencing Pierre Bourdieu's concept of "habitus." Because Sutpen internalizes various "habituses" that have formed in places far from the South and joined with each other to form a conglomerate,

Sutpen inevitably clashes with the Southerners, whose opinions and values have been crucially determined by a homogenous "habitus" (16–21).

5. Because slavery was legally abolished when Haiti became an independent Republic, enslaved people were not legally admitted in Haiti in the 1820s, to my knowledge. However, as Matthews mentions, under the Rural Code issued in 1826, a social circumstance that could be considered pseudo-slavery was restored in Haiti (253). Quentin and Shreve, the final narrators in *Absalom*, evaluate the truthfulness of various hypotheses about the Sutpen family, discarding what they think to be false and putting together what they deem correct in their effort to produce a plausible story. Kartiganer says that, with the aid of imaginative reconstruction, the story formed by Quentin and Shreve succeeds in capturing the truth in the case of the Sutpen family (92). I take the same stance in this paper regarding the discussion of how Sutpen took custody of the enslaved people who worked for him.

Works Cited and Consulted

Bate, Jonathan. "From 'Red' to 'Green.'" *The Green Studies Reader: From Romanticism to Ecocriticism*. Ed. Laurence Coupe. London: Routledge, 2000. Print.

Behrens, Ralph. "Collapse of Dynasty: The Thematic Center of *Absalom, Absalom!*" *PMLA* 89. 1 (1974): 24-33. Web. 20 Feb. 2012.

Bloom, Harold, ed. *Robert Penn Warren*. New York: Chelsea House, 1986. Print.

Brooks, Cleanth. "R. P. Warren: Experience Redeemed in Knowledge." *Robert Penn Warren*. Ed. Harold Bloom. New York: Chelsea House, 1986. 27–48. Print.

Buell, Lawrence. *The Future of Environmental Criticism*. Malden: Wiley-Blackwell, 2005. Print.

Clark, William Bedford, ed. *Critical Essays on Robert Penn Warren*. Boston: G.K. Hall, 1981. Print.

Duvall, John N. *Race and White Identity in Southern Fiction: From Faulkner to Morrison*. New York: Palgrave Macmillan, 2008. Print.

Faulkner, William. *Absalom, Absalom!* New York: Vintage Books, 1990. Print.

Foner, Eric. *Free Soil, Free Labor, Free Men: The Ideology of the Republican Party Before the Civil War.* London: Oxford UP, 1970. Print.

———. *The Story of American Freedom.* New York: W.W. Norton, 1999. Print.

Frye, Northrop. *Anatomy of Criticism: Four Essays.* Princeton: Princeton UP, 1957. Print.

Gates, Henry L., Jr. *The Signifying Monkey: A Theory of African-American Literary Criticism.* New York: Oxford UP, 1988. Print.

Gerend, Sara. "'My Son, My Son!': Paternalism, Haiti, and Early Twentieth-Century American Imperialism in William Faulkner's *Absalom, Absalom!*" *Southern Literary Journal* 42.1 (2009): 17–31. Web. 23 Dec. 2011.

Glissant, Edouard. *Faulkner, Mississippi.* Trans. Barbara Lewis and Thomas C. Spear. Chicago: U of Chicago P, 2000. Print.

Godden, Richard. "*Absalom, Absalom!* Haiti and Labor History: Reading Unreadable Revolutions." *ELH* 61.3 (1994): 685–720. Print.

Grimshaw, James A., Jr. *Understanding Robert Penn Warren.* Columbia: U of South Carolina P, 2001. Print.

Guterl, Matthew P. *American Mediterranean: Southern Slaveholders in the Age of Emancipation.* Cambridge: Harvard UP, 2008. Print.

Kartiganer, Donald M. *The Fragile Thread: The Meaning of Form in Faulkner's Novels.* Amherst: U of Massachusetts P, 1979. Print.

Madden, David, ed. *The Legacy of Robert Penn Warren.* Baton Rouge: Louisiana State UP, 2000. Print.

Matthews, John T. "Recalling the West Indies: From Yoknapatawpha to Haiti and Back." *American Literary History* 16.2 (2004): 238–262. Web. 22 Feb. 2012.

Murphy, Patrick D. *Ecocritical Explorations in Literary and Cultural Studies: Fences, Boundaries, and Fields*. Lanham: Lexington Books, 2009. Print.

Owada, Eiko. *Faulkner, Haiti, and Questions of Imperialism*. Tokyo: Sairyusha, 2002. Print.

Stanchich, Maritza. "The Hidden Caribbean 'Other' in William Faulkner's *Absalom, Absalom!*: An Ideological Ancestry of U.S. Imperialism." *The Mississippi Quarterly* 49 (1996): 603–617. Print.

Vickery, Olga W. *The Novels of William Faulkner: A Critical Interpretation*. Baton Rouge: Louisiana State UP, 1995. Print.

Warren, Robert Penn. *All the King's Men*. Restored ed. New York: Harcourt, 2001. Print.

———. *The Legacy of the Civil War*. Lincoln: U of Nebraska P, 1998. Print.

———. *Wilderness: A Tale of the Civil War*. New York: Random House, 1961. Print.

Weinstein, Philip. "The Land's Turn." *Faulkner and the Ecology of the South*. Eds. Joseph R. Urgo and Ann J. Abadie. Jackson: UP of Mississippi, 2005. 15–29. Print.

Françoise Buisson

From the Circle of Time and Memory to the Circus of Fiction: Bolton Lovehart and a Few Faulknerian Puppets

In *The Sound and the Fury*, Quentin's father underlines the reification of men's bodies, which he compares to "dolls stuffed with sawdust swept upon from the trash heaps where all previous dolls had been thrown away" (111). This phrase could also apply to the creatures shaped by Bolton Lovehart in "The Circus in the Attic" (1946), a novella published in the short-fiction collection, *The Circus in the Attic* (1947), which can be read as a parable on time and the absurd role played by men in history. In *Understanding Robert Penn Warren*, James A. Grimshaw refers to James Justus, who "rightly suggests that Warren's short stories demonstrate his ability to express abstract metaphysical concerns by creating compellingly distinct, historically specific narratives" (65). Warren's novella can be read as a historical narrative in which the circus is also a metaphor for more abstract concerns. The word "circus" has the same etymological roots as the word "circle" (*circus* in Latin and *kirkos* in Greek) and can also send us back to a spatial representation of Time as a *circulus vitiosus deus*, a ceaseless return of evil forces, as Nietzsche would put it. In *As I Lay Dying*, the return of evil forces is symbolized by the buzzards, which embody both movement and fixity: "Motionless, the tall buzzards hang in soaring circles, the clouds giving them an illusion of retrograde" (75). Such absurd circularity could also remind us of the philosophical essay written by the French philosopher Albert Camus, *The Myth of Sisyphus*: just as Sisyphus is doomed to push a heavy stone up a hill, only to have to begin again after it rolls back down, thus living in a petrifying, repetitive time, human beings also have to bear the burden of their past, their families, and their own selves: they are doomed to "fall into furious attitudes, dead gestures of dolls" (*As I Lay Dying* 164). One can wonder to what extent the circus designed by Bolton Lovehart, and whatever it may symbolize, can enable human beings to break out of the absurd circle and cycle of repetitions. Our aim in this article is to examine the intertextual echoes between the lives of Bolton Lovehart and a few Faulknerian characters who can be compared to puppets, such as

Emily Grierson in "A Rose for Emily," Benjy or Quentin Compson in *The Sound and the Fury,* and the Sutpens or Rosa Coldfield in *Absalom, Absalom!* If the analysis of the intertextuality can be built around the circle and circus metaphors, the dialogue between Faulkner's and Warren's texts goes far beyond the mere portrayal of characters. The extent of this dialogue has been noted by quite a few scholars, including Joseph Millichap who, in his article entitled "Warren's Faulkner," underlines the Mississippi writer's influence on the Kentucky writer's novella: "the first two selections in Warren's single short-fiction collection—the title novella (1947) and "Blackberry Winter" (1946)—were recent work; the county seat of Bardsville in the former and the white/black family patterns on a prosperous farm in the latter recall both Faulkner's Jefferson and Yoknapatawpha County" (358). As regards the genre itself, the short story cycle, Joseph Millichap also draws parallels between Warren's collection and Sherwood Anderson's *Winesburg, Ohio*, John Steinbeck's *The Red Pony,* and Faulkner's *These Thirteen* in another article dealing with the role of geography ("Robert Penn Warren and Regionalism" 36).

The first part of this essay focuses on the circle of time and memory and especially the ambiguous representation of time, whose apparently linear progression barely conceals its repetitive patterns: the circle itself, based on the cyclical vision of history, and especially personal history, conveys the feeling of confinement and insularity. The characters in Faulkner's and Warren's circuses of fiction are, indeed, often ensnared in repetitive patterns that deprive them of their freedom and turn them into puppets. The second part aims to highlight the role that fiction and imagination can play in the lives of such grotesque protagonists. Bolton's private circus provides a good example of the principles defined by Donald Woods Winnicott in *Playing and Reality*, for the circus can be likened to a transitional space, a way of facing up to the circle of time and entropy without being harmed. Yet the fact that the circus is a metaphor for the struggle against time and for the sublimation of reality also gives a metafictional dimension to the novella, which can be read as an illustration of what Linda Hutcheon calls "historiographic metafiction." Like *Absalom, Absalom!*, it gives the reader food for thought on the unreliable rewriting of history, and, like *The Sound and the Fury*, it seems to imply that all life ends in fiction, or even in farce, if one takes into account the comic dimension of Faulkner's short story "My Grandmother Millard," the parody of a romance rich in mock-heroic overtones aimed at debunking war.

The circle of time and memory

Paradoxically, the representation of time in "The Circus in the Attic" proves to be both linear and circular: the reader is presented with historical landmarks; the dates referring to personal or collective histories are intermingled, which contributes to the blurring of the chronology of events. Quite significantly, Bolton, who seems indifferent towards time despite—or rather because of—the few events of his life having occurred outside the orbit of his house or of his attic, perceives time as an accumulation of days: "And years are nothing but so many days laid end to end" (37). After the death of his father, who had taken part in the Civil War, he realizes that he has failed to build up an accurate and useful knowledge of his family's history and of his own roots: "But he knew that it was too late, he would never know those things, for they were slipping through his fingers like a handful of water dropping into dry sand" (29). The water and sand image can send us back to Quentin's experience of Time when he imagines his "murmuring bones and the deep water like wind . . . [his] bones upon the lonely and inviolate sand" (*The Sound and the Fury* 51). Like Quentin, who also associates sand with sexual isolation and thus barrenness, Bolton would like to find eternity through dissolution into water, which symbolizes the ebb and flow of Time, the cyclical succession of days and nights that lulls him to death: "He wanted to lie here forever, lapped in the long, soft rhythm of day and night, like a tide" ("The Circus in the Attic" 23). The dotted line of events inevitably leads to death and Time is personified as the Reaper, a skeleton standing for the triumph of Thanatos and entropy, which is the result of some cold, mathematical determinism: "the austere, logical articulation of fact with fact in the skeleton of Time" ("The Circus in the Attic" 28). This description of Time seems to be echoed in the portrayal of Dilsey and her body's degradation even if she "endures" through time: "her skeleton rose" (*The Sound and the Fury* 165), "her fallen cheeks . . . the myriad coruscations of immolation and abnegation and time" (183). Death is, nonetheless, part of the repetitive pattern of Time, and both Faulkner and Warren also comprehend temporality as a cycle of repetitions: the circus as a show is a symbol of cyclical returns, since, as a peripatetic performance, it usually comes and goes. In "The Circus in the Attic," the narrative includes a series of repetitive, even ritualized episodes, such as Bolton's acts of rebellion: his baptism performed by a Baptist preacher testifies to his iconoclastic attitude towards his mother's religion. He then decides to run away with the circus and the menagerie, which is his second subversive gesture, before his flight into literature and "circus-making," which is regarded as an attempt at "taking his own wings."

Despite such rebellious and carnivalesque episodes, there is nothing new under the sun and the Heraclitean flux of Time brings nothing but sameness and repetition, as is suggested by intratextual echoes: "Once back home, everything was as it had been before" ("The Circus in the Attic" 26); "Everything was as though nothing had happened" (35). The making of the circus results in his final confinement in the attic, the place of memories. He has come full circle: "Finally he had found his way back" (60). The frequent use of the iterative mode petrifies his actions and turns him into a puppet: "the show was on, he would slip to the door of the theatre and stand in the shadow, and peer through a crack in the heavy red curtain at the screen" (38). Ironically, the movie theatre, which seems to have replaced the circus as a form of entertainment, symbolizes, through the very kinetic quality of films, the flux of Time and modernity from which Bolton, hiding in the wings, is doomed to stand aloof. His voyeuristic attitude is ritualized and makes of him a monomaniac. The narrator's play with all tenses— past, present, and future—often conveys the ritualization of Bolton's movements, as well as his submission to repetitive patterns, and more generally, his lack of willpower. He is psychologically controlled by his mother and physically manipulated by his first girlfriend, Sara Darter. One of the major topics, betrayal, also causes the narrative to be built around repetitive effects: Bolton tries to "betray" his mother several times; when she dies, his mother feels betrayed by her own body, and especially her heart; as for Bolton, he is betrayed by his wife who dies with her lover in a car accident. His life is characterized by a to-and-fro movement between the attic and the outside world; he is both at the center and on the margins of the community. In *The Sound and the Fury*, Benjy also lives in ritualized time: at the end of the novel, he cannot bear the change in the circular movement around the statue of the Confederate soldier: "his [Benjy's] eyes were empty and blue and serene again as cornice and façade flowed smoothly once more from left to right, post and tree, window and doorway and signboard each in its ordered place" (199). In fact, the whole South seems to be caught in a petrifying, repetitive time. Both Faulkner and Warren depict frozen tableaux of their characters which give the illusion of permanence. In "A Rose for Emily," the eponymous heroine appears to be "framed" by her father into a rigid position, "her upright torso motionless as that of an idol . . . We had long thought of them as a tableau, Miss Emily a slender figure in white in the background, her father a spraddled silhouette in the foreground, his back to her and clutching a horsewhip, the two of them framed by the back-flung door" ("A Rose for Emily" 123). The daughter and her father can be respectively compared to a dancer or girl acrobat and to a tamer or ring master, which implies that they are locked in a kind of perverse incestuous relationship that proves quite similar to the relationship between Bolton and his mother. In "The Circus in the Attic," the reader is given a perfect, idyllic image of the Lovehart family, and the present tense reinforces this illusion of eternal happiness: "As we look back on them, down the sixty years, they scarcely seem to move at all, to be fixed there in a photograph in an album to prove something sweet and sure about the past" (17). The fallacious representation is thus obliquely denounced by the narrator. In Professor Darter's house, while being sexually initiated by Sara, Bolton feels spied on by "the serried eyes of dead grandfathers and grandmothers" (35). The ancestors' pictures also suggest sameness and repetition, as if the series of pictures had been designed by Andy Warhol. Warren was obsessed with both the Heraclitean flux of Time and the still moment: "You have the sense of the small becoming large in time, the large becoming small, the sweep of time over things. That, and the balance of the frozen, abstracted moment against violent significant action" (*Robert Penn Warren Talking* 41). This balance between stillness and movement is one of the tensions at work both in his fiction and Faulkner's, and is to some extent embodied by Emily Grierson, whose mask—that of the pure and vulnerable girl trapped in the past—conceals her violent nature. Repetition itself implies both sameness and movement, epitomized by Sutpen "galloping through avatars which marked the accumulation of years, time, to the fine climax where it galloped without weariness or progress, forever and forever immortal" (*Absalom, Absalom!* 231): the flux of linear time merges with circularity and results in the final frozen tableau conveying permanence and eternity.

The repetitive patterns most certainly lead to confinement and endogamy. Lem Lovehart, the pioneer figure, is one of Mrs Parton's ancestors; yet, Mrs Parton, a widow, has married Bolton. Such marriage bonds testify to the characters' inability to break out of the family circle: "For Lovehart blood was in her veins, too. She, too, was descended from old Lem Lovehart, by the daughter he had left when the Chickasaw scalped him" ("The Circus in the Attic" 48). Moreover, Bolton finds it impossible to break out of the grotesque circular— womblike— relationship that usually traps the mother and her child: "the powerful, vibrating, multitudinous web of life which binds the woman and the child together, victor and victim" ("The Circus in the Attic" 17). Such webs of life also weave secret relations between brothers and sisters in Faulkner's novels, Quentin, Benjy, and Caddy in *The Sound and the Fury*, or Henry, Charles, and Judith in *Absalom, Absalom!* John T. Irwin has studied the temporal consequences of "doubling and incest," which "evoke the way in which the circle of the self-enclosed repeats itself through time as a cycle, the way that the inability to break out of the ring of the self and the family becomes the inability of successive generations to break out of the cyclic repetition of self-enclosure" (59). Faulknerian characters cannot escape from the family ring that fences in each member and that is symbolized by Benjy waiting for Caddy behind the fence of the family's property. Neither can they escape from what they perceive as a curse on the successive generations. Space itself is circular and often consists of a shrinking dark house in which characters—the prisoners of time and memory—are secluded. At the end of Warren's novella, Bolton can no longer bear the ghostlike presence of the creatures he has shaped. Their eyes remind him of his mother's panoptic tyranny. Since they are slaves to repetitive time and ritualized events, the grotesque characters often behave as mechanically as puppets trying to pull one another's strings.

The circus of fiction and its grotesque protagonists

The circus in Warren's fiction was inspired by a real miniature circus designed by John Wesley Venable, born in the 1880s in Hopkinsville. "As a museum piece," Patricia Bradley mentions, "Venable's circus, which Warren evidently never saw, is singularly unprepossessing. Some of the figures are no more than magazine and newspaper cutouts mounted on pasteboard" (*Circus Aesthetic* 53). Because of the *collage* technique, one may reasonably assume that the figures are coarse-textured and thus distorted. Bolton's circus itself provides him with a grotesque vision of mankind which falls prey to anamorphoses. Patricia Bradley shows that the creatures shaped by Bolton are replicas of the main protagonists: Bolton stands for the clown (or a scarecrow); Mrs. Parton, his wife, embodies the girl acrobat through her sensuality, and her son, Jasper, is the "ring master come to life" (*Circus Aesthetic* 6). Bradley also underlines the relevance of the circus trope in *The Sound and the Fury*: Caddy and her daughter, Quentin, can be described as aerialists or fliers, whereas Jason is a kind of clown. She also mentions that the Jason section is "a struggle for identity within a circuslike hierarchy" (*Circus Aesthetic* 78). André Bleikasten has also defined *The Sound and the Fury* as "a burlesque Southern melodrama" (147), with Jason as the comic villain, Benjy as the drooling idiot, the sister and niece as trollops, the father and uncle as alcoholics, and the mother as the hypochondriac type. Such clownish features reduce their story to "the ludicrous proportions of a madhouse chronicle" (Bleikasten 148). These monomaniacs behave all the more as puppets since they are stranded in the past and cling to their rituals. Referring to Bergson, who "delineates the comic character as that which acts mechanically, predictably, single-mindedly," Fred Chappel concludes that the Compsons "are in fact so one-purposed that they *never* change" (385).

Some characters are even portrayed as if they were mechanical toys: Rosa Coldfield looks reified and her limbs have the rigidity of puppets': "her legs hung straight and rigid as if she had iron shinbones and ankles" (*Absalom, Absalom!* 3). She is compared to a doll living in a doll-sized house where she hides Henry, an act of resistance or even rebellion that is part of a repetitive pattern since she also hid her father during the Civil War. The reader is thus plunged into a labyrinth of embedded stories dealing with isolation and seclusion, which may be construed as an attempt at escaping from the chaos of History. The stories are literary *mises en abyme* of the different circuses of fiction peopled with grotesque figures: the cave-like or womb-like house, and the tomb-like chamber in "A Rose for Emily." The reference to the cave appears all the more relevant as the adjective "grotesque" comes from the Italian word, "grottes," which means "caves," because of the decorative elements found in grottoes (Cuddon 295). The attic—the transitional space—gives Bolton the opportunity to shape and dominate the world, at least symbolically, as if he were a demiurge. He is yearning to see the world with God's eyes. Looking at maps generates a feeling of omnipotence: by reducing the world to a circus, he can enjoy his own power over the world.

The circus is halfway between Apollinian order and Dionysian chaos, for it requires both discipline and subversion. It can also be perceived as the transitional space depicted by Winnicott in *Playing and Reality*. Games make it possible for the child to deal with reality obliquely, without being harmed, and to make up for a loss of omnipotence. Bolton's circus is a private space that gives him a feeling of bliss, which can be likened to the poet's epiphany in William Faulkner's short story, "Carcassonne": "he felt, for one moment, up there above the world, the peace and purity of spirit that comes when vision and cunning are commensurate" ("The Circus in the Attic" 42). The making of the circus can also be perceived as a quest for both entertainment and distraction, which, according to the French philosopher Blaise Pascal, consists in negatively turning away from reality. Whereas Bolton feels deprived in the real world, he fulfils himself in the attic and proves to have a true self—expressed in the attic—and what Winnicott calls a false self—expressed outside the attic—under the community's or the mother's eyes. Patricia Bradley asserts that Bolton Lovehart is somehow also Warren's self-projection, "something of a portrait of Warren as a young modernist" and that Mrs. Parton also "crafts her own image" ("Choosing Sides During the Culture Wars" 41) as a girl acrobat who aims at climbing the social ladder to some extent by resorting to popular art. This use of the trope conveys Warren's ambivalence towards the circus, which, Bradley shows, contributed to fuelling American conservative ideologies. As for Joseph Blotner, he thinks that Bolton is the projection of another self, for he yearns to be the historian Warren might have been: "Had Robert Penn Warren been submissive rather than powerfully self-assertive, he might have become a historian of Todd country" (235). The circus unmistakably symbolizes Warren's quest for a form of artistic sublimation which does not exclude history.

In Nietzschean terms, the making of the circus can be praised not only as a way of withstanding negative forces but also as a Dionysiac revenge against the order imposed by the mother and, to a larger extent, by religious and social convictions. The real circus is undoubt-edly associated with paganism and subversion: "a flame-streaked Dionysiac revelry" (24). Creativity enables Bolton, "a clever puppet" (16)—which sounds like a contradiction in terms—to face up to exter-nal reality. He later sells the circus and is thus led to share it with the community: "The death of Jasper had brought the secret circus out into the world to live, to be enjoyed, to be used and broken in the end" (55). The circus turns into a collective experience, as if Bolton had managed to adjust to reality. While it can be regarded as a form of redemption, as Bradley suggests, the dismantled circus can also symbolize "the most splendid failure," if one may use the famous phrase coined by Faulkner to describe *The Sound and the Fury* (*Faulkner in the University* 77): "The circus is broken up, parcelled out, and never really appreciated for what it has meant to Bolton's survival. Bolton's final return to his attic could very well signify that he has been defeated in his attempt to convert imaginative illusion into a lasting human reality" (Bradley, *Circus Aesthetic* 19). The end of the novella does tend to suggest that the tran-sitional space symbolized by the circus in the attic is actually a kind of deadlock or "terminal space". It proves ambiguous, since Bolton's private space seems to be literally "invaded" by his creation, which he no longer controls. He thus fails to become the puppet master and to come out of the attic. Undoubtedly Bolton enjoys some success when he decides to sell the circus and to give the money to the Red Cross; yet, artistic experience or at least artistic craftsmanship—which reminds us of Cash's craftsmanship in *As I Lay Dying*—cuts off the maker from the world, and Warren seems to imply that the artist figure cannot stay in his ivory tower. Bolton is the architect of a circus in which he is himself doomed to play the role of a puppet. Emily Grierson is also the architect of the stage on which she kills her lover, Homer Barron, but she also becomes a skeleton in the bedroom. Bolton and Emily are both "artistes manqués" in their own nooks and corners of fiction. The interest of such stories also lies in their metafictional dimensions, since the writer, whether Faulkner or Warren, is the master of his own fictional circus rich in histrionic figures, such as Thomas Sutpen, a would-be creator, "a madman who creates within his very coffin walls his fabulous immeasurable Camelots and Carcassonnes" (*Absalom, Absalom!* 129).

The circus metaphor and the metafictional dimension

Bolton is interested in the writing of history, and the fact that he is both interested in "the Pastime of Past Time" (Linda Hutcheon) and the making of his private circus has ironical overtones, turning the novella into a piece of historiographic metafiction. Bolton is a failed historian who never manages to write his book of local history. He only accumulates information but refrains from giving any interpretation to the facts he reports, and his vision of history proves to be shallow and distorted. For example, in a chapter ironically entitled "The Coming of the Fathers," he pays a tribute to the pioneers and founders of Bardsville, the poets' city, but his knowledge is quite biased and restrictive. He dodges all hermeneutic issues. His interest in geography is all the more paradoxical since, far from being a trailblazer, he does not even try to match geographical reality with its representation on maps, which is a kind of secondhand knowledge: "He had never seen mountains, only pictures" (27). Fleeing from reality and interpretation, he is mired in representation and empiricism, or he transforms any form of reality into his own fiction. Rosa Coldfield is also a failed artist: as a poetess laureate, she is a champion of the Lost Cause and she contributes to rebuilding the myth of the South. Yet the whole world is a stage on which Sutpen is compelled to wear "the mask in Greek tragedy, interchangeable not only from scene to scene, but from actor to actor and behind which the events and occasions took place without chronology or sequence" (*Absalom, Absalom!* 49). Sutpen is thus described as if he were a performer acting over and over again in a peripapetic circus of fiction, out of time and out of place. Human beings are dehumanized, dismantled puppets or dolls, "diffused and scattered creatures drawn blindly limb from limb from a grab bag and assembled" (71). Thomas Sutpen's design tries to imitate Southern fiction: to some extent, his achievement is a kind of architext, or even hypertext, juxtaposed upon the traditional Southern text. He aims to create his own dynasty, and the children he gave birth to are portrayed as mere fictional representations: "the three of us are just illusions that he begot, and your illusions are a part of you like your bones and flesh and memory" (277).

Memory is unreliable and "The Circus in the Attic" exemplifies the failure of memorialization. The attic is a dumping-ground for a lot of objects referring to different stages of United States history, such as arrowheads or the flag, as if the attic were a miniature or toy museum. The dark space represents a kind of "synchronic time" in which memories and souvenirs are juxtaposed in utter confusion, which reminds us once again of the *collage* technique. The impression of chronological chaos is conveyed by the end of the novella, with its catalogue of dead creatures, including the little kitten Bolton's mother killed when she was a little girl. This ironical detail reveals the narrator's intention to undermine the seriousness of his historical discourse. The narrative technique aims to show the unreliability of historical narratives—and of any narrative actually—for the heterodiegetic narrator throws an ironical light on the way the inhabitants of Bardsville rewrite their history: the United Daughters of the Confederacy are portrayed as "the repositories of the ignorance of history" (5).

Right from the start, the narrator highlights the fictional dimension of his narrative: "Let us assume that it is summer" (3). And then the novella begins with a travel sequence that clearly manipulates the reader's attention. He debunks some local celebrities' heroic dimensions: Cassius Perkins and Seth Sykes are two Civil War heroes whose glory is based on lies and misunderstandings; as young boys, they already behaved like "circus performers"; Seth Sykes was killed because he wanted to save his corn—he was probably more a champion of the Corn Cause than of the Lost Cause! Hence the bitter and ironical conclusion drawn by the narrator: "That was the truth about Seth Sykes and how he became a hero" (12). Ironically, the witness who knew part of the truth about the episode is an outcast, a tramp and a grotesque figure who "spat and sank back, silent for a moment, into the miasma of rotgut and time" (7). The zeugma, which incongruously combines time with cheap alcohol, sounds like a particularly subversive desecration of the past. History, far from being a cycle of heroic achievements, is just a circle of fictions: even the fighters look like toy soldiers (5). As Joseph Millichap puts it, "Warren's vision of history is a circus. The Battle of Bardsville, Bolton's baptism, Bardsville's picture show, its Armistice night, 'nigger town,' the home front, and newsreels of the Second World War—all are described in vivid circus imagery" (Millichap, *A Study of the Short Fiction* 15). The monument erected in 1917 to celebrate the local heroes' courage is founded on lies and blindness, which seems to have an intertextual connection with the Confederate Soldier's blind eye at the end of *The Sound and the Fury*.

Faulkner debunks Southern monumentalism, and through his choice of unreliable homodiegetic narrators, through monologues and contrapuntal narratives, he questions our ability to write history without undermining its possible truth. The reading of Faulkner's novels is quite often both linear and circular, since the end compels us to read the story over and over again: to some extent, they are a *mise en abyme* of the narrative pact because they dramatize the way narrators can play with readers, who are also handled as if they were puppets. Yet, according to Jonathan Cullick, whose study is devoted to Warren's historical constructions, "Warren demythicizes the historical figure while he also expresses the need for something in history that appeals to the human need for meaning" (86): he establishes an interesting distinction between "debunking" and "demythicizing." The "demythicizing process" can be seen as a kind of humanistic re-creation: "The merely heroic becomes fully human. The demythicizing process reconciles the disjunction between idealism and realism" (156). The return to a realistic form of narrative through demythicizing can be perceived in Faulkner's short stories about the Civil War, such as "My Grandmother Millard." Symbolically, the children have to comply with a ritual consisting in bringing down the big trunk from the attic, which symbolizes the past once again, and then in hiding the silver in the trunk before burying it: they are rehearsing or "performing" before the Northern soldiers' arrival and, indirectly, caught in the cycle of rituals, they never stop burying the South. At the end of the short story, the grandmother, whose spectacles may convey her short-sightedness or lack of projection into the future, also decides to hide the clock in the trunk, which to some extent is a way of putting an end to the flux of Time and of locking the South into the circle of fiction.

Rosa Millard also rewrites Southern history: fiction meets reality since she compels General Forrest to write false reports so that a Southern soldier, "cousin Philip," unfortunately named "Backhouse," can be reported to be dead, change his name, and marry the stereotyped Southern Belle, "cousin Melisandre," who can be compared to "a mad woman in the attic" ever since she was the victim of an explosion in the outhouse. Ironically, the war hero, N.B. Forrest, invents a battle to account for the soldier's so-called death: "'Now I've got to have a battle', he said. 'Another sheet, son'" (696). Instead of waging a battle, he is "writing" it, actually writing fiction into history. By blurring the boundaries between history and fiction, Faulkner obliquely debunks the epic dimension of historical narratives whose protagonists, far from being heroes, are the playthings of absurd human violence. After her death, Rosa Millard is thus described as a puppet: "but now she looked like she had collapsed, like she had been made out of a lot of little thin dry light sticks notched together and braced with cord, and now the cord had broken and all the little sticks had collapsed in a quiet heap on the floor, and somebody had spread a clean and faded calico dress over them" ("Riposte in Tertio," *The Unvanquished* 107). The fact that Rosa was savagely murdered by men who have no ethics or obey no chivalric code shows that heroism is but a fallacious construct and a grotesque performance and that she herself was the victim of the fictions generated by the Old South.

This perception of historical narratives is close to what Linda Hutcheon has called historiographic metafiction. The circus metaphor implies that the text has to be perceived as a construct. In both "The Circus in the Attic" and *Absalom, Absalom!*, the past seems to be reduced to sheer theatricality, as Shreve suggests: "the South is fine, isn't it. It's better than Ben Hur, isn't it" (176). Bolton Lovehart, behind the scenes, is also watching Ben Hur, the epic movie or peplum (38). He lives vicariously, through fiction, which is symbolized by the circus itself. His universe includes many worlds of fiction in which he is doomed to play a voyeuristic part. "The Circus in the Attic" is a *mise en abyme* of different circuses: the novella itself with its puppet-like characters, the real circus that causes Bolton to run away, and the toy circus that leads him to create his own circus in the attic. These specular effects and echoing images blur the boundaries between reality and fiction. At the end of the novella, reality and real characters join the other figures in the attic, so that the circle of time merges with the circus of fiction.

Warren's circus in the attic is a reminder that reality is a stage and "life is just a tale told by an idiot" (*Macbeth*, Act V, Scene 5, lines 28-29). The fact that the novella ends with a reference to Jasper, Bolton's surrogate son—"And Jasper will be at home there" (62)—who is another avatar of the idiot, finds a parallel in the conclusions of *The Sound and the Fury* and *Absalom, Absalom!*, which both end with puppet-like idiot characters who may be compared to two clowns, respectively Benjy Compson and Jim Bond. In his introduction to

The Marionettes (1920), Noel Polk highlights Faulkner's fascination with *commedia dell'arte* characters and "fantoches"—also a reference to a poem by Paul Verlaine—a French word referring to puppets as "the playthings of fate" (xxx): "Unquestionably, Faulkner throughout his career was interested in the idea of fate, and in the image of men as puppets, particularly when they could be used to add classical and tragic dimension to his work" (xxxi). Yet, even if human beings seem trapped in a circular form of time, they may find the will or the ability to escape from the puppet master: "To whatever extent Faulkner's characters talk of fate, to whatever extent they comfort themselves by placing the responsibility for their entanglements on the shoulders of a puppet master, the reader must keep both the character and the circumstance in the ever-present moral context in which Faulkner places them; and he must hold characters individually accountable for their sins" (xxxii). Bolton Lovehart is also torn between his free will to escape from his dull life and the circumstances that seem to lead him back within the circle of his attic: indeed, his personal history is built around to-and-fro movements between reality and fiction. For Bolton Lovehart and Faulkner's characters such as Emily Grierson, Rosa Coldfield, or even Quentin Compson, who tries to reconstruct or recreate Sutpen's story, finding one's way back into fiction itself is the form of a Nietzschean will to nothingness or at least of a narcissistic withdrawal into a dark house, away from the turmoil of History and Time, which is the real puppet master.

Works Cited

Bleikasten, André. *The Most Splendid Failure: Faulkner's* The Sound and the Fury. Bloomington: Indiana UP, 1976.

Blotner, Joseph. *Robert Penn Warren: A Biography*. New York: Random House, 1997.

Bohner, Charles. *Robert Penn Warren*. New York: Twayne Publishers, 1964.

Bradley, Patricia L. *Robert Penn Warren's Circus Aesthetic and the Southern Renaissance*. Knoxville: U of Tennessee P, 2004.

———. "Choosing Sides during the Culture Wars of the 1920s, '30s, and '40s: Robert Penn Warren, the Weight of Agrarianism, and the Popular Audience." *Mississippi Quarterly*, 64.1 & 2, (Winter/Spring 2011): 25–57.

Camus, Albert. *The Myth of Sisyphus*. 1942. Trans. Justin O'Brien. Harmondsworth: Penguin Books, 2005.

Chappel, Fred. "The Comic Structure of *The Sound and the Fury*." *Mississippi Quarterly* 31 (Summer 1978): 381–386.

Cuddon, J.A. *A Dictionary of Literary Terms*. 1976. Harmondsworth: Penguin Books, 1979.

Cullick, Jonathan S. *Making History: The Biographical Narratives of Robert Penn Warren*. Baton Rouge: Louisiana State UP, 2000.

Faulkner, William. *Absalom, Absalom!* 1936. New York: Vintage International edition, 1990.

———. "A Rose for Emily." *The Collected Stories of William Faulkner*. 1930. Harmonsdworth: Penguin Books, 1985.

———. *As I Lay Dying*. 1930. Harmondsworth: Penguin Books, 1963.

———. "Carcassonne." *The Collected Stories of William Faulkner*. 1931. Harmondsworth: Penguin Books, 1985.

———. "My Grandmother Millard." *The Collected Stories of William Faulkner*. 1943. London: Penguin Books, 1985.

———. "Riposte in Tertio." *The Unvanquished*. 1938. Harmondsworth: Penguin Books, 1988.

———. *The Sound and the Fury*. 1929. New York: Norton, 1994.

Grimshaw, James A. *Understanding Robert Penn Warren*. U of South Carolina P, 2001.

Gwynn, Frederick L., and Joseph L. Blotner, eds. *Faulkner in the University: Class Conferences at the University of Virginia, 1957–1958*. 1959. Charlottesville: U P of Virginia, 1995.

Hutcheon, Linda. "'The Pastime of Past Time': Fiction, History, Historiographic Metafiction." *Postmodern Genres*. 1988. Ed. Marjorie Perloff. Norman: U of Oklahoma P, 1989. 54–74.

Irwin, John T. *Doubling and Incest/Repetition and Revenge. A Speculative Reading of Faulkner*. 1975. Baltimore: John Hopkins U P, 1996.

Justus, James H. *The Achievement of Robert Penn Warren*. Baton Rouge: Louisiana State U P, 1981.

Millichap, Joseph. *Robert Penn Warren. A Study of the Short Fiction*. New York: Twayne Publishers, 1992.

———. "Robert Penn Warren and Regionalism." *Robert Penn Warren*. Spec. issue of *Mississippi Quarterly* 48.1 (winter 1994–1995): 29–38.

Polk, Noel. "An Introduction to William Faulkner's *The Marionettes* (1920)." The Bibliographical Society of the University of Virginia. Chalottesville: U P of Virginia, 1977: ix–xxxii.

Warren, Robert Penn. "The Circus in the Attic." *The Circus in the Attic and Other Stories*. 1947. New York: Harcourt Brace, 1975.

Watkins, Floyd C., and John T. Hiers, eds. *Robert Penn Warren Talking. Interviews 1950–1978*. New York: Random House, 1980.

Winnicott, Donald W. *Playing and Reality*. 1971. London and New York: Routledge, 2005.

Phillip Gordon

Naples Re-visited: A New Perspective on Same-Sex Desire in "Divorce in Naples"

As a scholar of gay and lesbian literature, I confess that turning to Faulkner can be somewhat frustrating. His works are full of suggestive material for queer readings and provocative hints that a homosexual presence may well reside in his fiction, but rarely does one find overt homosexual activity except in two key places: the lesbian themes of his early poetry and the short story "Divorce in Naples." The latter is also an early work—Faulkner wrote it either while he was in Europe or immediately after his return in 1925 under an older title, "Equinox." He failed to publish it, but in 1950, when he published *Collected Stories*, he chose to include it in the "Beyond" section under its current title. On more than one occasion, I have had a very basic conversation about homosexual themes in Faulkner's fiction. I explain to someone that "I'm interested in studying homosexuality in Faulkner's fiction," and, more often than not, I get as a reply, "Well, there's 'Divorce in Naples,'" followed by an uncomfortable silence as if to suggest that beyond this story, few would venture to suggest that there is more. Homer Barron, Bon and Henry, Quentin and Shreve, Gail Hightower, or really any other vaguely queer characters may merit spirited debates about their sexual identities, but at best, theirs is a closeted homosexuality, and readings concerning them rarely prove definitive. In "Divorce in Naples," the homosexuality is neither conjectural nor closeted. The conflict of the story centers around a threatened homosexuality that may or may not last, but it is homosexuality nonetheless. Carl and George are gay lovers, at least when they are at sea. "Divorce in Naples" is Faulkner's gay story.

I would like to offer a new perspective on this story to counter a succinct but nonetheless loaded reading of the story offered by Joseph Blotner. He summarizes and interprets it in three sentences in his one-volume biography:

> The story deals with two crew members on a thirty-four-day ocean crossing. George is a large dark Greek,

whose beloved Carl—a small blond eighteen-year-old Philadelphian of Scandinavian descent—betrays him with a female prostitute. *Their reconciliation is shadowed, however, by an indication of future heterosexual betrayals by Carl.* (175, italics added)

Notably, Blotner does not say the word "homosexuality"; rather, he leaves it to be inferred in relationship to the "future heterosexuality" supposedly implicit in the end of the story. But deep in the folds of this seemingly innocuous interpretation lies an unsubstantiated assumption about homosexuality and its "future" (an assumption that Blotner, who can be quite progressive at times on the subject of sexual orientation, is very likely not altogether conscious of). It is an *a priori* assumption, a kind of logical fallacy often made in literary criticism and beyond by even the most skillful and insightful readers.

I would like to challenge this assumption and offer a different interpretation of the end of the story based on evidence from Faulkner's life—particularly concerning his interactions with two gay men—and with a different, but no less valid, *a priori* assumption of my own about the "normal" progression of sexual development. I readily confess my reading is based on an assumption, but I hope to show that even a minor revision in an approach to a text can produce a vastly different reading. In no way should my reading be seen as supplanting Blotner's. Rather, I merely seek to explore a new reading in the hope that the more ways in which we can make meaning legible, the better our understanding of a text will be as a result.

"Divorce in Naples" is told from a third-person limited perspective by a fellow deckhand who observers the interactions between two other crew members, Carl and George. This perspective means that the narrator does not observe any sexual encounters, but he observes the fawning, petting, and intimacy between Carl and George, and though he does not use the word "homosexual," he does not leave any doubt as to the nature of their relationship. The protagonists of the story are Carl and George. George is older, "Greek, big and black, a full head taller than Carl" (877). Carl is eighteen, of Scandinavian descent (he's blond), and as the narrator says, "ha[s] yet to experience or need to shave" (880). George takes Carl in as his own and protects and watches over him. Monckton, another shipmate, calls Carl George's wife and his girl "even if he d[oes] wear pants" (878). The two have travelled together as cook and second cook for at least two years prior to their current residence onboard the ship in the story.

In Naples, on shore leave, George, Carl, Monckton, and the narrator go to a cafe where they meet three girls, all professional, who are "of that abject glittering kind that seamen know or that know seamen" (877). Faulkner refers to *seamen*, not *sailors*, surely for the sake of the pun. Carl "betrays" George by running off with one of these girls and not returning for the rest of shore leave. When he returns to the boat as it pulls out of port, the narrator describes the long reconciliation between the two as they negotiate separate spaces onboard but are finally observed "dancing again in their undershirts after supper on the after deck" (892) while a victrola plays jazzy love songs. The story ends with the narrator overhearing Carl say to George: "When we get to Galveston, I want you to buy me a suit of these pink silk teddybears that ladies use. A little bigger than I'd wear, see?" (893).

The basics of Blotner's summary is accurate: Carl betrays George with a woman (we never see Carl and the woman have sex, but we never see Carl and George have sex either—we have to use our imagination and our common sense to deduce what happens "off camera"). Where Blotner goes astray, or at least adds a bit of subjectivity to his objective reporting, is his assertion that this final scene signals another future betrayal by Carl. Blotner's inference here is actually based on a deeper premise—that if Carl and George are lovers, then Carl is young and both experimenting with what will ultimately be an inconsequential sexual affair with George and using his youth and sexuality for protection while he travels. Therefore, this affair is limited. Carl will grow up into mature (or "proper") heterosexuality. As Alfred Kinsey famously recorded, a lot of young men have homosexual encounters, particularly in their youth. Few grow up to be real homosexuals. Though the measure is somewhat out of vogue nowadays, we could say George is probably a 5 or a 6 on Kinsey's scale.[1] Carl, on the other hand, is young and maybe just a 3 or a 4 with a decent chance of reducing that number as he grows up. One could argue that Faulkner based Carl on a more adventuresome version of himself. Faulkner biographer Jay Parini goes as far as suggesting that "[i]t is not outlandish to suppose that Faulkner himself had homosexual feelings" (31) as a young man but outgrew them, as all *natural* young men do.

116

I disagree with the premise that homosexuality is an adolescent sexual experiment that one outgrows, and so naturally, I disagree with Blotner's interpretation (and am skeptical of Parini's biographical note). I do not disagree with the notion that one undergoes a sexual development that can include experimental stages and youthful recreation. I merely disagree with the privileging of heterosexuality as the natural end of that development. Herein lies the deeper assumption underlying Blotner's reading of the story—a valid reading, at least to the extent his assumption is valid. The problem is that, if one finds this assumption invalid, the rest of Blotner's reading begins to muddle up into a problematic conclusion that may not address all the realms of possibilities that the text allows. If we assume Carl is heterosexual, then his affair with George is a momentary experiment and the story ends with the shadow of future heterosexuality. On the other hand, if we assume Carl is a homosexual, then we reverse the terms—his affair in Naples is the experiment, his return to George the fruition of his maturation process into adult homosexuality. But is such a reading possible? What would it look like? And on what, besides my personal opinion, might it be based?

Two of the chief influences on Faulkner's life during the period from 1918–1929 were gay men. One, Ben Wasson, was his friend from his university days and would eventually work as Faulkner's first literary agent in New York. The other, William Spratling, was Faulkner's roommate in New Orleans from 1925 to 1927 and also his traveling companion for his 1925 European trip (which, we know from Faulkner's letters home, included a pilgrimage to Oscar Wilde's tomb in Pere LaChaise Cemetery in Paris). John Duvall, in his essay "Faulkner's Crying Game: Male Homosexual Panic," recounts the story of Faulkner tempting Ben Wasson out of his dorm room to sit in the pleasant shade of the Ole Miss campus "near one of the ubiquitous Confederate monuments" while Faulkner read aloud Conrad Aiken's *Turns and Movies*. Wasson, in his memoir, recalls other students "glancing questioningly at us" (33). Wasson fails to remind his readers that several of the poems in Aiken's volume describe varieties of homosexuality. Duvall uses the story to counter the notion that Faulkner was completely panic-stricken over homosexuality. Surely, Faulkner understood those questioning glances and knew that passing students were wondering if, perhaps, they were witnessing a same-sex courtship.

What students were less likely to witness directly were another series of meetings between Wasson and Faulkner, also recounted in Wasson's memoir. Wasson recalls evenings when he and Faulkner would slip away from campus and retreat to the house of Jim Stone (Phil Stone's father). Faulkner assured Wasson he was always welcome there, even when no one was home. Alone together, the two men sat in the family library, perusing the excellent collection of Victorian titles. Faulkner, though, was not content just to talk books. He promised Wasson a surprise one night—a victrola symphony of Beethoven's Fifth on a Red Seal record. The music moved both men; Wasson remembers, "We were caught up in the spell and surge of the great musical composition, a triumph of a master . . . We had several such music sessions when the Stone family was away" (35). We might glance questioningly at Wasson's rhetoric here. He paints a scene of intellectual communion over music and books and then offers a subtly erotic description of their sharing a private, intimate space. How romantic! To be "caught up in the spell and surge" of that intimacy and to repeat that intimacy "several" times. I am not arguing that Wasson and Faulkner were actually having sex in the Stone's house. The details do not quite warrant such a radical interpretation. But these two men—one a known homosexual—are clearly sharing something beyond mere friendship, and before we dismiss the implications of this scene, I would offer the rejoinder: let us not unto the marriage of true minds admit impediments.

These intimate encounters occurred between 1919 and 1922, while Wasson was a student at Ole Miss. In 1922, he moved home to Greenville, but he returned often to visit. On one visit, in 1924, Estelle and Cho-Cho were also in Oxford, one of a handful of visits she made home during her marriage to Cornell Franklin.[2] Wasson also recalls in his memoir that, after a party at the Oldham house, Estelle cornered him and kissed him. He wandered the streets of Oxford for some time after this kiss, clearly upset about it. But he was not upset that he had interfered with Faulkner's love for Estelle. Wasson actually claims he did not know Estelle and Faulkner had any feelings for each other at the time. Instead, he is worried about Estelle taking the encounter the wrong way, but he ends up explaining the kiss to Faulkner in a tone of outrage and apology. Strange that he would need to apologize to Faulkner when he claims that he does not realize he has even offended him . . . unless, of course, Wasson felt he had offended Faulkner for reasons not concerning Faulkner and Estelle's relationship but rather his own relationship with Faulkner from back in those collegiate days of poetry readings and musical sessions. Faulkner responded that Wasson needed to "[w]atch out . . . and remember, Bud, that Eve wasn't the only woman who handed out the apple, just the first" (81). Then Faulkner gave Wasson a poem he had been working on and never mentioned the incident again.[3]

A similar incident occurs with Faulkner's friend and gay roommate William Spratling. In 1925, the very night they arrive in Europe, in Genoa as opposed to Naples, Spratling and Faulkner got very drunk in a bar with two crew members of the ship they crossed on. As he recounts in his own memoir, Spratling decided a man and woman at the bar were a pimp and a prostitute, so he threw money at them and danced on their table in his reverie as a kind of taunting. His little drunken display put Spratling in jail, not for drunkenness, but for defacing the image of the king on the coins he had been dancing on. Spratling, far too jovial a character to see the Kafka-esque quality of his experience, takes his imprisonment in stride. In his memoir, he recounts some of the other characters languishing in his Italian jail. They are, of course, all men. In the two published versions of his memoir, Spratling never confesses to anything more than just conversing with a couple of them. Spratling does report that, in the morning when Faulkner came to retrieve him, he was "distant and gloomy" and seemed mad at Spratling. When Spratling pressed him about "seem[ing] a little sore," Faulkner rebutted that "why shouldn't he be sore, having missed such an experience himself" (33).

The evidence that lies below the surface of this story is somewhat more readily available than trying to siphon meaning from Wasson's rhetorical gestures in his memoir. Blotner, when he collected this story from Spratling, also noted that Faulkner wrote Wasson about the incident, but when Faulkner retold it, he, not Spratling, had been the one jailed. Blotner also adds, in his one-volume biography, that Spratling actually confessed to Faulkner when he came to bail him out that he had a homosexual encounter in the jail during the night. Spratling did not confess this in either printed version of his memoir, and Blotner's interview notes with Spratling, though colorful, do not contain reference to this encounter,[4] though Blotner cites that interview as his source for this information while also explaining, "Clearly, this fitted with the character of George" from "Divorce in Naples" (176). Actually, if Spratling's real life jailhouse encounter underpins any elements of "Divorce in Naples," Spratling should be Carl. Carl is the one who sneaks off for an affair; George is the one bruised and angry when Carl returns. Spratling admits to Faulkner that he had sex in jail; Faulkner gets cranky and mad that he was not involved. Of course, George is the more recognizable homosexual, the Kinsey 6, like Spratling. Carl, as I suggested earlier, is the novice and easier to align with a more adventuresome version of Faulkner who might experiment with homosexuality but, at least in one way of reading the story, turn straight eventually. The night in Genoa seems fundamental to the story "Divorce in Naples," but Faulkner did not transcribe its events in a 1:1 correlation into his story. He made the actual considerably more apocryphal than any easy allegorical reading can trace. He is, in a way, both Carl and George, they both manifestations of the complex relationships he carried on with Spratling and, earlier, with Wasson. Whatever was the case in actuality, in this story, we might say that Faulkner was apocryphally homosexual, even to the detail of the missing notes about Spratling's sexual encounter in Blotner's papers.

Despite the shifty and complex ways Faulkner transformed his real life experiences into fictional accounts, one basic pattern emerges from the relationships Wasson-Faulkner, Faulkner-Spratling, and Carl-George. In all three, two men engage each other directly as the principle players in the relationship. In all three, one of the two men also engages in an intimate act with a third party: Estelle, an anonymous prisoner, and a prostitute. In all three, the central act of reconciliation is between the two principle men. In the Wasson-Faulkner and Faulkner-Spratling relationships, Faulkner eventually does "betray" his partners by marrying a woman. But the fictional relationship is not so simple nor allegorical. Indeed, though perhaps we can all easily fall into the miasma of searching for the triangulated pattern of same-sex desire explicated by Eve Sedgwick in *Between Men*, we must pause before committing that fallacy. These relationships do not center on a woman's body as the safe site for the transference of same-sex desire. The "woman" in all three is a third wheel, never central to the core relationship nor a site for its safe practice. Both the real relationships and the story date from the 1920s. Sedgwick herself, in *Epistemology of the Closet*, disavowed her earlier formulation as not relevant in a twentieth-century context when "at least some versions of same-sex desire unmediated through heterosexual performance have become widely articulated" (15). What she means is that by the twentieth century, men had come to identify as homosexual and perform that identity in fuller and more complete ways than as acts of deferral that require a woman to mitigate their implications. Spratling and Wasson both performed their homosexual identities as more substantial and meaningful than fraught and frustrated heterosexual desires. So too does Carl.

At the end of "Divorce in Naples," just as the reconciliation between Carl and George is about the take place, the narrator describes Carl's purification ritual one night, as the ship pulls out of port:

> He undressed swiftly, ripping his clothes off, ripping off a button that struck the bulkhead with a faint click. Naked, in the wan light, he looked smaller and frailer than ever as he dug a towel from his bunk where George had tumbled his things, flinging the other garments aside with a kind of dreadful haste. Then he went out, his bare feet whispering in the passage.
>
> I could hear the shower beyond the bulkhead running for a long time; it would be cold now, too. But it ran for a long time, then it ceased and I closed my eyes again until he had entered. Then I watched him lift from the floor the undergarment which he had removed and thrust it through a porthole quickly, with something of the air of a recovered drunkard putting out of sight an empty bottle. (888)

Cleansed of his iniquity, Carl proceeds to find George and apologize, after a fashion, by returning to him and asking him for quite simply the most obvious gift he could request given his costly purification: he threw his "undergarment" overboard. Now he needs a new one. Of course, it is somewhat lewdly erotic that he wants his new underwear to be a little pink teddy, but he is asking his lover to buy it for him. George will be the one most likely to see Carl wear it, so let us not unto the marriage of these two minds admit any impediments either. Yes, Carl has had a tryst "off-camera" that bruised his lover. But what better way to amend for his transgression than to ask George to invest in an item for their mutual sex life. Carl has learned something from his escapade, and he is returning to George ready to grow into a more mature relationship with him. It is, after all, no minor detail that Carl needs the teddy to be slightly bigger than he is. He is young; he is small. But he will grow into it.

Notes

1. The famous "Kinsey Scale" was proposed by Alfred Kinsey in his ground-breaking 1948 study *Sexual Behavior in the Human Male*. Though more significant today as a cultural document than a credible medical study, Kinsey (and his co-authors Wardell Pomeroy and Clyde Martin) defined homosexuality not as an either/or category but as existing on a scale of experience and desires. Kinsey proposed that the vast majority of men have had, at some point in their lives, a "homosexual" fantasy, many have had some youthful homosexual encounter, and more than a few have experimented with homosexuality. Kinsey created a 6-point scale for homosexual identity, with a Kinsey 0 being the rare male who is exclusively heterosexual and a Kinsey 6 being the rare male who is exclusively homosexual. Points 1-5 mark stages of sexual incidences that fall in the middle ground between these two points (and ultimately represent the experiences of most men as they move towards sexual maturity).

2. For a full list of times between 1918 and 1927 when Estelle visited Oxford, see Judith Sensibar, *Faulkner and Love*. Though Wasson does not date the event in question, we can infer it occurred in 1924 because of the limited number of times Estelle visited and the description of her picking up Cho-Cho (her daughter Victoria), who would have been around five years old in 1924, still small enough to pick up but old enough to wander around the house by herself. None of Estelle's other visits would coincide with the appropriate age and size for the description of Cho-Cho Wasson gives in his memoir.

3. Wasson claims—and Blotner seconds—that this incident did appear in Faulkner's fiction, in 1927, in *Flags in the Dust*, when little Belle walks in on a similar moment of indiscretion between Horace and her mother, Belle Mitchell.

4. The Blotner papers are thorough and extensive, but despite repeated efforts, I have been unable to find the reference to Spratling's homosexual encounter Blotner includes in the revised one-volume biography (but did not include in the original two-volume version). Blotner cites his interview with Spratling, which proved to be his only interview with Spratling since Spratling would die in a car accident shortly after that interview and before the original biography was published. Blotner typed up his notes for that interview on six pages, none of which include reference to a homosexual encounter. The handwritten interview notes total nine pages and do contain information not found in the typed notes, but reference to any homosexual encounter in jail is not included there either. Blotner also jotted down interview notes in small, handheld notebooks, but his handwriting in these is quite simply illegible.

But that Blotner chose to add this detail does imply that he was not simply making it up. It is likely that Spratling confessed his homosexual encounter to Blotner in the interview, but Blotner did not write it down. Rather, he filed it away in memory only. Blotner died in the months between my delivering this paper and my submitting it for publication. I was never able to verify from him this detail.

Works Cited

Reference to the interview with William Spratling comes from research done in the Joseph Blotner Papers, part of the J.D. Brodsky-Faulkner Collection housed in Special Collections at the Kent Library at Southeast Missouri State University in Cape Girardeau, Missouri.

Blotner, Joseph. *Faulkner: A Biography, One Volume Edition*. New York: Vintage, 1991. Print.

Duvall, John. "Faulkner's Crying Game: Male Homosexual Panic." *Faulkner and Gender: Faulkner and Yoknapatawpha, 1994*. Ed. Donald M. Kartiganer and Ann J. Abadie, 1994. 48–72. Print.

Faulkner, William. *Collected Stories* (1950). New York: Vintage International: Random House, 1995. Print.

Kinsey, Alfred Charles, Wardell B. Pomeroy, and Clyde E. Martin. *Sexual Behavior in the Human Male*. Philadelphia: W.B. Saunders, 1948. Print.

Parini, Jay. *One Matchless Time: A Life of William Faulkner*. New York: Harper Collins, 2004. Print.

Sedgwick, Eve Kosofsky. *Between Men: English Literature and Male Homosocial Desire*. New York: Columbia UP, 1985. Print.

———. *Epistemology of the Closet*. Berkeley: U of California P, 1990. Print.

Sensibar, Judith. *Faulkner and Love: The Women Who Shaped His Art*. New Haven, CT: Yale UP, 2009. Print.

Spratling, William. *File on Spratling: An Autobiography*. Boston: Little, Brown and Company, 1967. Print.

Wasson, Ben. *Count No 'Count: Flashbacks to Faulkner*. Jackson: UP of Mississippi, 1983. Print.

Rebekah Taylor

Modernist Ecologies: Faulkner's Wilderness and Warren's Wasteland

Despite scholars' unanimous acknowledgement of Robert Penn Warren's attention to place and sensibility for the natural world—made obvious through detailed references to insects, spiders, trees, shrubs, cows, birds, and of course, the black snake, "old *obsoleta*" (*Brother to Dragons* 208)—no ecocritical approach to Warren's canon exists. Warren's bent for inquisitiveness and time on Grandpa Penn's farm in his formative years undoubtedly contributed to his views, just as Faulkner's annual hunting trips in the Mississippi Delta made him an "environmental amateur" (Buell 15). Certainly, as Southern writers and modernists, Faulkner and Warren occupy a specific, critical place in our nation's history, and it is no surprise that their works are infused with commentary on the changing landscape and world around them. Still, Faulkner's works have received considerably more attention in terms of his treatment of nature, including in Christopher Rieger's *Clear-Cutting Eden*, which considers the intersection of race, class, and gender concerns with attitudes toward nature; truly, much of Rieger's insight into Faulkner's post-pastoral, where the search for balance in nature characteristic of the pastoral tradition is paradoxically trumped by the "lure for profit"—profit attained through systems that require human dominance—applies to Warren as well (140). But, while Faulkner links degraded environment to degraded culture, sometimes literally and sometimes allegorically, Warren increasingly links external environment to the individual's ability or inability "to know"—to know the self and to know the world, and to know the self by knowing the world. The focus on "knowing," I argue, anticipates recent moves in literary theory and environmental studies and demands that we take a closer look at Warren's ecology. True ecological thought, Timothy Morton writes, "thinks big and joins the dots. It thinks through the mesh of life forms as far out and in as it can. It comes as close as possible to the strange stranger, generating care and concern for beings, no matter how uncertain we are of their identity, no matter how afraid we are of their existence" (*Ecological Thought* 18–19). Morton's scholarship, among others', provides a new lens through which to view Warren's web metaphor, for example: When Jack Burden of *All the King's Men* remarks that "the world is all of one piece . . . like an enormous spider web and if you touch it, however lightly, at any point, the vibration ripples to the remotest perimeter" (266), he is certainly ruminating on personal responsibility and action as critics have noted, but this passage might also represent Warren's awareness of interconnectedness amongst more than just human beings.

I want to begin with the specific elements Warren the critic observed in Faulkner's treatment of nature, elements that might offer one starting point from which to unpack the very complicated relationship between human and environment in these authors' works. In order to illustrate that these concerns are essential and central, I will provide a representative sample from Warren's canon while, for brevity's sake assuming Faulkner's influence is understood to some extent. For as Joseph Millichap notes, Faulkner's "monumental presence within the literary landscape of the South and 20th century" is "unmistakable and problematic" ("Warren's Faulkner" 351); or in Eudora Welty's words, like "living near a great mountain, something majestic" (qtd. in Millichap, "Warren's Faulkner" 352). However, as sons are wont to do, Warren would outlive and outgrow his literary father, so I will also discuss how the psychological quality of Warren's nature, specifically focused on this obsession with "knowing," is symptomatic of his late-capitalistic world. Finally, I will close with some introductory commentary about the place of the human mind in nature and, conversely, the place of nature in the human mind, as might be gleaned from modernist writers, including but not limited to Faulkner and Warren.

As Charlotte Beck notes in *Robert Penn Warren, Critic*, Warren's commentary on Faulkner and others reveals the "close and fruitful synergy uniting Warren's criticism with his own poetry and fiction" (8). David Wyatt, who deplored that Warren's critical mind interfere with the action of his novels, saying that Warren's novels talked about themselves too much, wrote in an early, spirited *Virginia Quarterly* article that "Warren the critic always shepherds us toward the destination the artist knowingly withholds" (480). I would add that Warren the critic also shepherds us toward destinations the artist *unknowingly* withholds. Hoping this is the case, I will begin with a sample from

Warren's "Cowley's Faulkner," the review of Cowley's *Portable Faulkner* published April 12, 1946, in *New Republic*. Robert Penn Warren, as critic, observes:

> The right attitude toward nature is, as a matter of fact, associated with the right attitude toward man, and the mere lust for power over nature is associated with the lust for power over other men . . . . But the rape of nature and the crime against man are always avenged. The rape of nature, the mere exploitation of it without love, is always avenged because the attitude which commits that crime also commits the crime against men which in turn exacts vengeance, so that man finally punishes himself. ("Cowley's Faulkner" 178–79)

Warren's use of "attitude" here supports a kind of Hegelian approach as outlined in *Phenomenology of Spirit*, but for this discussion of Faulkner-Warren connections, it is important to note the reciprocity that Warren highlights in Faulkner's "The Bear" is very much characteristic of his own treatment of nature, and especially the fact that all action (or attitude) toward nature ultimately leads back to the self. Like Faulkner's, Warren's fiction and poetry intimates Warren's belief that man's relationship with nature indicates his ability to negotiate his world while retaining a certain measure of morality. And, like Faulkner, Warren's nature is no passive backdrop; rather, the wilderness is often infused with the clairvoyant ability to judge the heart of man, promising vengeance just as it holds the potential for absolution and self-knowledge. This promise of retribution, then, reverses the roles of master/subordinate, challenging dominant ideology; truly, nature is older, wiser, larger, and it "knows" while man clings tenuously to truth. Warren's comment that "man finally punishes himself" points us to various places in his own fiction where these crimes are avenged. For Warren, this vengeance often manifests as a sort of naturalistic decline; many of his characters who "cross over" to a greedy world view lose everything, sometimes even their lives. But vengeance is also exacted on the psyche of not only the individual but also all who live in a fractured modern world where the chasm between self and natural world seems unbreachable.

What constitutes a "crime against nature" is not difficult to identify in Faulkner nor Warren. Faulkner directly condemns exploitation of natural resources in the South, particularly the lumber industry that was often dominated by Northern companies, likely to strip the land and leave. As Rieger notes, "in the 1930s the cut-and-get-out phase of lumbering in the South was nearing the end of an ecologically devastating fifty-year boom" (137). Rieger, along with Don H. Doyle, Lawrence Buell, and others note the very real, historical accuracy of the exploitation depicted in *Go Down, Moses* particularly, although in "Faulkner and the Claims of the Natural World," Lawrence Buell adds that "like most precontemporary people, [Faulkner's] knowledge of environmental cause-and-effect was spotty" (6). Still, environmental concerns are crucial to both authors' historical moments and artistic visions, and it is to our detriment not to devote attention to this obviously significant aspect of their work.

Faulkner's *Go Down, Moses* is the most recognized and explicit demonstration of the "right attitude" toward nature, which Ike learns is an attitude of humility and pride, achieved and sanctioned through the hunt. In "The Bear," before the machine invades, Faulkner's wilderness "soared musing, inattentive, myriad, eternal, green; older than any mill-shed, longer than any spur-line" (307). Then, the wilderness was "tremendous, primeval, looming, musing downward upon this puny evanescent clutter of human sojourn" (337). But time passes and the log train begins to run more frequently and with heavier loads, literally and figuratively. In *Dixie Limited*, Joseph Millichap discusses Ike's (and Faulkner's) ambivalence toward the logging train, noting that representations of the train are tied up with issues of race, gender, class, and progress, among other cultural elements. The train is a material and symbolic reminder of how Ike's own personal history is tied to the land, and of the Delta's changing landscape, where the train runs between the walls of disappearing wilderness (*Go Down Moses* 68). Ike reflects that the train "had been harmless once" (304) and "it had been harmless then" (305); in the beginning, "nobody bothered to listen for it or not" (306). This repeated idea refers to the increasing exploitation of the land for material gain—the use of "then" and "once" suggests the potential that modernization and the morality of the "old people" might coexist, but that potential has passed away along with Old Ben. Still, Ike is able to preserve a certain idea of nature through memory, and he differs from Warren's characters in that he does not take on the attitude of "the world" but maintains this "right attitude toward nature." This is possible because Ike's is not nostalgia, but memory—for he inherits and participates in a very real, mutually beneficial relationship with the natural world. He is "humble and proud that he had been found worthy to be a part of it too or even just to see it too" (217). Ike's initial proclivity for the "right attitude" is then reinforced by Sam Fathers's tutelage and by the natural world itself—in the way that the Big Woods essentially respond and condition Ike as he must "earn for himself from the wilderness the name and state of hunter provided he in his turn were humble and enduring enough" (185). But the old way will disappear with Ike, and future generations will learn, as Jack Burden learns in *All the King's Men*, one can only put off the world for a brief moment; for eventually one must "go into the convulsion of the world, out of history into history and the awful responsibility of time" (609).

Faulkner's characters literally witness the wilderness disappear in real time, and the growing gravity of the situation is echoed throughout Faulkner's canon. One might think of *Light in August*, where Lena reflects that "[a]ll the men in the village worked in the mill or for it. It was cutting pine. It had been there seven years and in seven years more it would destroy all the timber within its reach" (4). Visually, the diminishing wilderness is problematic as both Faulkner and Warren make repeated mention of wood-lines or log-lines, the distinct separation between wilderness and what has been taken. In both men's works, we witness a real or imagined clash. Even Faulkner's final novel, *The Reivers*, though ostensibly continuing Boon Hogganbeck's story in its present, recounts the action of relevant sections of *Go Down, Moses* through the oral history within the family and community, without providing a workable model for those who must carry on now that Sam Fathers and Ike have passed. The eleven-year-old Lucius Priest flippantly jokes "perhaps you will find wilderness on the backside of Mars or the moon" (20). For, as Rieger astutely notes, Faulkner does not "reveal what an ethical Southern post-pastoral relationship with nature might actually look like" (158), and I argue his failure to do so is in part because he does not dramatize the post-pastoral in the present. For a large majority of the commentary on nature either takes place before the wilderness disappears or reflects back on how it *was*.

In contrast, Warren dramatizes modern man's attempt to negotiate an increasingly unfamiliar world in multiple lengthy narratives. Still, while Warren plays out the post-pastoral, he also may not provide an ethical solution, perhaps due to the difficulty and near impossibility that there is one. For if "the end of man is knowledge," as Jack Burden famously declares, and "to know is always all" ("Holy Writ" 212), we have to be willing to accept where that knowledge brings us, and as Jack warns, it's not clear whether that knowledge can save us. But this does not mean that we do not try. No, Warren would never suggest that one turn away from knowledge, at any risk. Again, I find Timothy Morton's scholarship, particularly his discussion of "beautiful soul syndrome," extremely relevant and helpful here. Morton attributes a substantial proportion of the ecological crisis to the "beautiful soul," which he defines as someone who "washes his or her hands of the corrupt world, refusing to admit how in this very abstemiousness and distaste he or she participates in the creation of that world. The world-weary soul holds all beliefs and ideas at a distance" (*Ecology without Nature* 13). Morton advocates a "plunging in" that Warren certainly requires of his characters and personas to reach knowledge: R.P.W. of *Brother to Dragons* echoes once again, "and the only / knowledge worth the knowing is / The knowledge too deep for knowing" (99).

The aforementioned clash between wilderness and wasteland informs the central action and the formal structure of Robert Penn Warren's second novel, *At Heaven's Gate* (1943), which juxtaposes varying attitudes toward nature, as it alternates between the world of capitalist Bogan Murdock and the hill-country "Testament of Ashby Wyndham." What has gone practically unnoted about this novel is that Warren comments on very real, very specific "crimes against nature." One narrative strain in the novel centers on the Massey Mountain project, a large energy enterprise associated with mining, lumber, and mountaintop removal, which brings to mind even more devastating consequences of the exploitation of nature than Warren could have anticipated, given the collapse of Upper Big Branch mine in 2009 that killed 29 miners and the consequent lawsuit finding Massey Energy responsible. Notwithstanding his ignorance of this impending tragedy, Warren was prescient enough to the kind of destruction that is imminent when greed mixes with power. Still, Warren admits, it is impossible for someone like Wyndham to subsist completely outside of the global economic system that has taken over by the modern period. Ashby Wyndham, like others who begin outside of the system, is forced to assimilate or, it is implied, starve to death. Even moreso than Faulkner's, Warren's characters wrestle with the recognition that humanity is a part of nature while subscribing to practices that are counterintuitive to a symbiotic relationship between man and nature. This is the unfortunate case of Ashby Wyndham, who sells out his brother Jacob, saying "they's payin hard money at Massey. . . . and I ain't stayin here to rot and grabble" (93).

Jerry Calhoun in *At Heaven's Gate* is yet another example of one who is torn between the "right attitude" and the world. A trained geologist, Jerry Calhoun is educated in the history of the earth's composition. From an airplane—in a scenario reminiscent of the one that takes place at 38,000 feet in "Homage to Emerson"—Jerry meditates on the valley below, taking note of the rivers and fields that he recognizes and names, then he imagines thousands of years ago when the land had laid beneath the "epicontinental sea." He recalls chipping shells out of limestone with his hammer in the laboratory. From the plane, the land below is full of "cunning and laborious perfections" (10). But a letter from Murdock interrupts this meditation. As if on cue, the plane begins its descent and Warren writes, "But, presently, he would go down into this world" (10). As Jerry becomes more and more immersed in Bogan Murdock's world and more and more entangled with deals and speculations, the land holds less wonder and more apprehension for him. For example, on a visit to the family home, Uncle Lew spits "You know that Bogan, too, and you work for him. And you come when he hollers and you dance his gig when calls it" (89). Lew's rant is interrupted as Jerry looks to the land, but "[a]ll the sundrenched autumn landscape seemed, to Jerry, on the moment inimical, its bright stillness watchful and treacherous" (89). As the novel progresses, something is certainly happening in Jerry's "gut or soul" as he uses his training as geologist to persuade investors, "we just haven't scratched the surface in this section. The resources here aren't really touched" (130). Yet, even as the words come, Jerry is struck with a pang of guilt and "feels the deprecatory smile on his face" (130).

In the same year that Robert Penn Warren published his review of *The Portable Faulkner*, he put the final touches on his most celebrated novel, *All the King's Men*. There are many interesting "crimes against nature and man" in this novel, but most importantly when thinking of Faulkner and Warren, one might consider the opening passage where Jack reflects on the past and the present, imagining how the landscape has changed because of the lumber industry. For wilderness has given way to wasteland and the effects are felt for generations to come. Jack muses:

> There were pine forests here a long time ago but they are gone. The bastards got in here and set up the mills and laid the narrow-gauge tracks and knocked together the company commissaries and paid a dollar a day and folks swarmed out of the brush for the dollar and folks came from God knows where. . . . The saws sang soprano and the clerk in the commissary passed out the black-strap molasses and the sow-belly and wrote in his big book, and the Yankee dollar and Confederate dumbness collaborated to heal the wounds of four years of fratricidal strife, and all was merry as a marriage bell. Till, all of a sudden, there weren't any more pine trees. They stripped the mills. The narrow-gauge tracks got covered with grass. (3)

Again, later in the novel, while thinking of the past, a time even before his birth, Jack imagines the Scholarly Attorney courting his mother in a mill town in Arkansas. He imagines the "scream of saws like a violated nerve in the center of your head" (184). Although Jack admits he has "never even set foot inside the State of Arkansas" (185), he imagines a land of stumps where the trees used to grow, and his mother and the Scholarly Attorney are now left standing "in the middle of the ruined land" (185). Although there is never a shortage of flora and fauna in any of Warren's works, Jack and others like him are not privy to Faulkner's wilderness directly, like the one in *Go Down, Moses* where the great bear Old Ben roamed. By the time he is seventy, "Uncle Ike" is left in "Delta Autumn," remembering the land the way it used to be and thinking how he had watched the land retreat. Ike has seen the Delta, "his land, even though he had never owned a foot of it," become "deswamped and denuded and derivered in two generations" (*Go Down, Moses* 337). Jack Burden (and Warren's various versions of him) might imagine the land as it once was—we might sense a nostalgia for Faulkner's wilderness—but can never come to full knowledge of it. For Jack is born into a wasteland, and the wind pounds across the hills

> where the pine trees had stood once and moaned in
> the wind but where there wasn't anything to break the
> wind now . . . the wind would come down a thousand
> miles . . . and inside him something would be big and
> coiling slow and clotting till he would hold his breath
> and the blood would beat in his head with a hol-
> low sound like his head was a cave as big as the dark
> outside. He wouldn't have any name for what was big
> inside him. Maybe there isn't any name. (41)

This passage certainly evokes *The Wasteland* itself, where the "wind / Crosses the brown land, unheard" (177–78). "What are the roots that clutch, what branches grow / Out of this stony rubbish? Son of man, / You cannot say, or guess . . ." (19–21), Eliot's persona bemoans. Moments like this, where the gap between the natural world and modern man is impassible, are common in Warren as when, in the poem "What is the Voice that Speaks," the speaker demands, "Have you heard the great owl in the snow-pine? You know / His question—the one you've never, in anguish, been able to answer?" (11–12). The persona in "American Portrait: Old Style" "long[s] to know the world's name" (55) and lies watching the sky drift on "[f]rom *where* on to *where*" (120). Taken in the context of Warren's canon, and modernist literature more broadly, the prevalence of moments of disconnect, when connection is wanted and needed, point to Warren's warning that mistreatment of nature causes irreparable damage to humanity as well, so that indeed "man finally punishes himself" (Warren, "Cowley's Faulkner" 179). Aside from obvious questions of sustainability, Warren also suggests that mental "anguish" is a result of the wrong attitude toward nature.

If "Cowley's Faulkner" contains the germ of Warren's views on the interconnectedness of humanity and environment, that germ would never stop sprouting, flowering, and entwining across Warren's long lifetime. And, if Faulkner's works hint toward impending environmental devastation, Warren's fiction and poetry explore the results of the very practices Faulkner witnessed and commented upon. But, for Warren, man has more at stake than the depletion of natural resources. The chasm between man and world resonates deep within the psyche of Warren's human subjects. In a 1946 interview with Marshall Walker, Warren forewarned, "Man's role in nature, as being part of nature, is no longer felt . . . And we don't know the end of this story; but something is happening deep in the gut or the soul of modern man that we just don't know the meaning of now" (167).

Until the last, Ike clings to his "old order" ideals, for better or for worse. Warren's characters more often than not *begin* torn between opposing views of nature—between stewardship and exploitation, communion and domination—but end up in a psychological and/or physical wasteland. Jeremiah Beaumont of *World Enough and Time* is the epitome of this—he moves from the agrarian model into land speculation into politics and murderous revenge. His slow but sure immersion in the world takes him away from the "right attitude" toward nature. As land speculation takes Jeremiah further from home and deeper into the greedy mire of human degradation, he loses touch with the natural world and the *self.* By the conclusion of the novel, Jeremiah is at the ends of the earth in La Grand Bosse's swamp, where he becomes a syphilitic alcoholic detached from his personal past. From this wasteland, Jeremiah laments "I did not guess that all we need is knowledge. Knowledge is not redemption but it is almost better than redemption" (460).

Warren's dialectical treatment of nature deserves more extended critical attention than the introduction I have supplied here. Faulkner's wilderness seems to have informed Warren's wilderness, but Warren's canon is largely set in a world where the wilderness is not even a memory but a feeling, an attitude passed down from one of the millions of fathers to the son and read about in dusty newspapers or yellowed journal pages, just as the modern narrator of *World Enough and Time* opens the novel, saying, "I can show you what is left" (3). The fact that both Faulkner and Warren comment on very real, historically grounded environmental concerns invites an ecocritical reading where we might understand nature as external to the self in some way—misuse, exploitation, destruction; these things are happening *to* the natural world, undeniably. But, for Warren, nature is not only "over there" or "apart" from the self—it is simultaneously other and internal to us.

It is in our gaze and in our gut. One of the many values of studying Warren's concept of nature is a better understanding of the way in which modernism—and all that entails—creates a (troubled) psychic attachment to place. Considering Warren's intense focus on "knowing," current thinkers such as Timothy Morton are helpful for understanding the way attitudes and ideas—cognitive constructs on the part of the perceiver—ultimately shape reality and must be evaluated if there is any chance for environmental and social justice. Because while first-wave ecocritics took issue with anthropocentric views of nature, arguing for a more ecocentric view of the natural world as interrelated and codependent, with all human and nonhuman occupants playing a vital role, current scholarship brings into question the validity and practicality of an ecocritical approach that does not begin with the human (as observer, perceiver, creator), suggesting that it is impossible to divorce mind from matter, so that any representation of nature one might discover in art *is*, inextricably, human-centered. As theoretical approaches to literature and the environment expand beyond the obvious arena of "nature writing," analyses of more complex treatments of environment in literature—especially narrative, lyric, and psychological literature—offer rich insights into constructions and conditions of the natural world. Scholars from multiple (now converging) fields take a specific interest in psychological literature, and Warren seems to have anticipated this shift in his own meditations on what it means to know nature and know oneself, for "the world is a parable and we are the meaning" ("Internal Injuries" 246).

Works Cited

Beck, Charlotte. *Robert Penn Warren, Critic.* Knoxville: U of Tennessee P, 2006. Print.

Buell, Lawrence. "Faulkner and the Claims of the Natural World." *Faulkner and the Natural World.* Ed. Donald M. Kartiganer and Ann J. Abadie. Jackson: UP of Mississippi, 1999. 1–18. Print.

Eliot, T.S. *The Wasteland.* Ed. Michael North. New York: Norton, 2001. Print.

Faulkner, William. *Go Down, Moses.* New York: Vintage, 1990. Print.

———. *Light in August.* New York: Vintage, 1990. Print.

Millichap, Joseph. *Dixie Limited: Railroads, Culture, and the Southern Renaissance.* Lexington: UP of Kentucky, 2002. Print.

———. "Warren's Faulkner." *Mississippi Quarterly* 60.2 (2007): 351–67. *MLA International Bibliography.* Web. 1 April 2012.

Morton, Timothy. *Ecology without Nature.* Cambridge: Harvard UP, 2007. Print.

———. *The Ecological Thought.* Cambridge: Harvard UP, 2010. Print.

Rieger, Christopher. *Clear-Cutting Eden: Ecology and the Pastoral in Southern Literature.* Tuscaloosa: U of Alabama P, 2009. Print.

Warren, Robert Penn. "Cowley's Faulkner." *The New Republic* 12 April 1946. Microtext.

———. *All the King's Men.* Restored Edition. San Diego: Harcourt, 2001. Print.

———. *At Heaven's Gate.* 1943. New York: New Directions, 1985. Print.

———. "American Portrait: Old Style." *The Collected Poems of Robert Penn Warren.* Ed. John Burt. Baton Rouge: Louisiana State UP, 1998. 339–42. Print.

———. *Brother to Dragons: A Tale in Verse and Voices.* 1953. Baton Rouge: Louisiana State UP, 1996. Print.

———. "Internal Injuries." *The Collected Poems of Robert Penn Warren.* Ed. John Burt. Baton Rouge: Louisiana State UP, 1998. 242–47. Print.

———. *Talking with Robert Penn Warren.* Ed. Floyd C. Watkins, John T. Hiers, and Mary Louise Weaks. Athens: U of Georgia P, 1990. Print.

―――. *World Enough and Time*. 1950. Baton Rouge: Louisiana State UP, 1999. Print.

Wyatt, David. "Robert Penn Warren: The Critic as Artist." *The Virginia Quarterly Review* 53 (Summer 1997): 475–87. Print.

Conor Picken

"There Ought to Be a Law": Prohibition in Faulkner and Warren

Soberly biding his time among a throng of belligerent bootleggers, Popeye, the notorious corncob-wielding villain in William Faulkner's *Sanctuary*, snarls without the least bit of irony, "I told [Goodwin] about letting them sit around all night, swilling that goddam stuff. There ought to be a law" (96). Jack Burden, the first-person narrator in Robert Penn Warren's *All the King's Men*, recalls the time he remedies Willie Stark's hangover on the morning that Stark is to give an important campaign speech: "According to old folks . . . the best way is to put two shots of absinthe on a little cracked ice and float a shot of rye. But we can't be fancy. Not with Prohibition" (88). Each of these novels is (partially) set during Prohibition.[1] Despite this historical setting, however, Prohibition is barely mentioned. I argue that both Faulkner and Warren use Prohibition to contextualize their views that the Volstead South possessed a fundamental aversion to social and political progress, and their shared concern for the region's recalcitrant confrontation with modernity stems from how the literal and figurative economies of alcohol were reconfigured at this time. In both texts, drinking occupies a symbolic space concerning societal power structures, and these locations speak to how the South's culture of imbibing signifies social change (or a lack thereof). Faulkner warns of the fallout when morality is imposed through legislation. The brazen way that Jefferson's elite drink highlights the ethical divide between those wielding power in self-interest and those who suffer because of it. Warren shows how political corruption becomes normative in a Volstead-era South that so easily dismisses the law, and the unapologetic violation of Prohibition by prominent lawmakers implies that progressive ideological stances will not successfully unseat the conservative establishment that Willie Stark opposes with populist vigor.

Prohibition was meant to rescue America from its pandemic of overconsumption and save individuals from the pitfalls of drunken despair. The Eighteenth Amendment was largely the result of temperance movements in the late nineteenth and early twentieth centuries, emerging in response to a saloon culture that saw working class men squander what little money they had on liquor. Movements such as the Woman's Christian Temperance Union (WCTU) blamed moral and familial decline on drunkenness and "demanded personal and social purification to save the nation from cosmic catastrophe" (Chavigny 110). Such evangelical movements associated alcohol with sin, presenting the case for alcohol prohibition in strictly religious terms: "Impelled by religious fervor, evangelical temperance advocates were the radicals of the temperance movement. They excoriated moderate drinkers and liquor sellers for their sinfulness and campaigned for laws to end the sale of liquor" (110). As temperance gained momentum, the target of its directive became clear. Temperance reformers pled their case for Prohibition, as "dry reformers worked symbolically to inscribe particular configurations of class, ethnic, and religious hierarchy upon the body politic . . . to impose a moral code on laboring men who threatened bourgeois notions of discipline and order" (Rotskoff 26). Reform movements associated immoral drinking with particularities of social class—persons from the lower classes drank problematically, while others did not.

Broadly speaking, Prohibition was conceived as something inherently progressive in its ideological bent, both in the demographic it fought to protect (abused women, long underserved in society) and in the centrality of women to its becoming law. Prohibition's ultimate failure obfuscates this point and, perhaps fairly, paints Volstead America as ideologically static when this was in fact not intended to be the case. Women fought vigorously for national Prohibition, citing, among their many political reasons, the need to protect other women in the domestic sphere: "[Temperance reformers] wanted the right to divorce [drunken] men, and to have them arrested for wife beating, and to protect their children from being terrorized by them. To do all these things they needed to change the laws that consigned married women to the status of the chattel. And to change the laws, they needed the vote" (Okrent 15). The impetus behind temperance reform was progressive through-and-through, and other such political agendas (particularly suffrage) attached themselves to the movement. Wrapped up in the passage of the Volstead Act were old North-South antagonisms. Daniel Okrent notes that, "For many of the racially motivated prohibitionists of the South, whose populist anger was monochromatic but nonetheless real, [Prohibition] was a way to avenge Reconstruction by striking back at the economic and political imperialists of the North" (57). The popularity of the Temperance Movement invited other such "progressive" platforms seeking political alliance, the Ku Klux Klan among them: "The Klan, which supported woman suffrage on behalf of Prohibition, in turn supported Prohibition as a weapon against the immigrants" (86). In addition to attracting more dubious, decidedly anti-progressive ideological partners, Prohibition also catalyzed an era of lawlessness and corruption so widespread that the motivation driving temperance reform—to rescue America from its immoral drinking problem—was obscured by the more sensational fallout from illegal bootlegging. Lori Rotskoff states that "as long as Demon Rum was demonized as a grave social threat, the traditional gendered order seemed to mandate the Eighteenth Amendment," though as the law persisted, "repeal advocates began to sway public opinion against Prohibition, arguing that it caused problems worse than those it was intended to eliminate: a black market in liquor, organized crime, urban violence, and a general disrespect for the law" (34). These consequences bear profoundly in Faulkner and Warren, particularly since each author gives distinct versions of how Prohibition as a failure in legislative "progress," in turn, reflects back on a region with no real interest (or chance) to progress meaningfully.

Francois Pitavy remarks of *Sanctuary*: "Prohibition so saturates the narrative that it comes to inform it—to control its very writing. From subject matter, [P]rohibition becomes a governing concept ordering the narrative—at once what is told and what must remain untold" (1). Lost in some of the more sensational scenes is the fact that *Sanctuary* is unmistakably about Prohibition. The central plot—Temple's abduction by Popeye, Horace Benbow's recovery of her, and her perjury at Lee Goodwin's trial—relies on the outward signifiers of Prohibition, setting the text firmly within the cultural milieu of the Volstead Act. These dramatic events betray a region under the siege of corruption, and this state of affairs is more troubling given the manner in which liquor was made illegal. Indeed, that Prohibition arose from a groundswell of political and moral fusion by temperance reformers makes the outright flaunting of the law all the more egregious. Faulkner biographer Joseph Blotner is right in describing the world of *Sanctuary* as a kind of "wasteland" (269), and this decay is moral, social, and political, rotting church and brothel alike.

Nearly every character in the novel imbibes illicitly, revealing the depth to which the culture of drinking is entrenched in Faulkner's South. Jefferson's geographic and class divisions fall on either side of the bootlegging line—Lee Goodwin and his crew of roughneck moonshiners distill liquor at the Old Frenchman Place on the outskirts of town, while Jefferson's thirsty consumers anxiously await distribution into the city. This symbiotic relationship is illegal of course, though it exists peacefully since all are drinking and the arrangement remains mutually beneficial. Faulkner's indictment of legislative inefficiency does not rely solely on corrupt senators and police chiefs frequenting brothels, however. In *Sanctuary*, only a corncob suffices to symbolize how Prohibition's progressive bent fails miserably in a region preoccupied with outdated precepts of hierarchy and oppression. Herein lies one of the novel's most penetrating critiques of the Volstead Act, broadly speaking to the South's farsighted failure to embrace progress: Narcissa and the rest of the Baptists—the embodiment of "progressive" temperance, whose sole mission is to reform sinful sots—remain the lowest common moral denominator, saboteurs emblematic of the South's privileging of hegemony over progress and, for that matter, justice.

Like the temperance reformers with whom they share Dry sentiment, Narcissa and company couch their ideology in stark moral Right-Wrong terms and remain undeterred in achieving their version of a just society. The problem with this mentality, though, is that their covert manipulation seems more an act of self-preservation than benevolence or reform. Furthermore, their actions register as even more sinister given the increasingly porous class boundaries that now exist as illegal booze is transported to and from the backwoods. As these two Prohibition era worlds collide—city and country—Narcissa and her cohort pocket their moral compasses in order to reinforce social boundaries at the expense of justice. Horace Benbow understands the reaches of this mentality as Narcissa (his own sister!) and the Baptists sabotage his case, culminating in their bullying Ruby Lamar (former prostitute and current girlfriend of Lee Goodwin, who stands trial for murder) from the hotel in town. Benbow angrily confronts the hotel clerk for relenting to their demands:

"They come in this morning. A committee of them.

You know how it is, I reckon."

"You mean to say you let the Baptist church dictate who your guests shall be?"

"It's them ladies. You know how it is, once they get set on a thing. A man might just as well give up and do like they say." (Faulkner 180)

Underscoring the Baptist resistance here is that the moonshining economy arising due to continued demand for liquor inadvertently smears longstanding social class lines, threatening Jefferson's white social class hegemony. The Popeyes, born of Prohibition, exist solely to facilitate backwoods moonshine to hubs of urban consumption; they remain invisible as they shuttle back and forth. Thus, it is Lee Goodwin who is perceived as the threatening menace. Suddenly visible, he cannot be ignored, and Benbow's involvement with Ruby and Lee exacerbates the unease felt when moonshining country hicks provide opposition for conservative Drys. The social order being protected by Narcissa's morally contradictory behavior is meant to insulate Jefferson's most fragile demographic: women, particularly young women susceptible to the predations of dangerous men. While race traditionally plays a large part to engender such a fear, *Sanctuary* is relatively void of the Faulknerian racial interplay seen in other novels. Replacing the black threat to the preservation of southern womanhood, then, are men of the lower-class (i.e., Goodwin and others from the margins).

Intensifying this fear is the fact that, because alcohol is illegal, Prohibition reconfigures the social dynamic for young people who were curious to drink. This demographic seems particularly vulnerable to the newly emerging culture of illicit consumption. The intoxicating combination of drinking rituals and southern masculinity produces a dangerous amalgamation for someone eager to assert himself as the next generation of the South's elite—someone, of course, like Gowan Stevens. Although Temple Drake comes to embody Prohibition's myriad failures in the novel, Gowan represents how young drinkers during Volstead America dangerously resisted vacuous legislation. John W. Crowley notes that "Simply because it became illicit, drinking possessed a singular importance; drinking in defiance of Prohibition was a sign of solidarity with the rising generation's resistance to what it called 'puritanism' and to what it considered to be the oppression of bourgeois

American life" (37). Young and highly educated (just ask him), Gowan could potentially represent this socially conscious resistance, yet eludes such characterization through his phony posturing as a "Virginia gentleman." Rather than drink in political protest, as Crowley notes, Gowan imbibes under the pretext of an outdated southern caricature that no longer holds purchase in a socially progressing America.

What also negates Gowan as a potential figure of progress is the fact that he has a severe drinking problem, and the toxic combination of alcoholism and affected southern honor catalyze the violent convergence of city and country when Temple is abandoned and left to the predatory devices of Popeye and the Goodwin crew. Gowan's drinking assumes more nefarious significance when considering how drunkenness was tied to precepts of southern masculinity, something Stevens holds in high regard, boasting that "'I went to school at Virginia. Teach you how to drink, there'" (32). The deviance in his drinking is compounded by this purported gentlemanliness, as his masculinity not only becomes subsumed by his drunkenness but comes to represent the very (perceived) threat to the bastion of southern social stability. Susan Zieger traces this threat as it appeared in nineteenth-century temperance narratives: "Such stories made 'habitual drunkenness' and 'intemperance' bywords for the systematic depletion of white, middle-class, masculine subjective dynamism; the 'slavery of drink' metaphor ironically recast white men as figuratively black, disempowered, static, and emasculated," (21) all terms aptly relating to this Virginia Gentleman. Progressive though Prohibition purported to be, Faulkner's appropriation of it suggests otherwise, particularly in its southern manifestation. Volstead-era Jefferson becomes the locus of corruption unchained—not only are people profiting from illegal booze but Yoknapatawpha's conservative Drys, seemingly the only teetotaling demographic remaining, signify this legislative failure through a moral hypocrisy that privileges self-preservation over justice. *This*, Faulkner implies, is what happens when progress is understood in moral terms: the Temple is desecrated, the Virginia Gentleman emasculated, the innocent bootlegger lynched, and the city rumrunner escapes, all the while senators, judges, and police officers drunkenly patronize Memphis brothels. In Faulkner's Jefferson, illegal drinking remains closeted at best, encouraged at worst, laying bare the hypocrisy of a region that unapologetically gains from outlawed liquor while cleaving to the "progressive" ethos of temperance reform.

While *Sanctuary* and *All the King's Men* both rely on the context of Prohibition to facilitate a critique of regional stagnation, only *Sanctuary* was written during the Volstead reign, rendering its portrayal of a conflicted South fundamentally different from Warren's post-Repeal representation. To be sure, *All the King's Men* uses the Eighteenth Amendment to show corruption, but Prohibition is less foregrounded, rendering the context itself less important than how the novel's culture of illegal drinking symbolizes the futility in Willie Stark's progressive ideology. Warren's South—Wet or Dry—wrestles with the threat of literal annihilation, represented in Willie Stark's increasingly fascist political sensibility. Stark's alcoholic governance is closely tied to his consumption; in the novel, power exchange occurs while people are drinking (sometimes illegally, always problematically). As a populist response to the South's social and political inaction, Stark's power play seems well conceived (while corruption and power eventually erode his utilitarian political platform, his early intentions are indeed progressive in their motive to help the underprivileged), ruthlessly executed, though improperly managed, in many ways not unlike Prohibition. And where Prohibition fails to reform a nation of problem drinkers, Stark's populist vision also goes unfulfilled, both in its encounter with the region's old guard anti-progressive politicians and in his personal devolution from hick idealist to tainted megalomaniac. The disregard for legislated morality parallels the backlash against forcefully mandated collective welfare, and Stark couches his politics in an ethical dichotomy (Right-Wrong, Good-Bad) similar to that used by temperance reformers. A complete inversion of the entrenched ideological status quo proves impossible in the face of mounting unease at Stark's increasing radicalism. Thus, the blasé manner in which the novel's drinking characters violate the terms of the Volstead Act inadvertently undercuts any chance that Stark's political platform might succeed. Willie Stark's own foray into the culture of illegal drinking speaks presciently to how, in the end, he meets a violent demise.

Jack's first introduction to Cousin Willie Stark occurs in 1922 at Slade's place, a small-town speakeasy serving as the gathering point for local politicians and backdoor drinkers alike. At the time, Stark is the Mason County Treasurer, accompanying a colleague to a meeting with Tiny Duffy. Initially, Duffy is reluctant to engage in conversation with the two small-town politicians, since he "was never talkative in the morning before he had worried down two or three drinks" (War-ren 13). When Slade offers beer to the entire table, Willie politely refuses on account that "'[My wife] Lucy don't favor drinking . . . For a fact'" (17). When Tiny pressures Willie, he remains steadfast, prompting Slade to proclaim, "'I sells beer to them as wants it. I ain't making nobody drink it'" (17). This seemingly inconsequential episode is important in how it establishes the centrality of alcohol and drinking to Warren's critical concerns. In what becomes a hallmark of Stark's reign, he does not forget Slade's treatment, and this gesture receives recognition in time: "Well, anyway, when Repeal came and mailmen had to use Mack trucks to haul the applications for licenses over to the City Hall, Slade got a license. He got a license immediately, and he got a swell location" (17). Stark's payback assumes added significance in that it stems from an incident pertaining to alcohol, and Slade's post-Repeal success positions the novel's symbolic location of political action within the space of alcohol consumption. Once averse to drink because "Lucy don't favor [it]," the Boss now privileges both Slade's loyalty and his line of business, a sentiment touching on the convergence of politics and consumption, or more appropriately, the politics of consumption.

Stark's crossover into the realm of drinking and corruption pro-vides a nice example of how one part political power and many parts alcohol, when mixed, tastes of the region's tenuous relation to social and political change. While on the campaign trail during his first gubernatorial run, Stark's speeches bore audiences with, among other things, details about the tax code. While his ideas are rooted in a senti-ment opposing the political status quo, they fail to inspire. It is not until after learning from Jack and Sadie Burke that he has been put up solely to divide the vote that Stark transforms from teetotaling Cousin Willie to the ruthless, drunken Boss. What catalyzes this evolution is a spectacular binge followed by a dramatic transformation in Stark's political rhetoric, exemplifying an emerging political consciousness that emphasizes power over pragmatism, action over diplomacy. The irony in this episode should not go unnoticed: Willie's binge spurs his politics into action, but the booze required to cure his stage fright is consumed *illegally*, a flagrant violation of a law meant to protect soci-ety's vulnerable. In Warren's South, this segment of the population are those to whom Stark speaks with his populist sensibilities, yet Stark is only able to make his appeal upon breaking the law. Initially, this irony goes unnoticed, as Stark's surge of confidence and power radically challenge the state's hegemonic, anti-progressive institutions. But the further he pushes his agenda, the more that opposition mobilizes itself, and regardless of how well intentioned the politics are, they cannot survive the inevitable backlash. What begins as a simple drink snowballs into the radical subversion of the social-political status quo, proving it is no coincidence that Stark's ascendance commences in breaking the law while campaigning to be a lawmaker.

The morning after Stark's binge, he awakens in a horrible state. Jack coaches Willie through the hangover so that he can make his scheduled speech. After Willie vomits, Jack goes to the only means he knows to improve Stark's condition: "'More coffee?' [Stark] asked. 'No,' I said, and unstrapped my suitcase and got out the second bottle. I poured some in a tumbler and took it to him" (88). Jack repeatedly "give[s] a treatment," dosing no less than four drinks to Willie as he prepares for the speech. As they approach the fairgrounds by car, "Willie put out his hand and laid it on the flask. 'Gimme that thing,' he said." Jack's protestations against too much treatment go unrecognized: "But he already had it in his mouth by that time and the sound of it gargling down would have drowned the sound of my words even if I had kept on wasting them. When he handed the thing back to me, there wasn't enough to make it worth my while putting it in my pocket" (88). Having finished a pint of (highly potent) liquor on the heels of a considerable bender the night before, Stark is clearly intoxicated—"'Hair [of the dog], hell,' [Sadie] said, 'he must have swallowed the dog'" (90). Tiny Duffy also notices Willie's state, to which Jack tellingly replies, "'He never touches the stuff,' I said. 'It's just he's been on the road to Damascus and he saw a great light and he's got the blind staggers'" (89). Jack's ironic reference to the Apostle Paul's conversion conveys a deeper significance to the episode unfolding. Willie Stark has indeed been converted—a symbolic baptism by fire (water) that he conceives of in explicitly Biblical terms—and he sees himself in the midst of a moral conundrum where he represents good against the evil political establishment. The state's political situation is fundamentally imbalanced, requiring a dramatic moral-ideological fix, much like the national abstinence advocated for by divinely driven temperance reformers. Stark forcefully sermonizes, "'And it came to him with the powerful force of God's own lightning'" (91) that he was set up to divide the MacMurfee and Harrison factions. As Willie concludes, he identifies Tiny Duffy as the puppet master behind the whole scheme: "'There is the Judas Iscariot, the lick-spittle, the nose-wiper!'" (92). Stark shoves Duffy off the stage, before finishing the speech with what becomes the basis for his populist platform: "'Whatever a hick wants he's got to do for himself. Nobody in a fine automobile and sweet-talking is going to do it for him. When I come back to run for Governor again, I'm coming on my own and I'm coming for blood. But I'm getting out now'" (93).

True to his word, Willie exits the race, but not before cementing a new political reputation, anticipating a successful campaign four years later. But at what cost? Granted, his ascension provides the disinherited with a powerful and charismatic figure speaking on their behalf. What plagues this ideological benevolence, however, is the manner in which he bridges the gap between the old and new guards. When a supposedly progressive platform requires illegal maneuvering and thuggish intimidation, then perhaps "progress" in Warren's South need be re-examined. The dramatic inversion of existing power structures necessitates the irony in its implementation—Good and Bad, Moral and Immoral all resist sound categorical footing against the historical backdrop of a constitutional amendment that complicated any solid notion of right and wrong. As both politician and drinker, Governor Stark remains fundamentally different than Cousin Willie, and the fact that his transformation begins with a sustained alcoholic episode during Prohibition sets the stage for the novel's larger critique of social change in the South: if it takes someone like Willie Stark to facilitate change, and the inevitable results of such concentrated power are violence and death, then how might the region navigate the choppy waters of modernity, if at all? Like Faulkner before him, Warren locates Prohibition as the perfect historical moment through which to critique how the South's course of action *vis-à-vis* social progress is insufficient. Although neither author offers the prescriptive anodyne for the region's ideological stasis, they at least re-appropriate a common (and often celebrated) trope—the southern drinking man—to demonstrate the fallacy of such a cultural characteristic. Drinking during Prohibition in Faulkner's and Warren's Souths reconfigures the act into something symbolic of a fundamental hesitance to progress. As the region was forced to confront the swirl of change from outside, antiquated markers of cultural hegemony no longer sufficed. Prohibition's impetus at social and political reform proves ill-equipped, particularly in a region that unapologetically cleaves to the past at the expense of the future.

Notes

1. The Eighteenth Amendment to the Constitution, more commonly known as Prohibition or the Volstead Act, was ratified on January 16, 1919 and went into effect on January 17, 1920. Section 1 of the Eighteenth Amendment is worded as follows: "After one year from the ratification of this article the manufacture, sale or transportation of intoxicating liquors within, the importation thereof into, or the exportation thereof from the United States and all territory subject to the jurisdiction thereof for beverage purposes is hereby prohibited" (qtd in Okrent). Prohibition was repealed on December 5, 1933.

Works Cited

Blotner, Joseph. *Faulkner: A Biography*. 1974. Jackson: U P of Mississippi, 2005. Print.

Chavigny, Katherine A. "Reforming Drunkards in Nineteenth-Century America: Religion, Medicine, Therapy." *Altering American Consciousness: The History of Alcohol and Drug Use in the United States, 1800-2000*. Ed. Sarah W. Tracey and Caroline Jean Acker. Amherst: U of Massachusetts P, 2004. 108–123. Print.

Crowley, John W. *The White Logic: Alcoholism and Gender in American Modernist Fiction*. Amherst: U of Massachusetts P, 1994. Print.

Faulkner, William. *Sanctuary*. 1931. New York: First Vintage International Edition, 1993. Print.

Okrent, Daniel. *Last Call: The Rise and Fall of Prohibition*. New York: Scribner, 2010. Print.

Pitavy, Francois. "Prohibition in William Faulkner's *Sanctuary*: Motif and Metaphor." (1996): 1–8. Web. 15 Mar. 2011.

Rotskoff, Lori. *Love on the Rocks: Men, Women, and Alcohol in Post-World War II America*. Chapel Hill: U of North Carolina P, 2002. Print.

Warren, Robert Penn. *All the King's Men*. 1946. New York: Harcourt Brace
    & Company, 1996. Print.

Zieger, Susan. *Inventing the Addict: Drugs, Race, and Sexuality in Nine-
    teenth-Century British and American Literature*. Amherst: U
    of Massachusetts P, 2008. Print.

Jason Zerbe

"The only way a young man could earn money in school": "Wild Palms," The National Sporting Press, and the Professionalization of College Football

During his time at the University of Virginia, William Faulkner attended a number of Cavalier football games and often sat alongside his biographer, Joseph Blotner. On November 16, 1957, the two men watched a struggling Virginia team lose to South Carolina, despite Faulkner's ardent and rather vocal support from the stands. Perhaps perplexed by the reserved author's genuine excitement, Blotner asked Faulkner if he hadn't seen better football in his hometown of Oxford, where the University of Mississippi boasted a perennial national championship contender throughout the 1950s. In response, Faulkner claimed to "like this. This is real amateur sport. At home they got a tame millionaire and he buys a team for them. That's professional sports. This is amateur" (Blotner 646). Not surprisingly, this anecdote illustrates Faulkner's lifelong fascination with the game of football, which he reportedly played until his high school years and enjoyed watching on television (Blotner 47, 656). What is striking about Faulkner's statement, though, is that it is informed by the rigid binary influencing the better part of general discussion about collegiate football in the popular press of the early 1920s to the late 1950s: amateurism/professionalism. That Faulkner is even able to offer "inside dope" about the excessive disbursement of athletic subsidies at Ole Miss betrays his intimate awareness of the corruption of college athletics, as well as his engagement with a debate that played out on the pages of the same national magazines in which he published his short fiction.

In light of Faulkner's obvious interest in the debate surrounding the ethics of professionalization in an ostensibly amateur game, and football more generally, it is quite remarkable that very little scholarship explores the author's engagement with the sport in his fiction. The lack of scholarly attention paid to this issue is particularly notable, considering Faulkner's decision to devote an entire chapter of *The Hamlet* (1940) to Labove, an Ole Miss football star. Even in the scholarly discussion on this chapter, only Christian Messenger provides a significant reading of Labove *qua* football star, suggesting that Faulkner "relies heavily on the reader's knowledge of that *modern* stereotype from the athletic field" to parody popular culture's school football star by placing him in the Mississippi backcountry during the 1890s, a milieu in which no one holds any regard for his on-field achievements (220). Messenger's reading is certainly a valuable contribution to critical understandings of Labove, but what makes it even more intriguing is the way in which its focus on pop cultural texts parallels many scholarly treatments of *The Wild Palms* (1939), the novel which directly precedes *The Hamlet* in Faulkner's oeuvre.

While the critical discourse surrounding *The Wild Palms* typically centers on the connection between the alternating narratives of "Wild Palms" and "Old Man," scholars often attend to the myriad references to pop cultural artifacts in the two tales, and particularly those found in "Wild Palms." Certainly, the Tall Convict in "Old Man" disastrously attempts to live out pulp fantasies, but Cleanth Brooks and Thomas McHaney, both early commentators on the texts influencing the novel, argue that Faulkner draws on the popular literary tradition of romantic love in crafting Harry Wilbourne and Charlotte Rittenmeyer's tragic pursuit of an ideal love (*Beyond* 210; *A Study* 51). Anne Goodwyn Jones, who notes the novel's "almost obsessive" concern with popular culture, reworks Brooks's and McHaney's argument to suggest that "Wild Palms" is "a masculine popular romance plot written by men for men . . . that attempts to warn men away" from the illusion of perfect love permeating mass art forms (156). For Pamela Rhodes and Richard Godden, "Wild Palms" is a result of Faulkner's exploitation as a screenwriter in Hollywood and represents a reflection on how "the whole social metabolism has been invaded by the dominant commodity form" governing the products of popular culture (92).

Although these considerations of the popular forms penetrating "Wild Palms" are important and enlightening, scholars seem to have dismissed the national sporting press as an element of mass culture unworthy of serious inquiry. Indeed, Goodwyn Jones gives a sense of the critical consensus, as she claims to notice everything from "dance marathons to movies to pop fiction—romances, true confessions, westerns, and detective stories" in the tale, without broaching the issue to popular sport (145). I hope to add to the investigation into the popular texts infusing "Wild Palms," the story Faulkner claims he was "trying to tell" in *The Wild Palms,* by examining the extent to which the national press's discussions and representations of college football in the 1920s and 30s influence certain aspects of the narrative (*University* 171). More specifically, I posit that Harry Wilbourne is a character deeply affected by popular perceptions of excessive subsidies doled out to collegiate football stars and that the national press's treatment of the sport has a marked effect on Faulkner's characterization of several other men in the story.

Professionalism and the National Sporting Press

Although the professionalization of college athletics has been a topic of debate since the 1880s, when Ivy League institutions began accusing each other of hiring tramp athletes, discussions of college football did not center on the issue until the 1920s. The condemnation of college football's corrupting professionalism first found frequent attention in monthly and quarterly magazines of opinion, such as the *Independent, Outlook, New Republic,* and other publications read mostly by America's patrician class in the 1920s. Unquestionably, the most ardent defender of college football's "amateur ideal" was Harvard graduate and former Crimson tennis player, John R. Tunis, whose 1928 *Harper's* essay, "The Great God Football," was the first of his many scathing critiques of college football's unabashed commercialism. In this polemic, Tunis accuses universities of "making a regular profession of football" and turning the sport into "almost a national religion," as he ultimately urges institutions to realize "that what they have on their hands is a first-class octopus which is strangling many of the legitimate pursuits of educational institutions" (95–96). Tunis would disseminate this sort of rhetoric throughout his career, and he became so obsessed with what he viewed as the damaging professional ethos of college football that he would become a well-known figure in the American press by the 1930s.

However, Tunis's persistence rendered him an object of ridicule among his colleagues, rather than a celebrated champion of amateurism. For example, in a 1939 *Newsweek* article, John Lardner joked that "The evils of college football have been exposed officially, with names and numbers, for the eighteenth time in the last ten years, by John R. Tunis . . . The new revelations . . . have left America stagnant with excitement" (qtd. in Oriard 110). Such criticism certainly indicates the prevalence of Tunis's views in the national sporting press, but it also suggests that, as Michael Oriard asserts, "during the hard times of the Depression, the values of sporting gentlemen were an impossibly hard sell" (110). It is no surprise, then, that by the mid-1930s, the public discussion of college football was moving in a new direction on the pages of general interest publications, such as *The Saturday Evening Post*, which targeted a more middle-class readership.

In 1937, the same year Faulkner began to write *The Wild Palms*, Francis Wallace began writing his "Pigskin Previews" for the *Post* and regularly presented a view of athletic subsidies decidedly different from Tunis's. Instead of opposing the professionalization of college football, Wallace attacked college administrators and coaches for knowing "that the stork doesn't bring football players," yet still refusing to admit their institutions' disbursement of subsidies (qtd. in Oriard 112). For Wallace, even more disturbing than hypocrisy were the exploitative business practices it allowed for, as he illustrated in his 1936 *Post* article, "I Am a Football Fixer":

> They pay these boys and masquerade the payment . . .
> They train this talent using expert coaches and scien-
> tific equipment . . . They present the athletes in great
> outdoor stadia and charge all that the traffic will bear
> . . . Because they pay low prices for raw material and
> services, and charge high for the finished product, they
> make profit. (qtd. in Watterson 190)

By selling their highly professionalized, yet grossly underfunded players as amateurs, Wallace suggested, school officials sought to keep the paying public's interest focused on the high-quality, yet suppos-edly pure college game as an unabashedly professional brand of football began to gain popularity. Essentially, Wallace was upset with the false product he saw on the field each fall Saturday and pushed for big-time college football programs to openly acknowledge the funds they granted to athletes.

Despite Wallace's espousal of open athletic scholarships, he dis-played the Northern bias typical of many national sportswriters in his condemnation of the Southeastern Conference (SEC), which became the first conference to openly offer athletic subsidies in 1935. Faulkner, of course, spent most of his life in the heart of the SEC, and, as his comments to Blotner in 1957 suggest, would probably have been well aware of Wallace's reasons for finding a general movement "definitely away from excess, except in the South," in national recruiting practices during the 1939 season (qtd. in Oriard 115). Indeed, in 1936, former Ole Miss assistant coach Russell Crane boasted to Bob Zuppke, the head coach of a struggling Illinois program, that "The Southern schools are getting it down to a science," and claimed that many were even beginning to fund clinics for high school coaches in an effort to develop more in-state talent (qtd. in Watterson 184). So, although the wide-ranging debate surrounding the professionalization of college athletics was certainly a national one, it often centered on the South and, as I hope to show, was something that the Faulkner of "Wild Palms," a Southern writer deeply concerned with contemporary popular culture, could simply not ignore.

What if Harry Wilbourne Strapped on a Helmet?

One of Harry Wilbourne's more intriguing characteristics in "Wild Palms" is his seemingly constant need to understand his quest for perfect love with Charlotte Rittenmeyer, as the consequence of his innocence or sexual inexperience. Though he tells his friend McCord that his relationship with Charlotte "lasted as long as it did because I waited too long . . . twenty seven is too long to wait to get out of your system what you should have rid yourself of at fourteen or fifteen or maybe even younger," he eventually looks to his medical school years as he ruminates on missed opportunities to lose his virginity (137). For example, after he learns that Charlotte has become pregnant in Utah, forcing him to struggle with her demands for an abortion, he thinks that *"this is the price of the twenty-six years, the two thousand dollars I stretched over four of them by not smoking, by keeping my virginity until it damn near sapped on me"* (208). Clearly, Harry has come to understand that a deferral of sexual pleasure was necessary for him to progress through medical school on the two thousand dollars left to him in his father's will, and that such a suspension of gratification has rendered him susceptible to the ill-fated journey to live out the sort of romantic love story only "read in books" (48).

Considering Harry's reflections, the explanations as to why he is unable to supplement his father's two thousand dollar outlay seem particularly significant. Soon after the first section of "Wild Palms," in which it is evident that Charlotte's life is in jeopardy, presumably because of something Harry has done, the narrator begins the second section of the story by describing the early years of a man whose lover now has reason to call him a "bungling bastard" (21). In this interesting exposition, the reader learns that Harry's father entered medical school "when an education could be paid for in kind or in labor . . . and had completed his four year course at a cash outlay of two hundred dollars" by heating dormitories and waiting tables (31). Though the "elder Wilbourne" leaves his only son two thousand dollars for a medical education, "*believing that the aforesaid sum will be amply sufficient for that purpose*," Harry discovers that it "was not much more than his father's two hundred had been. It was less, because there was steam heat in the dormitories now and the college was served by a cafeteria requiring no waiters and the only way a young man could earn money in school now was by carrying a football or stopping the man who did carry it" (31–32). Certainly, modern technology has replaced the menial jobs his father held in medical school, but Harry is a student whose legitimate academic aims are primarily complicated by an excessively professionalized brand of college football, which, according to Tunis, had "tentacles all over the educational world" (qtd. in Watterson 398).

Because the subsidies-obsessed Tunis never mentions Harry's educational struggles in his writings, it is safe to assume that he never read *Wild Palms*, but it is important to note that education is not the only aspect of university life that a lack of funds complicates for Faulkner's protagonist. Harry's poverty also forces him to abstain from even the simplest pleasures, but even after "stopping tobacco for a year," he still has "nothing left over for squiring girls . . . as he balanced his dwindling bank account against the turned pages of his books" (*Palms* 32). Such an inability to court co-eds can be interpreted as a direct result of the university's disbursement of athletic subsidies in place of medical scholarships. Furthermore, the reasons Faulkner offers for Harry's non-existent love life seem to function as a response to "a new formula in 1930s football fiction and film, in which the shady ethics of subsidization served as the backdrop for conventional romance," and any criticism was silenced as the campus hero invariably got the girl (Oriard 102). In his treatment of Harry's experience in medical school, then,

Faulkner clearly turns to the pervasive issue of athletic subsidies to suggest that the corrupting professionalism hotly debated in the nation's sporting press, yet ambivalently depicted in popular fiction and film, can have a devastating effect not only on the "amateur ideal" but also on the average student who must pay for an education at the expense of youthful romance. Indeed, Faulkner seems to suggest that Harry could only have avoided his ultimate plight if he were able to strap on a helmet and display a certain level of athletic prowess.

Bradley, Callaghan, and the Corruption of College Athletics

In 1939, readers of "Wild Palms" would have most likely seen Faulkner as an avowed Tunisite after his description of Harry's Wilbourne's four years in medical school. While Faulkner may consciously avoid Tunis's infamous octopus metaphor, he does seem to share the sportswriter's view that all aspects of the professionalized college game, including scholarship players, adversely affect the academic aims of individual students and the university as a whole. In May of 1947, shortly after visiting a number of English courses at the University of Mississippi, Faulkner even wrote to the Ole Miss English department to demand that his classroom visits not be mentioned in the same "high-pressure ballyhoo" that boasted of how "our football team almost beat A&M" in an effort to lure students to Oxford (*Letters* 249). Later, in 1958, Faulkner responded to a question on the higher education of African Americans by suggesting that black students were more amenable to education while "the white man says . . . I've got to have a good football team or I ain't going there. I've got to have cheerleaders or I may not like it" (*University* 220). Although these statements indicate the extent to which Faulkner ultimately upheld Tunis's views, "Wild Palms" reveals a certain ambiguity in his thoughts regarding the status of the college athlete. Specifically, near the end of the story, he seems to move toward Wallace's view of the professionalized college athlete as an under-subsidized laborer duped into doing grunt work for a corrupt and corrupting business run by college administrators.

Perhaps to emphasize the significance of Harry's time in the university, the narrator of "Wild Palms" often attempts to give some sense of how a number of other men in the story experienced college life. This occurs most noticeably with Francis Rittenmeyer, but it also occurs with Bradley, whom Harry and Charlotte meet after they leave

Chicago to spend the autumn months in the Wisconsin wilderness. Bradley's appearance in the story is rather brief, but it is clearly worth considering, as his "crass and insolent confidence" is both unsettling and threatening for Harry, reminding him, as Charlotte says, "that I divide at the belly" (107). What is striking about Bradley's confidence is that the narrator leaves little doubt that it was developed over four years at "an Eastern college," where he presumably acquired the eyes that "did not laugh, the assured, predatory eyes of the still successful prom leader" (*Palms* 106–7). These details, along with the "hard violent bone-crushing meaningless grip" with which Bradley greets Harry, certainly characterize him as what Mary C. McComb identifies as the conventional campus hero "of the 1920s—star football players, captains of sports teams, smooth talkers, and prom leaders" (*Palms* 106; *Depression* 60). Furthermore, in a 1941 letter to Random House editor Saxe Commins, in which he bemoans Ole Miss's late-season loss to Mississippi State, Faulkner clearly links athletic ability to sexual prowess, claiming that if members of the Rebel team "are still fumbling at their other two avocations like they were doing last at football they have been chaste since and must be about starved by now" (*Letters* 147). It is no wonder, then, that Harry is more than a little discomfited in Bradley's presence, for it must seem to him as though the star athlete who received his scholarship money is now in Wisconsin to win his lover. Ironically, though, Bradley introduces himself to offer a box of extra food, which Harry tries to reject as a belated and meager form of compensation.

That Bradley seems to possess all of the attributes of a campus sports hero provides, at least for the narrator, a fairly clear indication of the sort of work he does for a living. Specifically, what could be described as the rather athletic handshake noted above betrays him as "a broker's front man," who has been out of college for only two years (*Palms* 106). Though Bradley has done nothing to suggest that he works to conceal the questionable business practices of his employer, it is as if the "Bad Smell" of professionalized college athletics still follows him (107). For the narrator, Bradley is the same sort of "front man" in the business world that he was on the college gridiron, where he presumably cloaked his professional status under the widely invoked "amateur ideal" in order to boost the profits of his "Eastern college."

While Bradley is certainly tainted by a corrupting professionalism, the most deplorable "front man" in "Wild Palms" is Callaghan, the man who "hires" Harry to oversee the unpaid immigrant workers at his Utah mines. Like Bradley, Callaghan appears only briefly, in his office in Chicago, where he is unsurprisingly introduced as a man with "the body of a two-hundred-and-twenty-pound college fullback gone to fat, in a suit of expensive tweed which nevertheless looked on him as if he had taken it from a fire sale at the point of a pistol" (128). Here, Callaghan is the corrupted athlete turned business administrator, and his strict negotiations with his voluntary medical prospect seem to mimic the unfair dealings of university officials attempting to lure valuable athletic talent.

Faulkner seems to highlight the athlete's powerlessness in such negotiations, as Harry accepts an incredibly low salary, which Callaghan does not even intend to pay. More interestingly, Harry proves valuable enough for Callaghan to pay for two train tickets to Utah, and the transportation, lodging, and food that he does eventually receive from his employer mirror the "wages" paid to college athletes after their tuition was waived. For example, as one college coach claimed, after "greeting and hand shaking," college officials saw that incoming football recruits had "a place to eat, a place to sleep, often they pay the travelling expense for better boys" (qtd. in Watterson 184). Ultimately, in Harry's dealings with Callaghan, Faulkner's own ambivalence regarding the status of the professionalized college athletes is most evident. Harry is rendered a voluntary recruit who is exploited by an employer, but that employer is a former player whose "four-year course in deception," as Wallace puts it, has made him more than willing to sell false prospects, just as he helped to sell a false product on the gridiron (qtd. in Oriard 111).

Faulkner's ambivalence on this issue is also evident after Harry assumes his unpaid post at the mine in Utah. Buckner, the mine's acting manager, informs Harry that "there hasn't been a payroll here" in nearly four months and suggests that the crew of Poles still working at the mine are there simply because they cannot "understand dishonesty" (*Palms* 188). That the Poles are the only group left working for Callaghan is especially relevant to this discussion, as young men of Polish descent, most notably the University of Minnesota's Bronko Nagurski, were widely celebrated for their exploits on the athletic field throughout the 1920s and 30s. Indeed, by the late 1930s, Polish stars, such as

Nagurski, Creighton's Charlie Klem (Klemaszewski), Fordham's Ed Danowski, and Bill Ozmanski of Holy Cross, "had become so numerous that an air of retrospective complacency settled over the Polish press," which had fervently lauded its gridiron stars since the early 1920s (Oriard 266). But a number of national sportswriters pointed to Polish players to highlight the corruption of the college game, with Tunis even creating "Slats Miskowitch, the Power House of East Dakota" as a prototype for the professionalized player destroying the "amateur ideal" (qtd. in Oriard 273). As Oriard points out, "Poles from Chicago playing for the University of Washington might be a source of pride in the Polish American press but evidence of professionalism in an article in *Collier's*" (273).

In light of this treatment of Polish players in the popular press, Faulkner's presentation of the workers at the Utah mine is particularly intriguing. For Harry, whose alienation from the ideal college hero has been illustrated above, the Poles seem to be school sports stars stripped of their pads and removed from Saturday afternoon's spectacle. For example, he initially perceives the Poles as "giant-seeming men" working in an athletic sort of "frenzy," but comes to realize that "none of them were the giants they seemed, that the illusion of size was an aura, an emanation of that wild childlike innocence and credulity which they possessed in common" (*Palms* 186–7). In Utah, then, Faulkner presents the college athlete, more specifically the ethnic athlete, as little more than an abused laborer unaware of his own exploitation. But perhaps because of Tunis's marked influence on his own thoughts concerning professionalization, which appears to preclude Faulkner from betraying his sympathy for subsidized football stars, the author is either unable or unwilling to explicitly link his Poles with the likes of Nagurski and other Polish gridiron stars. Instead, Faulkner turns to a sport that had been openly professional since the 1890s, as his narrator notes the Poles' "tongue which Wilbourne could not understand almost exactly like a college baseball team cheering one another on" (*Palms* 187). Regardless of what type of athletic team the Poles resemble, though, it is clear that Faulkner at least acknowledged a number of sportswriters, namely Wallace, who suggested that professionalized college athletes constituted a cheap and willing workforce that could be exploited to generate huge profits for universities across the country.

"Rat" Rittenmeyer and "Football's Public"

As pointed out above, the national debate on athletic subsidies often focused on the enormous proceeds universities enjoyed by staging weekly football contests. These profits, however, were perhaps more a result of the spectacle surrounding the game than the product on the field. As Oriard notes, beginning in the 1890s, newspaper accounts of Harvard-Yale and Yale-Princeton matchups centered on the social elites in attendance, thus "confirming for readers the social importance of the new sport" (163). Throughout the 1920s and 30s, as college football spread across the country, national magazines such as *The Literary Digest* and *The Saturday Evening Post* placed on their covers not players or coaches but what *Time* called "Football's Public," or the mass of "undergraduates, parents, alumni, their wives, sweethearts, cousins . . . every element of the country" sitting in the stands (qtd. in Oriard164). Most importantly, membership in "Football's Public," Oriard suggests, "had become a mark of upwardly mobile middle-class status" and signified "the best of what up-to-date America offered" (170).

If there is a character in "Wild Palms" who can be identified as a member of "Football's Public," it is certainly Francis Rittenmeyer. It is, after all, his middle class "respectability" that Charlotte seeks to escape. Also, Harry clearly views Francis as a man who wants only the best of what modern America has to offer, as he imagines the outrage elicited by the Charlotte's potential medical treatment on "*The Mississippi coast? Why in God's name the Mississippi coast? A country doctor in a little lost Mississippi shrimping village when in New Orleans there are the best, the very best—*" (*Palms* 225). Indeed, Faulkner offers a number of indications that membership in the nation's football community is an aspect of Francis's bourgeois pretensions, but he also suggests that his relationship to this community may run far deeper than the "double-breasted suits" with an "impeccable shirt and tie," which characterized the game-day attire of a successful alumnus (*Palms* 39, 55; Oriard 228).

As both Harry and the reader are introduced to Francis, Charlotte reveals that he is an alumnus of the University of Alabama. More specifically, "He is the senior living ex-freshman of the University of Alabama." In 1935, then, the twenty-seven-year-old Francis, who is Harry's "own age about," apparently looks back fondly on his time at the university, probably because he was an undergraduate when the Crimson Tide defeated the University of Washington to win the 1926

Rose Bowl title, and went on to tie Stanford in the same game the following year (*Palms* 38). The Tide's performances in Pasadena were monumental events in the South because, according to Andrew Doyle, Southern progressives were able to celebrate them as "proof that the region was every bit as modern as the rest of the nation" at a time when "industrial cities with skyscrapers and streetcars" were quickly becoming integral parts of the Southern landscape (117). Little wonder, then, that Francis, a man who has cultivated the modern bourgeois identity that is so suffocating for Charlotte, wishes to cling to his days as a freshman in Tuscaloosa.

Just as interesting as Francis's alma-mater is the nickname he earned during his years as a student. Expressly because of his designation as "the senior living ex-freshman of the University of Alabama," Charlotte claims, "we still call him Rat" (40). This appellation, perhaps inexplicable to modern readers, is richly pertinent in the context of Francis's collegiate career, which began just as a nationally distributed newspaper article, "The Story of a Graduate Manager," brought the term "rat" into the national sports lexicon in 1925.[1] This article, penned by an anonymous graduate assistant at an unspecified "big-time university," was essentially a behind-the-scenes look at the systems put in place to monitor the actions of subsidized football players. In it, the author reveals that students known as "'widows' made certain that athletes found their way to the right classes, while 'rats' trailed the laggards to report on their class attendance and hours of study" (Watterson 161). In light of this usage of the term, Charlotte's ostensibly jocose suggestion that her husband "still is sometimes" a "Rat" is interesting, for her husband does indeed hire a detective to trail and report on her and Harry while they are in Chicago and has presumably taken similar measures on other occasions (*Palms* 40). Furthermore, Francis's nickname clearly suggests that he is not only a member of "Football's Public" but one of its privileged members who have undergone what Oriard calls an "initiation into the game's subtle mysteries" (164).

Though it may seem a bit of stretch to suggest that Faulkner meant so much by designating Charlotte's husband as "Rat," it is important to point out that the author seems to have carefully considered the name this character. In the initial typescript of the first chapter of "Wild Palms," Charlotte, bleeding profusely after her botched abortion, cries "John! John! John!" after Harry tells her to "cover yourself up with something" (Rowan Oak). In the published version, of course, "it was 'rat,' the noun, which the doctor believed he heard" as a delirious Charlotte says, "You promised, rat. That was all I asked and you promised" (*Palms* 21). And once again, in the final chapter of the published story, Charlotte speaks to her absent husband, telling him to "Listen, Francis—See, I called you Francis. If I were lying to you do you think I would call you Francis instead of Rat?—Listen, Francis. It was the other one. Not that Wilbourne bastard" (228). This interesting shift from "John" to "Francis" (Wallace) and "Rat" should by no means be overlooked, as both the names in the published version shed light on the centrality of the sporting press in "Wild Palms."

Before ending this discussion of Francis, it is intriguing to consider a curious image that seems to be Faulkner's attempt to mimic weekly magazine covers with his prose. Immediately after Francis wishes "to make a plea" at Harry's trial, the crowd gathered in the courtroom becomes outraged, and the narrator describes "the separate screaming voices, the officers of the Court charging into the wave like a football team: a vortex of fury and turmoil about the calm immobile outrageous face above the smooth beautifully cut coat" (322). Obviously, this scene does not take place in a football stadium, but the football simile used to describe the officers, and more importantly the description of Rat as a composed spectator, is incredibly suggestive of two *Time* covers from 1930 and 1935, on which "Football's Public" is celebrated. Though the two *Time* covers are the only ones to give a label to "Football's Public," Faulkner would certainly have been familiar with the image of a well-dressed man, or group of men, surrounded by the crashing and flying bodies of competing football teams, as weekly magazines returned to it each fall throughout the 1920s and 30s (Oriard 164–70). This image of Francis in the courtroom, one of the final images of him offered in "Wild Palms," emphasizes his place among America's rising middle class and firmly entrenches him as a privileged member of "Football's Public" who enjoys the benefits of his inclusion in such a group.

Conclusion: "Wild Palms" and Frenchman's Bend's football star.

As I mentioned at the outset of this discussion, the critical insights into the plethora of pop cultural text in "Wild Palms" has been truly illuminating, but I hope to have shed new light on the significance of the sporting press in the story. My broader aim in carrying out this investigation, however, has been to encourage other scholars to reconsider the role of sport in Faulkner's fiction, for it is an area of inquiry that has been shockingly ignored in what is a massive body of scholarship. Specifically, I hope this study allows the Faulkner interpretive community to understand Labove's football talents in *The Hamlet* as more than a curious anomaly tacked on to a comic novel in order to parody popular pulp heroes. Labove's story, as Christian Messenger has illustrated, certainly is a parodic rewriting of the exploits of Frank Merriwell and others, but it also seems to be born out of the more serious issue of athletic subsidies that Faulkner engages with in "Wild Palms."

To give some indication of the intimate relationship between "Wild Palms" and Labove's chapter in *The Hamlet*, I want to briefly return to Harry Wilbourne. As Harry is penning his pulp stories in Chicago, the narrator describes his process as

> one sustained frenzied agonizing rush like the half-
> back working his way through school who grasps the
> ball (his Albatross, his Old Man of the Sea, which,
> not the opposing team, not the blank incontrovertible
> chalk marks profoundly terrifying and meaningless as
> an idiot's nightmare, is his sworn and mortal enemy)
> and runs until the play is completed—downed or
> across the goal line, it doesn't matter which. (*Palms*
> 121)

In this passage, it is as though Harry's thoughts, which become commodities the second he sets pen to page to compose his next "moronic fable," are directly compared to the athlete's body, which is little more than a piece of merchandise when he grasps a football on game day.

Considering the argument I offer above, the comparison Faulkner makes between a pulp writer and a college athlete may not be so surprising in "Wild Palms." In the comic world of *The Hamlet*, however, it is striking to read of Labove during "Saturday's climax when he carried a trivial contemptible obloid across fleeting and meaningless white lines" (109). Aside from its much more humorous tone, this passage bears a striking resemblance to the simile used to explain Harry's pulp writing and establishes a link between "Wild Palms" and *The Hamlet* that cannot be considered a mere coincidence. Indeed, such an evident connection between the two works can allow for richer interpretations of Labove, as it suggests that athletic subsidies, professionalization, and particularly the commodification of the athletic body are all central to a fuller understanding Faulkner's perplexing, and seemingly anomalous, sports hero.

Notes

1. It is worth noting that Ole Miss head coach C.R. Noble, who coached the team during the 1917 and 1918 seasons, used "rat" to refer to each of his freshman players (Sorrels and Cavagnaro 76).

Works Cited

Blotner, Joseph. *Faulkner: A Biography*. New York: Random House, 1974. Print.

Brooks, Cleanth. *William Faulkner: Toward Yoknapatawpha and Beyond*. New Haven: Yale UP, 1978. Print.

Doyle, Andrew. "Turning the Tide: College Football and Southern Progressivism." *The Sporting World of the Modern South*. Ed. Patrick B. Miller. Champaign: U of Illinois, 2002. 101–26. Print.

Faulkner, William. *Faulkner in the University: Class Conferences at the University of Virginia, 1957–1958*. Ed. Frederick L. Gwynn and Joseph Blotner. Charlottesville: U of Virginia, 1959. Print.

———. Letter to Alton Bryant. 12 May 1947. *Selected Letters of William Faulkner*. Ed. Joseph Blotner. New York: Vintage, 1977. 249–50. Print.

———. Letter to Saxe Commins. 7 Dec. 1941. *Selected Letters of William Faulkner*. Ed. Joseph Blotner. New York: Vintage, 1977. 147. Print.

———. *The Hamlet*. 1940. New York: Random House, 1964. Print.

———. The Rowan Oak Papers. Archives and Special Collections, The University of Mississippi.

———. *The Wild Palms*. 1939. New York: Vintage International, 1966. Print.

Jones, Anne Goodwyn. "'The Kotex Age': Woman, Popular Culture, and the Wild Palms." *Faulkner and Popular Culture*. Ed. Doreen Fowler and Ann J. Abadie. Jackson: U of Mississippi, 1990. 142–62. Print.

McComb, Mary C. *Great Depression and the Middle Class: Experts, Collegiate Youth and Business Ideology, 1929–1941*. New York: Routledge, 2006. Print.

McHaney, Thomas L. *William Faulkner's* The Wild Palms: *A Study*. Jackson: U of Mississippi, 1975. Print.

Messenger, Christian K. *Sport and the Spirit of Play in American Fiction: Hawthorne to Faulkner*. New York: Columbia UP, 1981. Print.

Oriard, Michael. *King Football: Sport and Spectacle in the Golden Age of Radio and Newsreels, Movies and Magazines, the Weekly & the Daily Press*. Chapel Hill: U of North Carolina, 2001. Print.

Rhodes, Pamela, and Richard Godden. "Wild Palms: Degraded Culture, Devalued Texts." *Intertextuality in Faulkner*. Ed. Michel Gresset and Noel Polk. Jackson: U of Mississippi, 1985. 87–113. Print.

Sorrels, William Wright, and Charles Cavagnaro. *Ole Miss Rebels: Mississippi Football*. Huntsville, AL: Strode, 1976. Print.

Tunis, John R. "John R. Tunis on College Football, 1928." *America between the Wars, 1919–1941: A Documentary Reader*. Ed. David Welky. Malden, MA: Wiley-Blackwell, 2012. 94–97. Print.

Watterson, John Sayle. *College Football: History, Spectacle, Controversy*. Baltimore: Johns Hopkins UP, 2000. Print.

Daniel Anderson

"Long Years Ago, in Minneapolis . . .": The Late Resurfacing of Robert Penn Warren's Minnesota Years

While fame and fervor surrounded Robert Penn Warren during his years in Minnesota (1942 through 1950), that time is most often discussed today in context of his revision of a previously written (but unpublished) play, *Proud Flesh*, into his most celebrated novel, *All the King's Men* (1946).[1] As a result, Warren's experience in Minnesota has largely been described as one defined by a teaching position that resulted in a few friendships and offered temporary perspective on his "real" interests in the South, the East Coast, and Europe. However, an examination of primary and secondary sources (including the archives of the University of Minnesota's English Department)[2], suggests that this characterization is limited, if not shortsighted. Late in his life, Warren wrote two poems and a new introduction to *All the King's Men* that recalled his Minnesota years, exploring the sudden surfacing of lost memories. "Minneapolis Story" (1981), for example, recalls a random incident on a snow-swept street, causing the aging speaker to "ponder / The mystery of Time and happiness and death" (*Collected Poems* 459). Such explorations into the "upper reaches" (as Warren also described the library room in which he completed his novel) of the mind and memory have wide-ranging resonance in Warren's work; they also point to an "attic" motif, emblazoned by Warren's novella "The Circus in the Attic" (1947) and suggested by Patricia L. Bradley in her book-length analysis of Warren's "circus aesthetic." This attic motif, though not as replete throughout Warren's work as his use of "circus" tropes and imagery, specifically connects Warren's writing from the late 1970s and the early '80s with that of his Minnesota years.

Indeed, it was at the University of Minnesota's Walter Library that Warren completed his best-known work. In 1943, he began to rework the novel from a draft of *Proud Flesh*, a verse play he had written six years earlier. In a 1981 essay, published in *The New York Times* and adapted from an introduction he had written for the thirty-fifth anniversary edition of the novel, Warren recalled that while he had previously stored the play away, one day he retrieved it "out of a drawer." In the introduction to the Modern Library edition of 1953,

Warren recalled that he drew the manuscript "out of its cupboard" and continued: "The book was finished in the fall of 1945, back in Minneapolis, the last few paragraphs being written in a little room in the *upper reaches* of the Library of the University of Minnesota" (Warren, "Introduction" vii-viii, emphasis added). Three decades later, Warren revisited these "upper reaches," if not of building then of mind, as images and incidents from his Minnesota years resurfaced in his writing. "That old white bubble now arises, bursts / On my dark and secret stream," he observes in "Minneapolis Story," exploring again the interconnectedness of experience and memory through time, a theme that haunts, perturbs, and defines Warren's first-person narrator in *All the King's Men*. Fittingly, just as the novel's completion famously defines his Minnesota years, Warren's experiences and memories of that period re-emerge and in many ways define the wider exploration of this defining theme in his later work.

* * *

Upon his arrival in Minneapolis, Warren was better known as a poet than as a novelist, and perhaps even better known as an academic and a New Critic. His second book of poems, *Eleven Poems on the Same Theme*, had been published in April of 1942, while his second novel, *At Heaven's Gate*, largely written before he moved to Minnesota, was published in 1943. In 1942, Minnesota's department chair, Joseph Warren Beach, had lured Warren to Minnesota from Louisiana State University, which failed to match Beach's offer (a full professorship and $4,000 a year). At Minnesota, Warren split duty teaching the writing seminar with Sinclair Lewis, as Beach established creative writing as a central aspect of the English Department.

At Minnesota, even before *All the King's Men* became a bestseller in 1946, Warren's classes were celebrated on campus for their popularity. In the fall of 1945, the total enrollment in his three courses—Interpretation of Poetry, Twentieth-Century Literature, and the Seminar in Writing—totaled nearly two hundred students. While Warren modestly attributed this groundswell to the expansion of the university after the end of the war, the university's student paper singled him out for notoriety. In October, *The Minnesota Daily* observed: "Sardines who know anything about the University have a joke going around about people. This time it's on the large number of students packed, crammed and crowded into the three English courses taught by Robert

Penn Warren" (qtd. in Blotner 220). During the war, incidentally, his workload had been even heavier: he had taken on one extra section of Air Corps men, in addition to one night per week of barracks study supervision and responsibility for scripting a radio show on great works of literature: three hours—or 12,000 words—every week (e.g., *Brooks & Warren* 74).

The writing courses Warren taught at Minnesota were creative in nature, but his approach was steeped in practices, such as regular conferences with students, that are now staples in the teaching of composition. James Shannon, the former president of the University of St. Thomas in St. Paul, earned a Master's degree in English (as well as a doctorate at Yale) with Warren as his adviser. In an interview for *The University of Minnesota, 1951–2001*, Shannon recalled Warren's approach to teaching: "He was just superlatively good, and deeply, deeply, courteous to the students. I learned as much also from Robert Penn Warren about how teachers should treat their students as I learned about how novelists should treat their readers" (Shannon 3). Similarly, in an earlier history of the university, James Gray called Warren "a part-time saint" who spent hours in his Folwell Hall office, holding conferences with his students (Gray 30).

In 1946, of course, *All the King's Men* became a bestseller. In the Twin Cities, Warren's celebrity grew beyond the lecture halls of the university and reached the society pages of the local press. The *St. Paul Pioneer Press* observed, somewhat provincially, "Minnesota Faculty Man Does Impressive Novel" (Barry 10). Brenda Ueland, the writer of the "What Goes on Here" column in the Minneapolis *Daily Times*, described Warren for the general public as a "red-haired, Leslie-Howardish-looking man; teaches English at the University; reads Dante continuously; likes to swim back and forth across Lake Calhoun, tacking like a sailboat" (Ueland). In the fall, the *Sunday Tribune* featured the English Department's creative writers in a photo essay centered on Warren ("New Best Seller").

The ensuing events in Warren's tenure at Minnesota are fairly well known. While Warren won the Pulitzer Prize for fiction and sold the film rights to the novel, he also gave the manuscript of *Proud Flesh* to the University Theatre for a staging in the spring of 1947. Meanwhile, he continued with his previous workload of 3 courses and 190 students in each of the fall and winter quarters; he relayed these numbers in a letter to Cleanth Brooks in the fall of 1948 in less charitable terms than he had used in his earlier statement to the student newspaper (*Brooks & Warren* 148). Warren spent most of 1948 in Italy on a Guggenheim fellowship and then the summer of 1949 on the set of *All the King's Men* in California. Back in Minnesota, the publication of *World Enough and Time* in June 1949 landed Warren on the cover of the *Minneapolis Tribune's* Sunday Magazine, which ran a dramatized "photo synopsis" of the novel along with a feature on the author.

Meanwhile, Warren had begun to explore other job offers, including some outside of academia altogether. He admitted in his letters that the prospect of leaving Minnesota saddened him, but his wife found the climate difficult, and their marriage was disintegrating for various reasons. Warren resigned his position in the English Department in 1950 and accepted a position in the Yale School of Drama.

* * *

Warren's tenure in Minnesota remained lodged deep in his consciousness, however, and in the late 1970s he published two narrative poems, "Minnesota Recollection" and "Minneapolis Story," that explored the sudden surfacing of lost memories. The first of these two poems is something of an outlier in Warren's later poetry, in that it seems to rework a story from another source, though its overall emphasis on "recollection" aligns it with many of the themes Warren was interested in at the time. The second poem, on the other hand, is more pertinent to my interests here.

"Minneapolis Story" was published first in the *New York Review of Books* in 1981 and then in his collection *Rumor Verified* that same year. The poem looks back, after more than thirty years, at a seemingly minor and random incident from his time in Minneapolis, recalled ostensibly involuntarily as Warren is mourning the recent death of a friend. Certainly, the poem falls in line with some well-established themes in Warren's work, as well as with some prevailing critical approaches to his late poetry. For example, the interconnectedness of Time is here: The enormous spider web, as Robert Hamblin examined in his plenary presentation at the 2012 Faulkner and Warren Conference, has rippled from the forgotten past to the unpredictable present; we can easily imagine the speaker of this poem surmising, as the narrator of *All the King's Men*, Jack Burden, does while lying on the bed in a hotel room in Long Beach, that "I had not understood then what I think I have now come to understand: that we can keep the past only by having the future, for they are forever tied together" (310–11). Similarly, we can place the poem in critical context by considering it as an example of the "life review" aspect of the *Alterswerk*, or age-work, that Joseph R. Millichap explored in his discussion of influence and intertextuality, which opened the same Faulkner and Warren conference. Millichap also cites the poem's significance in his analysis of Warren's ruminations on "space" as well as time, as he looks from East to West in Part III of *Rumor Verified* (Millichap 118).

Beyond these thematic and critical contextualizations, however, I would like to focus on the remembered incident in the poem. The poet (I will consciously conflate Warren and his speaker here) begins by remarking on the involuntary memory and its yearning to grope toward meaning: "Whatever pops into your head, and whitely / Breaks surface on the dark stream that is you, / May do to make a poem" (*Collected Poems* 459). After some more rumination, the poet recounts the incident:

> Long years ago, in Minneapolis,
> Dark falling, snow falling to celebrate
>
> The manger-birth of a babe in a snowless latitude,
> Church bells vying with whack of snow-chains on
>
> Fenders, there I, down a side street,
> Head thrust into snow-swirl, strove toward Hennepin.
>
> There lights and happiness most probably were—
> But I was not thinking of happiness, only of
>
> High-quality high-proof and the gabble in which
> You try to forget that something inside you dies.

It is ironic that in a poem that sets out to explore the strange power of memory, the narrative should center first on a moment in which the speaker is trying to forget something. Significantly, that "something" is not only physiological, deadened by alcohol, but emotional or even aspirational: the mere thought of happiness. It may seem surprising to anyone who is not steeped in the details of Warren's biography (or stereotypically cynical about writers and their predilections for booze) that the speaker is out looking for a bar on Christmas Eve (good liquor and the "gabble" of the bar are his "only" concerns). Assuming the poet is close to home as he walks down a side street "toward Hennepin" (still one of the primary "nightlife" streets in Minneapolis), and judging from the Warrens' home addresses, one would date this "incident" in December of 1946 or '48. For example, in a letter to John Palmer dated December 26, 1948, Warren wrote dourly: "Things brighten a little at the moment, or at least there is a breathing space, or judging from Christmas Eve, I should say drinking space, before things crowd in again" (*Letters* 319). As already mentioned, Warren's marriage was disintegrating.

This interplay between involuntary memory and willful forgetting, however, primarily provides context. The incident that followed is the one that popped into the poet's head: he stumbles into a drunk passed out on the sidewalk and runs, still "toward Hennepin," where he finds an ambulance. The poet knows nothing more about the incident or its aftermath: "'Gonna live?' I ask. 'Not if he's lucky,' the paramedic / Says. Slams door. Tires skid. That's all" (l. 23–24).

The implied question, of course, is "Why this memory?" Warren then moves to the conclusion the poem, pondering "The mystery of Time and happiness and death" (29). He wonders, again, why this incident has emerged through the surface of his memory, and why he should specifically recall

> The nameless, outraged, upturned face, where, blessed
> In shadow, domed architecture of snow, with scrupu-
> lous care,
>
> Is minutely erected on each closed eye.
> I had wiped them clear, just a moment before.
> [*Collected Poems* 460]

The aging poet is left no more certain of its meaning than is the young Jack Burden of the end of the Cass Mastern episode, when he grasps the enormous spider web and ponders the mystery with a similar reverie on eyes and what can be seen: "For him the world then was simply an accumulation of items, odds and ends of things like the broken and misused and dust-shrouded things gathered in a garret. Or it was a flux of things before his eyes (or behind his eyes) and one thing had nothing to do, in the end, with anything else" (*All the King's Men* 189). The emphasis on eyes, whether they are wiped clear but still closed, or focused on something "behind" them altogether, is rich with connotations of memory-grasping and emergence—especially in the study of Warren, who lost an eye in his youth (e.g., Runyon 230 fn1; Bloom xxv). However, I want to draw attention instead to the "garret" where these things have gathered.

I would like to suggest a garret or "attic" motif that prevails in the work of Warren's that is connected to his Minnesota period. I am admittedly springboarding here off of Patricia L. Bradley's extended study of Warren's "circus aesthetic," particularly her thoroughly persuasive analysis of "The Circus in the Attic," the novella that Warren wrote in 1946. As Bradley points out, in that 1981 introduction of the novel Warren recalls finishing *All the King's Men* in "an attic room of the library of the U of M" (as opposed to his more general reference in 1953 to the "upper reaches"). Bradley cites the attic as a place of refuge or retreat—for Jack Burden in *All the King's Men* as it is for Bolton Lockhart in the novella—and, as the locus of a "safe world of artistic illusion," for Warren as well (20).

The attic is for Warren, as it is for most of us, a place of storage: not just as a psychoanalytic metaphor for memory and the "upper reaches" of the subconscious—although it certainly can be that—but also as a repository of things for which the writer has not yet found a use. The reference shares much with the "lumber room" to which Faulkner famously referred in an interview at the University of Virginia, in which Faulkner combined the metaphor of memory with a storage space: "the writer reaching into the lumber room of his memory" (*Faulkner* 72, 117). The term, more widely used in Great Britain, has little to do with our contemporary American connotation of wooden building materials and much more in common with our notion of an attic: a space where random things are stored. As Nicholson Baker has pointed out in a wide-ranging exploration of "lumber" in all its connotations, Faulkner also cited his use of a "junk box" in the same interview (*Faulkner* 116, Baker *passim*).

Warren uses the term more extensively—that is, both as a

metaphor for memory and as a physical storage space—in his poem "Red-Tail Hawk and Pyre of Youth."[3] In this poem from 1977, he describes accidentally coming upon a stuffed hawk that he had shot years earlier and since forgotten:

> That night in the lumber room, late,
> I found him—the hawk, feathers shabby, one
> Wing bandy-banged, one foot gone sadly
> Askew, one eye long gone—and I reckoned
> I knew how it felt with one gone. (*Collected Poems* 349)

After acknowledging his kinship with the one-eyed bird and his self-consciousness about encroaching age, the speaker comes across a trove of old books and poems and prints as a result of the accidental encounter (he has gone home after his mother's death and sleeps in the room one last time). Although the things he finds had been consciously forgotten, they have been present in his life and work nonetheless ("all relevant items I found there"). Their sudden reappearance serves to help the memory connect different moments in time.

In the 1981 essay introducing *All the King's Men*, Warren wrote, as he often has, of memory and time:

> Time does not necessarily improve memory. But in the course of time, strange odds and ends—or even funda-mental facts not recognized in the noonday sun—may, out of blank idleness of a later mind, rise up, trailing God knows what, like a half-rotten log disturbed in a creek bed trailing algae, patched with moss, clung to by some strange, snail-like creatures, with a rusty length of barbed wire still nailed to it. What rises so gratuitously out of the deep of time may be a set of relationships and connections of which you had been unaware when things were fresh. The unconscious thing may, years later, become startlingly conscious, seemingly by accident. That is why it is always hard to say precisely when and how a book—or anything else—"began." ("In the Time" 1)

Here Warren is going up into the attic for some recognizable things (some tropes, we might say): the surfacing from underwater, the sudden ability or attempt to see clearly. But he also uses some other things (images, if you will) he wrote, while living in Minneapolis more than thirty years earlier, in "The Circus in the Attic." In this passage, Bolton has just retreated from a relationship with Sara Darter, who then leaves town forever:

> That last encounter with him had not been part of
> the plan. Or if it was a part, it was a part that had not
> showed itself above the surface of the stream, where
> the trivial debris and drift moiled and spun in the
> light, but wallowed in the dark central depth of the
> current, like an old log, black and waterlogged, sucked
> up from the mud, and borne in secret to the rock-
> tossed rapid narrows where the waters boiled over with
> a last fury into the placid reaches below. . . . ("Circus"
> 36)

Warren does not say in his 1981 essay whether he is consciously using or re-using (perhaps recycling) the same imagery he used in "The Circus in the Attic," but no matter—just as in "Minneapolis Story" a year earlier, he is clearly returning to his Minnesota period. Indeed, he wrote much of his novella over four days of his Christmas vacation in Minneapolis in 1946, as he wrote to his editor Lambert Davis, "despite several bottles of Old Forester which a friend gave me for the celebration of the birth of Our Lord" (*Letters* 228).

Writing his essay in 1981, Warren was in a particular corner of the attic, where stuff from the Minnesota years had apparently been stored. Like Bolton Lovehart, he climbed back up when other Minnesota memories, such as the one that inspired "Minneapolis Story," apparently sent him up there. As a longtime investigator into the meanings of time and memory (and Faulkner), he knew how to reach back to find those things. Sometimes, like the poet in "Red-Tail Hawk and Pyre of Youth," we happen upon things we have long forgotten, even though they were important; other times, though, we know just where things are, waiting and ready to be used.

Notes

1. *Proud Flesh*, which Warren began writing in the late 1930s, was never published during his lifetime, although Eric Bentley staged the play at the University of Minnesota in 1947. That version was published in 2000 as part of *Robert Penn Warren's* All the King's Men: *Three Stage Versions* (Grimshaw and Perkins 11 & *passim*).

2. Some of the original archival research used in this essay was done for a story that appeared in the University of Minnesota English Department's newsletter, commemorating Robert Penn Warren's centenary in 2005 (http://english.umn.edu/assets/pdf/sum05newsletter.pdf).

3. I am indebted to Patricia L. Bradley for drawing my attention to this connection between Faulkner and Warren. I would like to thank Dr. Bradley for her insights, and for her kind words, at the 2012 Faulkner and Warren Conference at Southeast Missouri State University.

Works Cited

Anderson, Dan. "Robert Penn Warren." *English @ Minnesota* 6.2 (2005): 4–5. Print.

Baker, Nicholson. *The Size of Thoughts: Essays and Other Lumber.* New York: Vintage, 1997.

Barry, Josephine. "Minnesota Faculty Man Does Impressive Novel." Rev. of *All the King's Men,* by Robert Penn Warren. *St. Paul Pioneer Press Magazine* 18 Aug. 1946: 10. Print.

Bloom, Harold. Introduction. *The Collected Poems of Robert Penn Warren.* Ed. John Burt. Baton Rouge: Louisiana State UP, 1998. xxiii-xxvi. Print.

Blotner, Joseph. *Robert Penn Warren: A Biography.* New York: Random House, 1997. Print.

Bradley, Particia L. *Robert Penn Warren's Circus Aesthetic and the Southern Renaissance.* Knoxville: U of Tennessee P, 2004. Print.

Grimshaw, James A., Jr., and James A. Perkins. Introduction. *Robert Penn Warren's* All the King's Men: *Three Stage Versions*. Ed. James A. Grimshaw, Jr., and James A. Perkins. Athens: U of Georgia P, 2000. Print.

Gray, James. *Open Wide the Door: The Story of the University of Minnesota*. New York: Putnam, 1958.

Gwynn, Frederick L., and Joseph L. Blotner, eds. *Faulkner in the University*. Charlottesville: U of Virginia P, 1959. Print.

Hamblin, Robert. "'The world is like an enormous spider web': The Contrasting Legacies of Thomas Sutpen and Cass Mastern." Southeast Missouri State University. Faulkner and Warren Conference, Cape Girardeau, Missouri. 25 Oct. 2012. Plenary Presentation.

Millichap, Joseph R. *Robert Penn Warren After Audubon: The Work of Aging and the Quest for Transcendence in His Later Poetry*. Baton Rouge: Louisiana State UP, 2009. Print.

———. "William Faulkner, Robert Penn Warren, and Walker Evans: Influence, Intertextuality, and Ekphrasis." Southeast Missouri Stat University. Faulkner and Warren Conference, Cape Girardeau, Missouri. 25 Oct. 2012. Plenary Presentation.

"New Best Seller." *Minneapolis Tribune* 13 Oct. 1946: Women's News 1. Print.

Runyon, Randolph. *The Braided Dream: Robert Penn Warren's Late Poetry*. Lexington: UP of Kentucky, 1990. Print.

Shannon, James. Interview by Clarke Chambers, 1995. English Department Archives, University of Minnesota. Elmer L. Andersen Library, Minneapolis.

Ueland, Brenda. "What Goes On Here." *Minneapolis Daily Times* 29 Aug. 1946. English Department Archives, University of Minnesota. Elmer L. Andersen Library, Minneapolis.

Warren, Robert Penn. *All the King's Men*. 1946. New York: Harcourt, Brace & Company, 1985. Print.

———. "The Circus in the Attic." *The Circus in the Attic and Other Stories*. 1947. New York: Harcourt, Brace & World, Inc., 1962. 3–62. Print.

———. *The Collected Poems of Robert Penn Warren*. Ed. John Burt. Baton Rouge: Louisiana State UP, 1998.

———. "In the Time of 'All the King's Men.'" *New York Times* 31 May 1981: Book Review 1. Print.

———. Introduction. *All the King's Men*. New York: Modern Library, 1953. Print.

———. *Selected Letters of Robert Penn Warren: Triumph and Transition, 1943-1952*. Vol. 3. Eds. Randy Hendricks & James A. Perkins. Baton Rouge: Louisiana State UP, 2006. Print.

Warren, Robert Penn, and Cleanth Brooks. *Cleanth Brooks and Robert Penn Warren: A Literary Correspondence*. Ed. James A. Grimshaw, Jr. Columbia: U of Missouri P, 1998. Print.

Benjamin J. Wilson

Approaching the Other Through Aesthetics: Faulkner, Warren, Native Americans, and Modernism

Race, history, literature: these three signifiers carry significant weight, living as we are in the post-postmodern moment. Starting with the work of the great "discourse-makers" such as Marx, Freud, and Nietzsche and the modernist art forms that arose at the turn of the last century, race, history, and literature have become complicated entities that undergo constant interrogation by artists and critics alike. These three words and all they represent background the careful examination of Native American representation in the work of William Faulkner and Robert Penn Warren. Race, of course, has been dealt with at length in studies of both authors, but primarily *vis-à-vis* their representation of African-American characters. History is also a major theme of their respective bodies of work. Previous critics that have examined their portrayal of Native Americans have engaged in anthropological, historical, and ethnographic studies, but I would like to consider the way that aesthetics may account for their construction of Native American characters. This is significant for both authors, as they both operated under a largely modernist aesthetic, though one that struggled with and was tempered by Romantic tendencies.

Faulkner, influenced as he was by the oral culture he was raised in, approached history more through storytelling than through careful research. As C. Ben Wright observes of the many characters attempting to recreate the story of Thomas Sutpen in *Absalom, Absalom!*, "Like historians reconstructing the history of a particular event, these characters may agree on the 'facts' . . . but they seldom agree on the meaning of the facts. By using multiple narrators, Faulkner suggests that no one point of view, or interpretation, is adequate for an understanding of history" (568). Although Wright's point is that Faulkner's presentation of these competing accounts of Sutpen's history is similar to debates concerning proper historiographical method, he underlines the fact that these narrators are engaging in storytelling, first and foremost, and the concern for the facts in such storytelling may not be as important as the interpretation of events. This attitude carries over into stories involving Native American characters, such as "A Justice," which is told as a reminiscence of Sam Fathers to a young Quentin Compson, or "A Courtship," which, although a recollection by its narrator, is full of those remarkable superhuman feats of achievement that are added as adornment to tales as they pass from storyteller to storyteller, through the generations.

Furthermore, as Howard C. Horsford has pointed out, the historical veracity of Faulkner's fictional Chickasaws and Choctaws is largely moot (311); these figures are conjured up partially from local myth and Faulkner's limited historical knowledge, but mostly from his creative capacity as an artist. Although some scholars have attempted to defend Faulkner's work as legitimately "historical" in some narrow sense, this is undermined by his explanation to Malcom Cowley that "the line dividing the Chickasaw and Choctaw nations passed near my home; I merely moved a tribe slightly at need, since they were slightly different people in behavior" (qtd. in Horsford 312).[1] It seems that Faulkner has more faith in his own genius to tell a story than historical realism, and at any rate, some of the facts would have ill-suited his purposes. For instance, Faulkner places great importance on the patriarchal lineage that gives Doom his power, when in reality, matrilineal relationships were more significant in Chickasaw tribes (Horsford 315); even more, "certainly in neither [the Chickasaw or Choctaw tribes] did a chief have the kind of autocratic power that Faulkner supposed for his" (Horsford 316). Instead of basing his Ur-Yoknapatawpha and its natives in historical research, he created his own alternative history, which allowed him the poetic license to craft the story of Yoknapatawpha in a mythological, as opposed to historical, vein. This invented history of Faulkner's serves as necessary background to the conversation in the commissary between Isaac McCaslin and McCaslin Edmonds in "The Bear."

Isaac's argument for repudiation of the land is deeply concerned with history—his own interpretation of it—but also hinges on his deep attachment to Sam Fathers's way of life, which he taught to Ike as a young man. Significantly, Sam Fathers is the most prominent Native American character in Faulkner's fiction; however, at the same time that he is Faulkner's most fully drawn Indian character, it must be said that the blood of African-Americans also runs in Sam Fathers's veins, as well as white blood, inasmuch as his mother was a "quadroon." Yet it is his Indian blood that Ike and Faulkner focus on, because his identity as a Native American helps forge an almost mystical connection with the land. This owes more to a popular sense, right or wrong, of Native Americans as connected to their homelands in a way unfathomable to non-natives, as opposed to historical reality; however, it is an important functional part of Faulkner's mythology. As Jay S. Winston has pointed out, "Faulkner conveys not only a sense of [Native American] cultural genesis in the landscape, as well as a convenient vanishing, but also the manner in which the ancestral people . . . and their history actually *became* the land" (131). In short, the desire for whites in Faulkner to be connected with the land, whether in the exploitative way of a Thomas Sutpen or in the almost Gnostic spiritual repudiation of Ike McCaslin, is bound to involve a reckoning with the land's past as the Native Americans' home; indeed, Native American identity in Faulkner is necessarily tied to the land, and vice versa. Winston elaborates:

> Isaac's attempt to achieve unity, by grasping toward a people who, within his own narrative, are viewed as "obsolete," and who are extinguished by modernity like the wild land itself, is ultimately doomed, and this doom is essential to Faulkner's own narrative. The Indians remain tragic, as do those, such as Isaac, and perhaps Faulkner himself, who attempt to grasp at them. In other words, the Indian in these texts is valued only in terms of what he means to the white man, who, according to the American myth, must naturally supplant him. (140)

Faulkner sees the darker, tragic side of the notion of manifest destiny and all the suffering that it would entail, but he also presents it as inevitable, even fated: consider the self-named "Doom" and his moniker's portent of the eventual eclipse of his people by white settlers.

I have argued that Faulkner's modernism is essential to his representation of Native Americans. Though their presence is not a major aspect of his work, Native Americans are typically evoked, as opposed to presented outright, to underpin the mythological nature of Faulkner's fictional landscape. The complication of understanding history and identity that accompanied modernism are present in the fragmentation of his work, as well as in the storytelling aspect: for instance, "A Justice" presents the story as told through at least two filters, that of Quentin Compson and Sam Fathers, putting us at great remove from the strange events of that story, which subtly undermines the "truthfulness" of Sam Fathers's account. However, there is something undeniably Romantic about Faulkner's Native Americans, their tragic fate, and the myth of white ascendance. This is troubling to my thesis: how can I defend Faulkner's modernism if his Native Americans are rooted in a Romantic conception of their lives and their connection to the land? Consider McCaslin Edmonds's description of Sam Fathers in "The Old People":

> He was a wild man. When he was born, all his blood
> on both sides, except the little white part, knew things
> that have been tamed out of our blood so long ago
> that we have not only forgotten them, we have to live
> together in herds to protect ourselves from our own
> sources. (GDM 161)

As both Horsford and Patricia Galloway point out, the real Choctaw and Chickasaw tribes had complex societies, which Faulkner smoothes out to a more-or-less popular sense of "Indianness," in which one tribe is indistinguishable from another (Horsford 313, 318, 321; Galloway 28). In this way, all of the tribes in Faulkner's world share a common "wildness" that sets them apart from the whites, and even African Americans to some extent—a crude approximation of the "noble savage" myth. Granted, what Faulkner actually thought of the Native American societies may not be in agreement with McCaslin Edmonds's take on it. Regardless of whatever his personal opinions may have been, Faulkner's fictional world portrays a white society that wrests control of the land from its native inhabitants through predatory financial bargains, then minimizes their tribal and cultural differences through a uniform understanding of their cultures that serves to further marginalize them, leading to their eventual absorption, through intermarriage, into either white or black culture. This is essentially the Native Americans' eradication, a historical injustice, writ in miniature in Faulkner's mythological rendering.

Portraying as it does the mythology of the Native American eclipse through which white America ascends, "The Bear" has come to be read as the equally Romantic tale of Ike, doomed to fail, fiercely following his conscience despite the fate it entails for him. Faulkner's flirtation with Romanticism deserves to be taken seriously; indeed, Robert Woods Sayre, considering the intersection of Faulkner's Native American characters and his Romantic tendencies, highlights the relationship to Faulkner's modernism: "[Romanticism is] a refusal of the multifaceted alienations of modern society in the name of values drawn from the past" (33). Thus, given Sayre's definition of Romanticism, it would follow that:

> The romantic posture emphasizes an irreconcilable contrast between the "civilized" values of modernity and the "primitive" culture of the Indians, to the detriment of the former, and experiences the advance of modernity as an irredeemable *loss*. (35)

The mythology of the Romantic Native American, the "noble savage," predates Faulkner, and was something that he had to deal with in portraying Native Americans in his work. In certain aspects, *Go Down Moses* utilizes this mythology as part of its many narrative lines, not merely in regard to its Native-American character, Sam Fathers. Faulkner was actually tapping into a larger Romantic myth, that of the frontier and manifest destiny. As Sarah Gleeson-White has shown, there was a fascination with "frontier images and rhetoric . . . [that] moved to the forefront of US culture and politics during the 1930s, when Faulkner was writing the stories that came to make up *Go Down, Moses*" (392). She reads the novel against the background of this reenergized frontier myth, which not only works against the grain of the typically South-centric readings of Faulkner's work but also adds an additional dimension to understanding the figure of Sam Fathers in the novel. Faulkner's work writing scripts for Western films directed by Howard Hawks and John Ford, as well as through his engagement with the work of James Fenimore Cooper, influenced his portrayal of Sam Fathers. As Gleeson-White points out: "The Indian is almost synonymous with the wilderness in *Go Down, Moses* and Cooper's [*The Deerslayer*], in the way in which he serves one sole purpose: to enable the initiation of the white man" (398). In other words, powerful Romantic currents ran through the work that seemingly influenced Faulkner most as he wrote *Go Down, Moses*.

Despite his fascination with Romantic themes, I would argue that "The Bear" demonstrates Faulkner working against Romanticism, at least in part through his use of modernist literary techniques. Chiefly he does this through the use of irony. What could be more ironic than the ultimate pointlessness of Ike's repudiation? Consider young Ike's reaction to General Compson and Walter Ewell's plan to "corporate themselves . . . and lease the camp and the hunting privileges of the woods":

> Even the boy, listening, recognized it for the subter-
> fuge it was: to change the leopard's spots when they
> could not alter the leopard, a baseless and illusory hope
> to which even McCaslin seemed to subscribe for a
> while, that once they had persuaded Major de Spain
> to return to the camp he might revoke himself, which
> even the boy knew he would not do. And he did not.
> (301)

Ike's repudiation of the land is likewise an attempt to "change the leopard's spots when [he] could not alter the leopard," and the effective impotence of his act is symbolized in the sexual encounter with his wife. He becomes an "uncle to half a county and father to no one" (3), denied the double legacy he would like of heroic repudiator of the land as well as father. This irony demonstrates Faulkner's basic anti-Romantic and modernist sense at work in "The Bear": Isaac aims for a sort of sainthood through his repudiation, but instead becomes a symbol to be pitied, a man whose attempt at a noble gesture failed because of his limitations.

Ike sees the injustice he attempts to fight through the lens of slavery and ownership rather than the tragedy of the Native American's fate at the hand of the white colonialist, but the sense of the injustice to the Indian is also present in his statement to McCaslin:

> It was never mine to repudiate. It was never Father's
> and Uncle Buddy's to bequeath to me to repudiate
> because it was never Grandfather's to bequeath to them

to bequeath me to repudiate because it was never old
Ikkemotubbe's to sell to Grandfather for bequeath-
ment and repudiation. (GDM 246)

Although Faulkner presents Ike's repudiation as failed from the
start, we do recognize that Ike understands something about the way
the land was obtained, controlled, and exploited that speaks to our
latter-day concerns about our nation's legacy of colonialism and displacement and slaughter of Native Americans. Gleeson-White, arguing
from a transregional perspective, demonstrates how Sam Fathers, with
his white, black, and Native American blood, works to destabilize
facile understandings of America's historical racial issues such as those
held by Ike:

> Fathers is crucially . . . a figure of instability, a figure
> difficult to contain textually, historically, and critically.
> The black-Indian body—the very site of the forma-
> tion of the Republic—returns us to the moment of
> colonization and its trauma; that is, to the wound at
> the heart of the nation. Father's multiracialized body
> must be subsumed within the signifier of the Indian,
> so that the romance of the white-Indian encounter
> might be played out nationally and textually in order
> that the Native American might be subsumed by the
> native American—or, to put this the other way around,
> in order that the European might become American,
> indeed *native* American. (402)

Sam Fathers then serves not just to "initiate" Ike into manhood,
nor to merely represent "Indianness" with his wilderness existence, but
to complicate the white-black axis that has dominated racial thinking in the United States. In the historical chronology of Faulkner's
Yoknapatawpha, we clearly have moved from the distinctly Native
American characters such as Ikkemotubbe to Sam Fathers, whose
"Indianness" springs from his mythical connection with the woods
and the land. Although Faulkner did not move beyond this Romantic
understanding of the Native American, he began to problematize it
through his modernist examination of the received American myth.

Robert Penn Warren engages many of the same problems in his last long-form narrative poem, *Chief Joseph of the Nez Perce*. The Romantic conception of Native Americans again looms large in the poem, and how much Warren gives into the temptation of Romanticizing Chief Joseph is still a matter of critical debate. In addition, like Faulkner, he is concerned with national myth making, especially as related to the West and the frontier. Despite the fact that this is Warren's first lengthy engagement with colonialist Native American relations, many of his themes in this poem have been career-long concerns: as Joseph Millichap points out, Warren's look Westward has been there from his first book, the biography of John Brown (56), in addition to his lifelong concern with race, especially his mid-career repudiation of his previously segregationist views. Furthermore, it is not hard to see what qualities of the Nez Perce drew Warren to them: as he says in his historical note at the beginning of the poem: "The Nez Perce were a handsome and very vigorous people, but not basically warlike . . . They moved about with the offerings of the seasons . . . and were, for the most part, devoted to their homelands" (xi). Given Warren's one-time association with Agrarianism, it is natural that he would both extol and find poetic inspiration in the Nez Perce. What he attempts to do that the Agrarians failed to do in the essays gathered in *I'll Take My Stand* is to move beyond that book's Anglo-Saxon-centered perspective.

Whatever Romantic urges Warren may have struggled with (unsuccessfully or not) in writing Chief Joseph, his poetic technique is firmly modern, perhaps even gesturing toward the postmodern: he chooses to portray his mixture of historical recounting and imagined commentary from Joseph in a poem that is daringly intertextual in its interspersing of selected historical documents with poetic narrative. Warren's literary technique, apart from being mere artifice, is central to interpreting the poem. Quoting Millichap again:

> From his triple epigraph forward, Warren juxtaposes the historical documents themselves with his imaginative version of the story as well as with a multiplicity of narrative view points. Three voices predominate: Joseph's, telling his own tale, an impersonal narrator's voice of history, and Warren's own, telling how

he traced Joseph's footsteps through the wilderness. In turn, Warren's overall narrative divides into three realms: Joseph's inner life, the outer "history" of the period, and Warren's reaction to both, which contrasts past and present, youth and age, innocence and experience. (61)

Although the narrative voices and realms interpenetrate throughout the poem in a complex way, Millichap's sketch of their form and function provide an accurate anatomy of the poem. The various voices and realms serve to color the reader's interpretation as he or she proceeds through the poem, and this starts with the epigraph.

The tripartite epigraph—quoting Jefferson hoping for peace and brotherhood between whites and Native Americans, quoting Sherman advocating either the killing or unending poverty of the Native Americans, and quoting Chief Sealth of the Duwamish warning us that "these shores will swarm with the invisible dead of my tribe . . . the White Man will never be alone," (ix)—becomes the focal point around which turn the three voices and the three realms of the poem. In terms of literary technique, this tripartite epigraph introduces the intertextuality of Warren's poem, which he continues throughout in these three narrative voices, interspersed with quotes from historical documents and sources, such as oral testimonies of Nez Perce soldiers, newspaper clippings, writings from military personnel, and more. The interwoven poetic voices juxtaposed with the historical documents create a heteroglossic poem that serves to refract and complicate historical understanding in a way that relates to Faulkner's use of techniques such as stream-of-consciousness and multiple narrators; Warren, however, moves beyond the high modernist aesthetic of Faulkner, one he employed early in his career, into a subjective questioning of identity that approaches postmodernism.

This shifting of Warren's poetic technique is not something unrelated to his lifelong engagement with racial issues, according to Anthony Szczesiul in his book *Racial Politics and Robert Penn Warren's Poetry*.[2] As Szczesiul points out, Warren had shifted his aesthetic and racial perspectives more or less concurrently earlier in his career:

Warren was a poet who was immersed in the contemporary political moment, and his aesthetic transformation reflects his changing political views as much as it reflects these trends in American poetry. Warren's reimmersion in the issue of race [in the 1950s] coincided with his return to poetry; similarly, his new willingness to place himself in his own poetry corresponded in method with his willingness to deal with race in a frankly personal manner. (108–109)

Indeed, Warren's move from a high modernist to a neo-Romantic aesthetic in the 1950s coincided with his repudiation of segregation, as well as an outright championing of the Civil Rights cause. Something of the reflection on racism that lead Warren to write *Brother to Dragons* around that time may have influenced his fascination in the 1980s with Chief Joseph and the Nez Perce War. In the 1970s, Warren had been reading some Native-American literature (Koppelman 69 n.9), and it is not a stretch to imagine that the same sense of injustice that lead to his involvement in Civil Rights may have precipitated the composition of *Chief Joseph*.

Furthermore, although Warren was recounting and reconstructing, poetically, an historical event and the accompanying historical personages surrounding it, throughout *Chief Joseph* he complicates the understanding of "history," both within the poem and through literary technique. This is underscored in the final section, where the poem shifts to the present day and Warren visits the site of the final battlefield and takes note of the historical markers that dot the landscape:

There is the map
Large, enamel on metal, weatherproof:
Analysis of the action. And then,
The large bronze plate on granite propped
By the Republic to honor the name
Of every trooper who, in glory, had died here. (59–60)

After the deprivations suffered by Chief Joseph and his people as recounted in the previous sections of the poem, these historical markers can be read only ironically by Warren as well as the poem's reader. Warren also interrogates poetically the nation's tendency to engage in myth making to justify things like manifest destiny, as his use of the terms "the Republic" and "troopers" bring a Romanesque mythological accent to the "official" recounting of the battle on the battlefield markers.

Warren's questioning of accepted history was a part of his poetry for a long time before *Chief Joseph*, but as Szczesiul points out, it took on an increasing importance in his last poetic phase, especially in light of his ever-growing concern with subjectivity:

> While Warren contemplated the nuances and complexities of memory throughout his canon, his late poetry increasingly foregrounds the view that truth cannot be discovered from historical facts—that even our memories are interpretations of factual events, not the events themselves. And this shift in emphasis in turn alters the way we define the self. (154)

Szczesiul has already demonstrated that Warren's aesthetic and political changes occurred together; even in *Chief Joseph*, Warren deals with subjectivity alongside the vagaries of historical understanding, putting these words in the mouth of Chief Joseph:

> You stand in the sun. You think: 'Am I Joseph?'
> You find yourself watching the white man's horse-
> soldiers
> How they ride two-by-two, four-by-four, how they
> swing
> Into line, charge or stop, dismount. (12)

In Chief Joseph's struggle to preserve his land and way of life for his people in the face of white encroachment, Warren imagines him questioning his own sense of identity. But of course: as Warren points out in the "Note" preceding the poem, not only were the Nez Perce "devoted to their homelands," but "the lands where the fathers were buried were sacred, and, in their version of immortality, the fathers kept watch on sons to be sure that truth was spoken, and that each showed himself a man" (xi). Throughout the poem, Joseph is concerned almost to obsession with both speaking the truth and behaving like a man, quests that in their own way animated Warren's career.

Despite Warren's attempt to imaginatively deal with the historical injustice of the Nez Perce War, some critics have faulted Warren's portrayal of Native Americans as simplistic and ham-handed. The description of the Nez Perce early in the poem's first section does smack of an Edenic mythology that feels one-dimensional:

> Boys, bareback, ride naked,
> Leap on, shout "Ai-yah!" Shout "Ai-yee!"—
> In unbridled glory. Eagle wing catches sun.
> Gleams white. Boys plunge into water, gay as
> The otter at gambol, with flat hands slap water
> Like beaver tails slapping to warn, then dive,
> Beaverlike, to depth, toes leaving the shimmer,
> Uncoiling upward, of bubbles. On sandbars
> Boys stretch, they yawn, and sun dries the skin
> To glints gold, red, bronze. (3)

Robert Peters wrote in his review of the poem, "I can't imagine Simon Ortiz, Wendy Rose, Joy Harjo, or a host of other Native American writers will be please at seeing their magnificent history reduced to cardboard, to coloring-book history" (qtd. in Szczesiul 238). Although I do not have space to engage in whether or not Warren's characterization is accurate, or one-dimensional, it is worth noting that critics are divided on the issue of how to approach Warren's portrayal of Chief Joseph. Warren's description of the Nez Perce boys at play, more than merely a "cardboard" description, hews very close to Romantic myths of the noble savage, undermining Warren's examination of fragmented identity elsewhere in the poem. It is hard to imagine Warren, as canny as he was in seeing the instability of historical reconstruction, being unaware of the pitfalls of trying to imaginatively enter the thoughts of one so foreign, so "Other" to his own experience, and not having it come out either one-dimensional or overtly Romantic.

One aspect to Warren's technique in the poem that may bring some clarity to this issue is his evocation—through language—of an oral culture. Much of the language and voice that Warren uses throughout, but especially in the sections narrated by Chief Joseph, self-consciously echo the rhythms of an oral culture. Whether this was an accurate evocation of Native American language or simply Warren's approximation of it is an issue that must be settled elsewhere by others; importantly for my thesis, Robert S. Koppelman has brought attention to how the oral culture of the Nez Perce, filtered through Warren's poem, stands as a direct challenge to a hegemonic American discourse of manifest destiny, which may have, in turn, played into Warren's continuing skeptical attitude towards American mythology. As Koppelman writes:

> In the end, we may ponder the extent to which Robert Penn Warren, in this poem at least, recognized the oral tradition, as represented by Chief Joseph, as more intimately engaged with the interconnected forces of time, nature, and history than was the very literary tradition with which Warren had identified for decades in the pursuit of these very issues. (68)

Although Warren's portrayal of the Nez Perce may fall short of our current notions of racial representation, Koppelman is right to point out that their lifestyle, as represented in the poem, offers an inherent critique of the history of colonialism in this country, a history that has lead to the modern disconnection from the environment. Whether Warren must romanticize the Native American to arrive at this conclusion about our fragmented national identity and our complicity in the racial and ecological sins of the past is still a question very open to debate.

Either way, we along with Warren clearly see the Nez Perce War as both tragedy and injustice. Where injustice against Native Americans exists in Faulkner's texts, it is presented as corollary to the great sin of slavery, but his Choctaws and Chickasaws too are guilty of slave ownership—in fact, it could be argued that Sam Fathers is presented as both black and Native American by Faulkner to save him from the taint of slavery that would haunt a full-blooded Indian in his moral economy. Faulkner's themes are less historically specific than Warren's and speak less to the historical injustices of white/Native-American relationships. And why not? Faulkner did not see himself redressing historical wrongs but rather portraying the "human heart in conflict with itself" (*Essays* 119). Warren, however, in *Chief Joseph,* as in the more celebrated *Brother to Dragons,* self-consciously struggles to convey the ways in which the United States has fallen short of its great promise of equality. As Hugh Ruppersburg writes:

> Underlying ["Chief Joseph"] is the premise that the
> Indian heritage is slipping quickly from our national
> memory, primarily because it does not belong to the
> white Anglo-Saxon ancestry traditionally perceived as
> the central component of the nation's ethnic heritage.
> Warren seeks to remind his mostly white, Anglo-
> Saxon readers that such a reason does not justify
> committing to oblivion an essential, and represen
> tative, episode of American history. Indeed, that
> memory's preservation becomes all the more impor
> tant. (77)

Compare this with the myth of Native Americans' tragic decline, allowing for the glorious ascension of white America. What Jay Winston sees as a "convenient vanishing" in Faulkner is dramatized by Warren as a tragic vanishing that should not have been allowed to happen. Warren, in *Chief Joseph,* struggles to understand a dark moment in the history of the United States as being somehow representative of the nation's history. Flirting with postmodern literary technique in the poem's final section, Warren ends by saying that he and his friends left the battlefield and drove largely in silence, thereby inviting the reader to join him in this appropriately reverential silence, forcing us to ponder—with Warren—the meaning of the historical events underpinning this poem.

Notes

1. Horsford points out that "[this statement is] only partly true and otherwise misleading" (313), further complicating Faulkner's evocation of Native Americans. He delves into the historical record that Faulkner was either unaware of or ignored, important information worthy of mention that I regrettably do not have the space to discuss.

2. Thanks to Dr. Patricia Bradley for recommending this text after I presented the conference version of this paper.

Works Cited

Faulkner, William. *Essays, Speeches, and Public Letters*. Ed. James B. Meriwether. New York: Modern Library, 2004.

———. *Go Down Moses*. New York: Vintage International, 1990.

Galloway, Patricia. "The Construction of Faulkner's Indians." *The Faulkner Journal* 18.1 (2002): 9–31.

Gleeson-White, Sarah. "William Faulkner's *Go Down, Moses*: An American Frontier Narrative." *Journal of American Studies* 43.3 (2009): 389–405.

Horsford, Howard C. "Faulkner's (Mostly) Unreal Indians in Early Mississippi History." *American Literature* 64.2 (1992): 311–330.

Koppleman, Robert S. "Warren and Oral Narrative: The Case for *Chief Joseph of the Nez Perce*." *RWP: An Annual of Robert Penn Warren Studies* 4.1 (2004): 61–76.

Millichap, Joseph R. "Robert Penn Warren's West." *The Southern Literary Journal* 26.1 (1993): 54–63.

Ruppersburg, Hugh. "Discovering America's History: Robert Penn Warren's *Chief Joseph of the Nez Perce*." *South Central Review* 5.1 (1988): 75–86.

Sayre, Robert Woods. "Faulkner's Indians and the Romantic Vision." *The Faulkner Journal* 18.1 (2002): 33–49.

Szczesiul, Anthony. *Racial Politics and Robert Penn Warren's Poetry*. Gainesville: U P of Florida, 2002.

Warren, Robert Penn. *Chief Joseph of the Nez Perce*. New York: Random House, 1983.

Winston, Jay S. "Going Native in Yoknapatawpha: Faulkner's Fragmented America and 'the Indian.'" *The Faulkner Journal* 18.1 (2002): 129–142.

Wright, C. Ben. "William Faulkner as History Teacher." *The History Teacher* 9.4 (1976): 567–574.

Dennis Negron

William Faulkner's Dilsey, Robert Penn Warren's Manty, and Race Politics

Much criticism has been written about the "Negro" presence in both William Faulkner's and Robert Penn Warren's canons. Their racial politics have also been the topics of intense critical focus, often, though not always, in conjunction with an analysis of their black characters. Anthony Szczesiul, Michael Kreyling, Forrest G. Robinson, and Hugh Ruppersburg have written seminal and insightful works on the topics, with Szczesiul's *Racial Politics and Robert Penn Warren's Poetry* currently considered to be the final word on Warren's views and poetry on race. Because the Negro presence is more prolific in Faulkner's works than in Warren's oeuvre, scholarship on the topic is more abundant. Thadious Davis, Gloria Jean Austin, Charles Nilson, James Baldwin, Irving Howe, and Charles D. Peavy are just a few of the scholars who have addressed Faulkner's intersection with the race question.

Little, however, has been said about the similarities between these two American literary giants and their experiences with race. Indeed, Joseph Millichap's pronouncement that "Warren's initial fiction stands in marked distinction to his early social criticism, a relationship which parallels that between Faulkner's finest creative writing and his often perplexing cultural commentary" (353) is one of the few statements that underscores the reality that both men include Negroes in prominent positions in their fiction, make public statements about their views on race relations in the United States, and become the focus of denigration because of those statements. Though Warren's career highlights the transformation he made from segregationist to integrationist, Faulkner's novels suggest he always was a proponent of integration. The young Warren is often discussed in terms of his advocacy of racial segregation in the 1930 essay "The Briar Patch," a position affirmed in his poem "Pondy Woods," which he penned in 1928. The young Faulkner is also known for his writings on race. About the same time that Warren is publicly supporting segregation, Faulkner is creating one of the most memorable Negro figures in all of American literature:

The Sound and the Fury's Dilsey. Indeed, the critical view, as Warren himself notes, is that "[the] actual role of the Negro in Faulkner's fiction is consistently one of pathos and heroism" ("Faulkner" 75), an apt description of Dilsey.

Yet the trajectory of Faulkner's career, as Frederick L. Gwynn and Joseph L. Blotner observe, eventually finds him defending himself against accusations "that despite his sympathetic treatment of Negroes in his fiction, [he] was at heart just another old-guard Southerner" (85). Those accusations are the result of two events. In its March 5, 1956, issue, *Life* publishes a "Letter to the North" by Faulkner. The missive advocates a "Go Slow" policy towards racial segregation. Two weeks later, *The Reporter* publishes an interview Faulkner had granted Russell Warren Howe in February of the same year. In an effort to underscore his position on state's rights versus federal rights, he makes during the interview his most inflammatory statements on integration: "But if it came to fighting I'd fight for Mississippi against the United States even if it meant going out into the street and shooting Negroes. After all, I'm not going out to shoot Mississippians" (qtd. in Peavy 70).

While the mid-fifties are a time when Faulkner is attempting to salvage his reputation as an integrationist, the period is a time of transformation for Warren. In 1955, he publishes *Band of Angels,* a novel in which a Negro woman is the protagonist. And in 1956, while Faulkner is battling racist accusations, Warren is publishing *Segregation: The Inner Conflict of the South*, an expanded version of an article he has published in *Life* in its July 9, 1956, issue. The article and the book further separate him from the conservative views of his former Agrarian colleagues.

Thus, in the nearly thirty years between the late-twenties and the mid-fifties, the two writers' careers reveal similar tensions. During the 1920s, Faulker reveals in his fiction and public statements a sensitivity for the Negro psyche unparalleled by any other white American author, while Warren is publicly supporting the "separate but equal" doctrine. Then in the 1950s, Faulkner is making public statements that suggest a racist bias while Warren is repudiating his past segregationist views. At the beginning and end of this near thirty-year period stand two Negro females: Faulkner's Dilsey and Warren's Amantha. The characters, in essence, then, become symbols of the authors' more idealized, liberal positions on race. But the symbolism does not stop there. If Dilsey is representative of where Faulkner stood on race politics and where Warren eventually would be, then Amantha characterizes the flawed beings they actually were.

Except for in a few of his poems, Negroes play no major role in Warren's early works. The poem that is often cited as evidence of Warren's racist tendencies is "Pondy Woods." Composed in 1928 and included in his 1936 collection *Thirty-six Poems*, the work tells the story of a runaway slave trying to elude a lynch mob:

> Big Jim Todd was a slick black buck
> Laying low in the mud and muck
> Of Pondy Woods when the sun went down
> In gold, and the buzzards tilted down
> A windless vortex to the black-gum trees
> To sit along the quiet boughs,
> Devout and swollen, at their ease. (7–13)

Eventually, a buzzard coughs the line that is most often quoted: "Nigger, your breed ain't metaphysical" (33). Critics disagree on whether this representation reflects Warren's own views on race since a bird, not the narrator, invokes it. Anthony Szczesiul positions Hugh Ruppersburg, Porter G. Raper, and Aldon Nielsen on one side of the debate. They argue for an ironic reading of the poem, "an extreme example" of the Negro as "hopelessly fated man" (17). Sterling Brown's sardonic commentary on the poem succinctly summarizes the opposing side of the debate: "Cracker, your breed ain't exegetical" (qtd. in Szczesiul 9). For Szczesiul, however, two particular aspects of the composition of the poem are of major import. One, "Pondy Woods" is part of a poem sequence that, taken as a whole, exhibits Warren's racial assumptions about the hierarchical structure of the South. Moreover, the poem is written almost at the same time that the poet is affirming his support for the 1896 Supreme Court decision in the *Plessy v. Ferguson* case (17–25). Szczesiul concludes that the poem merely "informs [Warren's] defense of segregation in *I'll Take My Stand*" (25).

The 1931 Agrarian manifesto was the group's polemic against the industrialization of the South as an obvious manifestation of the North's encroachment upon the values of that region. Warren's essay, "The Briar Patch," discusses the role of the Negro in an agrarian

South. It was a piece he volunteered to write. Early on in the essay, he contends the Negro is most comfortable in the United States: "They [Negroes] might be mobbed from their farms in Ohio or be forced to spend their days in the cotton-fields under a blazing Mississippi sun, but America, after all, was home. Here they knew where they stood; the jungle, though not many generations behind, was mysterious and deadly" (246). Warren then notes what he believes one of the egregious effects of Reconstruction to be: "Always in the past he [the Negro] had been told when to work and what to do, and now, with the new-got freedom, he failed to understand the limitation which a simple contract of labor set on that freedom. . . . Now he had to find a place, and the attempt to find it is the story of the negro since 1865" (247).

Warren continues his essay with his solution for the Negro presence in the South, evoking the name of one Negro he believes understands racial politics:

> Booker T. Washington realized the immediate need
> of his race; he realized that the masses of negroes,
> both then and for a long time thereafter, had to live
> by the production of their hands, and that little was to
> be gained by only attempting to create a small group
> of intellectual aristocrats in the race. The most urgent
> need was to make the ordinary negro into a competent
> workman or artisan and decent citizen. (250)

Therefore, vocational training of the Negroes is the appropriate approach to making them independently and economically viable. And this training must be in agrarian arts: "Without capital, without education, and with only the crudest training in agricultural methods, the negro has demonstrated his capacity to achieve a certain degree of happiness and independence on the land, and there is every reason to expect that the process will be accelerated from year to year" (261). From this reasoning, he concludes: "Let the negro sit beneath his own vine and fig tree" (264). This line is the one most often cited as evidence of Warren's racial bias. It is his succinct support of a segregated South.

"The Briar Patch" has three basic tenets: that Negroes deserve the same rights as whites, but within the framework of a segregated society; that Northern industrialization of the South would only victimize blacks even further and thus worsen their relationships with whites; and that the Southern black is best suited for an agrarian lifestyle. Interestingly, despite Warren's tacit support for the status quo, his essay did not sit well with his Agrarian colleagues: "Donald Davidson . . . refused to believe Warren had written the essay, accusing it of 'progressive' implications, with a pretty strong smack of latter-day sociology" (Ruppersburg 30). Yet Davidson's criticism is not indicative of the reception the essay, and the collection as a whole, received. For the most part, the critical view of *I'll Take My Stand,* when it was published, was that it was a reactionary and romanticized defense of the Old South, not a progressive polemic on race politics. But because Warren emerged as the most accomplished of the Agrarians, his essay has received the most critical attention.

"The Briar Patch" is a piece Warren would often have to address during his illustrious career even though he retracted the position he takes in the work. Joseph Blotner notes that even during the composition of the essay, Warren did not feel right about his conclusion: "I was just very uncomfortable with the piece, but it was this. My position was exactly that of the Supreme Court. Equal, you see; 'different but equal' was the view of the Supreme Court and of 99 percent of white people in the country" (106). Three books Warren wrote after his tenure as Poet Laureate from 1944–45—*Segregation: The Inner Conflict of the South* (1956), *The Legacy of the Civil War: Meditations on the Centennial* (1961), and *Who Speaks for the Negro?* (1965)—all support the idea that the more mature Warren would have never written "The Briar Patch." He himself says as much. Indeed, when *Legacy of the Civil War* was favorably reviewed for its "brilliance, insight, and beauty of the work" (Blotner 344), Warren took issue with one of the reviews that excoriated it. *The New Republic* accused him of the same biases in *I'll Take My Stand*: "Furious, Warren wrote the editor that he wished the reviewer had taken the trouble 'to glance at explicit repudiation, some time back, of what I said in 1929'" (Blotner 344).

Yet these retractions are not convincing to a number of critics. Forrest G. Robinson, arguably Warren's most vociferous critic on the issue of race, invokes Toni Morrison in the epigraph to his essay "A Combat with the Past: Robert Penn Warren on Race and Slavery": "We can agree, I think, that invisible things are not necessarily 'not-there';

that a void may be empty, but is not a vacuum. In addition, certain absences are so stressed, so planned, they call attention to themselves; arrest us with intentionality and purpose, like neighborhoods that are defined by the population held away from them" (511). For Robinson, that absence is most apparent in Warren's fiction, especially in *All the King's Men*, a work that the critic states is an indictment of Warren's evasiveness on the race question. Referring to Jack Burden's failure to acknowledge the race problem—an absence that is particularly glaring in light of Burden's uncovering of the details behind Cass Mastern's death—Robinson sees "[this] conspicuous omission . . . [as] evidence of an underlying ambivalence, shared by Jack and his maker, on the score of race and slavery. . . . Jack's silence is profoundly telling. And so is Warren's" (512). In the same essay, Robinson excoriates Warren's *Band of Angels* for its subordination of its racial themes to the explorations of self-knowledge and identity.

Michael Kreyling sees a similar omission in Warren's failure to recognize W.E.B. DuBois's and Malcolm X's vision for the Negro American. Indeed, central to Warren's argument for a future of racial integration is the idea that American identity must usurp racial identity, an idea antithetical to DuBois and Malcolm X:

> Warren's peroration [the book *Who Speaks for the Negro?*] would seem to exclude Malcolm X and DuBois—those who came to the conclusion reluctantly or readily that a flawed culture could not be corrected from within. Warren's project was to keep the system in the hands of the insiders, having both the sin and the penance in one cultural liturgy "developed and elaborated here." This is either/both a sincere act of contrition or/and a strenuous act of appropriation, for as courageous as Warren could be in confessing his own "cowardice" or "defensiveness" or "callowness," he was not about to surrender "here" nor the identity that functioned as his title to it. (292)

Thus, despite Warren's apparent transformation from segregationist to integrationist, he could never live down the statements he had made in "The Briar Patch." For a large number of critics, his support for early-century race relations informed all of his subsequent works. As Kreying concludes, "Warren might have recanted the comparatively simple racist perspective of 'The Briar Patch,' but it did not get him out of a thornier one" (285).

In like manner, though William Faulkner's "Letter to the North" appears in print closer to the end of his career, to a large number of critics the article informs much of what he had written on race relations prior to its publication in *Life*. In the letter, Faulkner reminds his readers of his commitment to integration. He then asserts his commitment to state's rights: "Now I must go on record as opposing the forces outside the South which would use legal or police compulsion to eradicate that evil overnight. I was against compulsory segregation. I am just as strongly against compulsory integration. Firstly of course from principle. Secondly because I don't believe compulsion will work" (51). Rapid change of race relations, he believes, will result in open violence. He references Miss Autherine Lucy, whose enrollment into the University of Alabama had been suspended out of fear for her life. He refers to a letter he had received from a Negro woman who asserts Emmett Till had gotten what he deserved. He reminds his readers of a lesson learned from the Civil War:

> The Northerner is not even aware yet of what that war really proved. He assumes that it merely proved to the Southerner that he was wrong. It didn't do that because the Southerner already knew he was wrong. . . . What that war should have done, but failed to do, was to prove to the North that the South will go to any length, even that fatal and already doomed one, before it will accept alteration of its racial condition by mere force of law or economic threat. (52)

And then he concludes by urging his readers to cease and desist: "Stop now for a moment. You have shown the Southerner what you can do and what you will do if necessary; give him a space in which to get his breath and assimilate that knowledge" (52).

Faulkner's letter was attacked by a number of different personalities, both the well known and the uncelebrated. James Baldwin published a denunciatory response in the Fall 1956 issue of *Partisan*

Review. A Presbyterian minister, Dr. Carl R. Pritchett, who at the time was still a relative unknown, condemned the contents of the letter at the March 22 National Civil Liberties Union Clearing House. The NAACP and the Southern Regional Council also saw fit to denounce the article and its author. W.E.B. Dubois challenged Faulkner to a debate on the topic of integration. Faulkner declined as he stated that Dubois's and his opinions on the topic were the same. Instead, Faulkner responded to the criticism by writing another letter to *Life.* In this letter he outlines his motivations for writing the former one. He explains that his primary motivation was a fear for Miss Lucy's life.

Yet Faulkner failed to convince a large number of readers that the March 5 letter did not reveal his true colors. Despite strong statements in his fiction about the racial crisis in the South, his 1950 public condemnation of bigotry in the miscarriage of justice during the Turner-Whitt Murder Trial, and a number of letters to the editor of the Memphis *Commercial Appeal* criticizing Mississippi's maintaining of two public school systems, Faulkner was now perceived to have always been an old guard Southerner. The most obvious reason for this conclusion is his comments to Russell Warren Howe, a correspondent for the London *Sunday Times.* Though the interview occurred on February 21, 1956, it was published on March 4, 1956. Its appearance in print, then, occurred one day before the publication of Faulkner's "Letter to the North." In the interview, Faulkner, as he does in the letter, professes his disdain for both "enforced integration" and "enforced segregation." However, his remark about "shooting Negroes" is what chafes readers. Though Faulkner denies ever making such a statement, even writing several letters to the editor of *The Reporter* asserting that he never would have made such a statement, the interview and the *Life* letter suggest otherwise to their readers.[1] James Baldwin encapsulates the general tenor of the criticism of Faulkner. To Baldwin, Faulkner "seemed to be a fallen idol who was unable to match his words with action, itself a profound form of respect" (qtd. in Inge).

The symbols of Faulkner's and Warren's tension between their fictional and nonfictional works are the two female Negro characters that come to life during the periods that the authors are publishing their polemic statements on race. One year before *I'll Take My Stand* is published, *The Sound and the Fury* hits the stands. Though Dilsey appears throughout the novel, the fourth chapter, despite being told by an omniscient narrator, is generally called "Dilsey's chapter." Moreover, in a work that obfuscates narrative authority, Dilsey's point of view is considered to be the most reliable. The reasons are several. She is a strong female character as evidenced by her exchange with Jason at the breakfast table:

> "Well, we're going to change all that," Jason said. "Go up and tell her breakfast is ready."
> "You leave her alone now, Jason," Dilsey said. "She gits up fer breakfast ev'y week mawnin, en Cahline lets her stay in bed ev'y Sundayh. You knows dat."
> "I cant keep a kitchen full of niggers to wait on her pleasure, much as I'd like to," Jason said. "Go and tell her to come down to breakfast."
> "Aint nobody have to wait on her," Dilsey said. "I puts her breakfast inde warmer en she—"
> "Did you hear me?" Jason said.
> "I hears you," Dilsey said. "All I been hearin, when you in de house. Ef hit aint Quentin er you maw, hit's Luster en Benjy. Whut you let him go on dat way fer, Miss Cahline?" (346)

The exchange subverts the ideas of "placeness" so crucial to Southern racial politics; it is a Negro woman suggesting to her white employers what the appropriate response to Miss Quentin's insubordination is.

Dilsey is secure in her place, and while part of the reason is that she proves over and over again to be the strongest character in the novel, a more crucial reason is that her strength is anchored in her goodness, especially to Benjy. In the scene in which she takes him and her children to church, Frony challenges her not to take Benjy to church anymore because "Folks talkin." Her response reflects her subversion of the hierarchical nature of race: "'And I knows whut kind of folks,' Dilsey said, 'Trash white folks. Dats who it is. Thinks he aint good enough fer white church, but nigger church aint good enough fer him'" (362). When Benjy and Dilsey sit side by side on a church pew, they are equals before Dilsey's God: "In the midst of the voices and the hands Ben sat, rapt in his sweet blue gaze. Dilsey sat bolt upright beside, crying rigidly and quietly in the annealment and the blood of the remembered Lamb" (370–71). Dilsey's goodness is manifested not only to the helpless but also to the undeserving. Upon her return home from church, her concern is for Mrs. Compson. Her attempts to ease the matriarch's apprehension over Quentin's absence, her unsolicited query about the temperature of the water in the hot-water bottle, and her fishing for the Bible in the bed in which Mrs. Compson is currently lying all reinforce Dilsey's strength in goodness.

The trait has been noted by critics as well. Referring to the notation under Dilsey's name in the appendix of *The Sound and the Fury*, Christine Smith writes, "Faulkner distills Dilsey to a single word that, through our reading of 1 Corinthians 13:4–7, explains her character. By writing 'Dilsey. They endured,' Faulkner gives the highest compliment possible, for he means that Dilsey loves on the deepest possible level. (100–01). Smith does not fail to note that most critics see the appendix as an actual response to Ike's telling McCaslin in "The Bear" "three times that they will endure and that, by enduring, they will ultimately have their chance to succeed the failing southern community" (100). However, her explication is consistent with Michael Dean's reading of the note in the appendix:

> I think the words have additional meanings. They do indeed honor Dilsey and her kin, but I think that Dilsey and her kin can be interpreted to mean the Christian saints who endure and prevail even in a century like ours. And I would venture to suggest that the plural pronoun Faulkner seemingly misuses encompasses not just people but also those oft-mentioned virtues: love, honor, pity, pride, compassion, sacrifice, endurance, courage, hope. These virtues, because of saints who, like Dilsey, are their embodiment in this world, endure, and they will one day, let us pray, prevail. (358)

Dean's beatification of Dilsey notwithstanding, the character Dilsey was a favorite of her own creator. On at least three different occasions, he mentions her as one of his more adored characters (Dean 352). The reason, one might suggest, is that Faulkner infuses in her something that is missing in virtually all of his other characters—strength in goodness. Indeed, when Cleanth Brooks praises the female characters in *Light in August* and *The Hamlet,* one cannot help believing the critic had Dilsey in mind as well: "Was Faulkner able to depict his women characters with insight and give them vitality? In my opinion, Faulkner portrays women with great skill. I would like to think that a great artist's comprehension transcends the boundaries of sex just as it transcends those of nationality" (81).

In contrast, Amantha Starr, Warren's female Negro protagonist, does not fare well among the critics. James Justus calls the narrator of *Band of Angels* a "whiner and a nagger" (*Achievement* 237) and accuses her of being "not complex enough" to warrant telling her story as an extra-diagetic character (*Achievement* 238). Warren himself concedes these characterizations as apropos in an interview several years later: "One thing there [referring to *Band of Angels*]: the narrator is wrong. There's no richness and depth in the experience of the narrator—at least, it isn't brought out" (Watkins and Hiers 188). Overall, the book has been labeled "an ambitious failure and perhaps the least satisfactory of his novels" by his biographer Joseph Blotner (300).

But despite failing to create a well-rounded protagonist, he apparently succeeds in what appears to be his ultimate goal—to foreground his protagonist in an exploration of self-knowledge and identity. The novel begins with Manty's woeful exclamation, "Oh, who am I? For so long that was, you might say, the cry of my heart" (3). It then begins to detail her confusion as a light-skinned mulatta who at one time thought she was the white daughter of a "compassionate" slave owner. A little less than halfway through the novel, she concludes that "what you are is an expression of History, and you do not live your life, but somehow, your life lives you, and you are, therefore, only what History does to you" (134). When, in the end, her husband Tobias Sears calls her "poor little Manty," she responds with "Don't call me that . . . don't ever call me poor little Manty again" (373). Tobias, instead, calls her "Miss Manty." To this, she buries her face in joy, and tears of joy stream down her cheeks. The ending suggests she has come to terms with being the daughter of a slave owner and a slave. Indeed, though Justus calls her a "whiner," he does concede Amantha a place next to Jack Burden for having accomplished a viable self-identity ("Mariner" 120). And Margaret Jordan concludes that the novel "offers significant insight into the intricacies and confusions of the race" (30). Though Warren may have failed in fleshing out his protagonist, Manty's quest for identity is consistent with what the author has sought to do with his other literary characters; Jack Burden, Percy Munn, Willie Proudfit, and Jeremiah Beaumont all embark on journeys for self-knowledge. In this respect, he succeeds.

Beyond Faulkner's success at creating one of the most memorable African-American characters in all of American literature and Warren's apparent failure to replicate the task, both Dilsey and Amantha symbolize the tension that exists between the fictional and nonfictional production of these two authors. The saint-like Dilsey is a primary reason why [most] critics. . . have concluded that Faulkner has managed to overcome the racial prejudice of his region and has not only recognized the humanity of Negroes but has also often used them in his fiction to portray universal as well as racial problems (Peavy 12). Yet almost thirty years after she was created, Faulkner's dedication to racial integration was being questioned as a result of his statements to Russell Howe and in his "Letter to the North."

In the same year that *The Sound and the Fury* was published, Warren's *John Brown: The Making of a Martyr* went to press. Warren concludes that Brown's motivations at Harper's Ferry were not noble, that he was motivated by greed. This excoriation of an abolitionist's hero led to early beliefs that Warren was a racist at heart, a sentiment reinforced by his segregationist views in "The Briar Patch." Yet almost thirty years after the appearance of these works, Warren, already beginning to mend his reputation, creates a black, female character who, though flawed, is an appropriate symbol for who he was in 1955. Indeed, Amantha is emblematic of both authors. Forrest Robinson describes her narrative as "defensive on the score of race-slavery" (527), a description just as *à propos*, one could argue, of Warren and Faulkner. Convinced that they both were on the side of the black during the incendiary decade of the fifties, Warren's and Faulkner's nonfictional prose proves to be a defense for segregation yet defensive of their race politics.

In the Foreword to Charles Peavy's book *Go Slow Now: Faulkner and the Race Question*, Patrick Hogan assesses Faulkner's position on race in the following manner:

It must be remembered that the Faulkner who has been rightly acclaimed as one of the major literary creators of the present century was also a man who not only inherited a tradition but who lived, suffered, and achieved during a recent period which demanded serious and dramatic questioning of that tradition, along with several others—a process which continues after Faulkner's death. Therefore, Faulkner's own views cannot be expected to have remained static, and since the artist who produced the fiction was also a human being, both his fiction and his expository writings of all sorts must be considered if a given view is to be attributed to him as characteristic of his thought, particularly about the Negro. (6)

If one inserts Warren's name in the three places where Faulkner's is found in the paragraph, Hogan's conclusions are apt descriptions of the poet as well. A near thirty-year period produced tensions between both authors' fictional and nonfictional works. This tension is symbolized most appropriately by their two Negro protagonists—Dilsey, the saint Faulkner and Warren hoped to be for the Negro race, and Manty, the flawed protagonist they actually were.

Notes

1. Part of Faulkner's refutation of the "shooting Negroes" comments to assert that they were statements "no sober man would make, nor, it seems to me, any sane man believe" (qtd. in Peavy 71). Peavy states that in a letter dated March 7, 1965, Howe notes that about two weeks after the interview, Faulkner went into the hospital in Memphis. During his stay he allegedly told a reporter for *Time* magazine that during the week of the interview he was drinking so much, "I might have said anything" (73). Howe, however, remembers a Faulkner who "was slow-spoken as usual, but didn't slur, misconstruct sentences or do anything else associated with people who are drunk" (qtd. in Peavy 73). Yet Joseph Blotner, Faulkner's biographer, confirms Faulkner admitted to drinking a lot during the week of the interview in a letter to Joan Williams Bowen (618).

Works Cited

Blotner, Joseph. *Faulkner: A Biography.* New York: Random House, 1974. Print.

———. *Robert Penn Warren: A Biography.* New York: Random House, 1997. Print.

Brooks, Cleanth. *On the Prejudices, Predilections, and Firm Beliefs of William Faulkner: Essays by Cleanth Brooks.* Baton Rouge: Louisiana State UP, 1987. Print.

Dean, Michael P. "Faulkner's Dilsey: A Saint for Our Century." *Southern Studies: An Interdisciplinary Journal of the South* 22 (1983): 351–58. Print.

Faulkner, William. "A Letter to the North: William Faulkner, the South's Foremost Writer Warns on Integration—Stop Now for a Moment.'" *Life* 5 (Mar. 1956): 51–2. *Google Books.* Web. 22 Apr. 2011.

———. *The Sound and the Fury.* 1929. New York: The Modern Library, 1956. Print.

Gwynn, Frederick L., and Joseph L. Blotner. eds. *Faulkner in the University: Class Conferences at the University of Virginia 1957–1958.* New York: Vintage, 1959. Print.

Inge, M. Thomas. "Faulkner's Enduring 'Dixie Limited.'" *Cosmos Journal* 10 (2000). Cosmos Club. Web. 1 Feb. 2013.

Jordan, Margaret I. *African American Servitude and Historical Imaginings: Retrospective Fiction and Representation.* New York: Palgrave Macmillan, 2004. Print.

Justus, James H. *The Achievement of Robert Penn Warren.* Baton Rouge: Louisiana State UP, 1981. Print.

———. "The Mariner and Robert Penn Warren." *Critical Essays on Robert Penn Warren.* Ed. William Bedford Clark. Boston: G. K. Hall, 1981.

111-21. Rpt. from *Texas Studies in Literature and Language* 7 (1966): 117-28. Print.

Kreyling, Michael. "Robert Penn Warren: The Real Southerner and the 'Hypothetical Negro.'" *American Literary History* 21.2 (2009): 268–94. *Project Muse.* Web. 14 Apr. 2011.

Millichap, Joseph. "Warren's Faulkner." *Mississippi Quarterly: The Journal of Southern Cultures* 60.2 (2007): 351–367. *MLA International Bibliography.* EBSCO. Web. 21 Apr. 2011.

Peavy, Charles D. *Go Slow Now: Faulkner and the Race Question.* Eugene: U of Oregon, 1971. Print.

"Robert Penn Warren: An Interview." *Journal of American Studies* 8.2 (1974). Rpt. in *Robert Penn Warren Talking: Interviews 1950–1978.* Ed. Floyd C. Watkins and John T. Hiers. New York: Random House, 1980. 173–95. Print.

Ruppersburg, Hugh. *Robert Penn Warren and the American Imagination.* Athens: U of Georgia P, 1990. Print.

Smith, Christine. "Faulkner's *The Sound and the Fury.*" *Explicator* 66.2 (2008): 100-01. *MLA International Bibliography.* EBSCO. Web. 24 Apr. 2011.

Szczesiul, Anthony. *Racial Politics and Robert Penn Warren's Poetry.* Gainesville: UP of Florida, 2002. Print.

Warren, Robert Penn. *Band of Angels.* 1955. Baton Rouge: Louisiana State UP, 1983. Print.

———. "William Faulkner." *Selected Essays.* New York: Random House, 1958. 59-79. Print.

Fadia Mereani

The Inadequacy of Language in William Faulkner's *As I Lay Dying* and Robert Penn Warren's *Brother to Dragons*

With the introduction of the Freudian subconscious, early twentieth-century writers witnessed a change in the view of one's mental capacity of perception and how one expresses it through language. The subconscious proved the limitedness of the conscious and the inadequacy of almost all different means of expression to convey the meanings that go beyond human perception. Early twentieth-century writers, familiar with the Freudian oeuvre and experiencing the impact of the changes of the view of human perception on other non-verbal artistic expression, realized the limitedness of the verbal means of conveying meaning as well, particularly in light of how language was used in the rhetoric of the age in connection to some bombastic words and mottos that idealize World War I. In his introduction to *The Flesh and The Word*, Floyd Watkins explains that the distrust in language came as "a reaction to an age of verbomania and logorrhea" when "slogans, glorified statements, magniloquent claims of virtue and victory idealized and sentimentalized the War . . . ruined the language" (5). Watkins shows how major twentieth-century writers—who include T.S. Eliot, Ezra Pound, Edith Wharton, Ernest Hemingway, William Faulkner, Katherine Anne Porter, and Robert Penn Warren—have reflected the inadequacy of language in their attempt at redefining the role of "the man of letters" and in their writings through their devotion to "the fact, the thing, the image" and through their emphasis on the self-reflexive limitedness of language when it works against itself in their style and characterization (7–10). In this study, Watkins focuses on Eliot, Faulkner, and Hemingway as representatives of that period to show the similar style and techniques these authors used to illustrate the shift from "objectiveness to abstraction, from the flesh to the word" in their treatment and attitude toward human perception, language, and meaning (4). This essay will focus on Faulkner's *As I Lay Dying* and Warren's *Brother to Dragons* to demonstrate how this theme has persisted to be one of the main concerns of twentieth-century authors as they move toward the end of the century and how both authors treat it similarly, yet with their distinctive styles.

Language has failed miserably to fulfill its communicative function in Faulkner's *As I Lay Dying*. In fact, the failure of verbal communication dominates the world of the novel and spreads its web among its inhabitants. Watkins states that language has failed to "communicate love" in *As I Lay Dying* (185). He adds:

> Those who articulate their interpretations of acts use meaningless words. Those who know and understand do not speak the words. Most of them remain silent in the novel, and emotion and truth are apparent in their deeds. Some reject empty words so much that they not only refuse to speak them but also reject them even in their internal monologues, their stream of thought. To know Faulkner's themes, his meanings, his characters, therefore, one must recognize the difference between truth and statement in each of the characters. Faulkner's techniques enable him to treat each character's relationship to love, fact, deed, and abstract word. The failure of language and meaning of object and act are keys to the most important ironies and meanings. (185–86)

In addition to the failure to communicate love, language fails to convey a meaning of life and death in *As I Lay Dying*. Faulkner illustrates this failure in two significant ways: he uses the semantic and syntactic aspects of language to show its limitation to convey meaning and depends heavily on non-verbal means of communication to show the characters' avoidance of verbal communication, out of their conscious or unconscious understanding of the limitedness of their language to express love or to understand life and death. Non-verbal means of communication include a general richness in sounds, artificial or natural, human, man-made or animalistic, which include a heavy use of personification of natural elements and animals, looks, which include descriptions of eyes, eye movements, and head movements and other bodily gestures and language. Other significant non-verbal means of communication emphasized in the novel are singing and music and laughter.

Faulkner shows the inadequacy of the semantic and syntactic features of language as he shifts between the grand poetic language of Darl to the simplistic, childish language of Vardaman and as he shifts between the philosophical, intellectual language of some of the characters (or perhaps an implied author and narrator) to the vernacular.

As I Lay Dying is full of sounds that fill the spaces of words wherever words fail to convey meaning. In his description of his brother while he is sawing and making the coffin for their mother, Darl describes how the wood is making sounds that are deep and expressive of a meaning of death, and perhaps of life, which goes beyond the perception of the characters in the book. Darl describes how "the planks" are making "long clattering reverberations in the dead air as though [Cash] were lifting and dropping them at the bottom of an invisible well, the sounds ceasing without departing, as if any movement might dislodge them from the immediate air in reverberant repetition" (75–76). This is juxtaposed to a description of the rain in which the sound of rain becomes "a long sigh, as though of relief from intolerable suspense" (76). Wood will become more communicative toward the end of the novel to add to those reverberations Darl's and Vardaman's ability to "hear" their mother through her coffin under the apple tree and as she becomes one with the coffin (214). Water in the form of the river this time will also "[talk] up to us in a murmur become ceaseless and myriad" and the surface of the water will be "silent, impermanent and profoundly significant, as though just beneath the surface something huge and alive waked for a moment of lazy alertness out of and into light slumber again" (141). Through these images, Faulkner establishes a connection between life depicted in different states of awareness, perception, understanding, and knowing and the ability to communicate without words. He then establishes a connection between death and sleep with the inability to communicate, except in the case of Addie where some kind of communication happens across the boundaries between the living and the dead. Fire also makes communicative sounds that join the sound of the falling barn to make a "sound like an interminable train crossing an endless trestle" (219). As "the sound of the flames" is pronounced loudly, the human voices become "thin and high and meaningless and at the same time profoundly wild and sad" (219). Wood, rain, and fire express through the different sounds they make a meaning of life and death that goes unperceived by most of the characters in the novel because of their dependence on the arbitrariness between sounds and meanings in their limited linguistic abilities. Where natural elements and their sounds relatively succeed in expressing meaning, human beings fail.

As a part of the natural elements in the novel, animals and their sounds are used to reveal the inadequacy of language. Faulkner compares human beings to animals: Addie is a fish and a horse, and Jewel is almost always compared to his horse, for instance, as if to reduce their linguistic abilities to express themselves in words to those of the animals. Like those animals, their silence expresses their mistrust of words and their lack of understanding of love, life, and death. However, animals, Faulkner suggests through his animal imagery, do understand and perceive meaning but cannot express it in words. Before launching into the river, Jewel's "horse is trembling, its eye rolling wild and baby-blue in its long pink face, its breathing stertorous like groaning" (142). The horse does understand danger and expresses it through its eyes and groan. At the moment of crisis, the mules are described as "breathing now with a deep groaning sound; looking back once, their gaze sweeps across us with in their eyes a wild, sad, profound and despairing quality as though they had already seen in the thick water the shape of the disaster which they could not speak and we could not see" (146–47). In this passage, the mules communicate with water, another natural element, to arrive at meaning they both understand but cannot express in words.

As language and words fail, expressions, glances, and head movements play important roles in expressing meaning and revealing the emotions and feelings of characters in spite of their silence. Because the deeds and acts are more important than words in the world of *As I Lay Dying,* a slight movement of the eye expresses volumes of meaning. In almost every instance in the novel in which characters fail to express themselves or refuse to use words to express meanings, they use their eyes to communicate their emotions. As characters looking up, down, or aside, they convey emotions that are different from the emotions expressed by the act of "watching" intently with fear or anger. They also blink or shut their eyes frequently every time communication fails as they withdraw into themselves.

Communication can be carried across in singing and music. When Addie passes away, the community comes together to sing and express their sadness (91–92). Through the act of singing, a meaning of grief and sadness is shared by the attendants of that scene. The voice of the singer becomes a voice separate from his identity. Faulkner suggests that this ability to convey meaning through a song goes beyond the human capacity to express meaning through language. When one is separate from one's voice, the voice takes an identity of its own and acquires the ability to convey meaning. This comes into a sharp contrast with the song Cora sings on her way home (92). Her song has words attached to it. Because her voice cannot be separated from her religious identity, the song becomes as meaningless as language itself. Faulkner ironically uses images of music when Anse goes into the house of his wife-to-be to show the inadequacy of language to convey meaning. The music keeps playing on and off and stops completely when Anse and the woman start talking, as if the musical notes were trying to tell the children something about their father's relationship with that woman. Even music here fails the children because an actual conversation has taken the place of music in the air, and music is forced into silence.

When music and other non-verbal means of communication fail to convey meaning, Darl's laughter expresses meaning in abundance. His laughter comes to signify an understanding of the futility of human emotions and, at the same time, of the futility of language to express these emotions. It suggests that perhaps insanity, the state in which the unconscious takes control of the human mind, allows meaning to be felt and perceived fluidly and without words.

Like Faulkner, Robert Penn Warren has also realized the inadequacy of language as communication. Randy Hendricks explains that Warren, in his attempt "to understand the past in its relation to the present," finds that this is "a painful process because of the limitation of words" (135). He also believes that "[n]o poem in American literary history that [he is] aware of treats history as a problem of language more rigorously than Warren's own great *Brother to Dragons*" (136).

Indeed, as the characters in *Brother to Dragons* struggle to communicate with each other, to articulate their ideas, and express their feelings, they show indirectly how language has failed to serve its purpose. *Brother to Dragons* shows how this inadequacy of language might eventually lead to a greater failure when the characters lose their battle to find a proper definition for the meaning of their lives. Like Faulkner in *As I Lay Dying*, Warren has successfully shown the inadequacy of language verbally and non-verbally in *Brother to Dragons* through the form, semantics, and syntax of the text, in addition to the characters' actions and reactions to each other and to the brutality of the murder committed in their past.

Brother to Dragons's form indirectly points out the inadequacy of language, as it defies classification.[1] The subtitle of the work says it is "a tale in verse and voices," making it look like a novel written in verse. When the reader focuses on the language used, he notices that it is actually a narrative poem with lively dialogue and rich images. Joseph Blotner explains how Warren "would variously employ blank verse and free verse" and how "[t]he tone and diction would be alternately poetic and literal, rhetorical and colloquial" (285). Marshall Walker describes *Brother to Dragons* as a poem in which:

> The blank verse, often Eliotesque in its rhythm and cadences, is regular enough to sustain the flow of high fleeing, but loose enough to preserve the spontaneity of narrative action and energetic argument, accommodating the colloquial speech of Aunt Cat, the Brother and Isham Lewis as well as the tense brooking of Thomas Jefferson. (118–19)

In the encyclopedic entry on "Robert Penn Warren" in *American Writers*, *Brother to Dragons* is described as "a vivid, lavish parable" that has "no direct action" and a poem that "consists of events recapitulated during lunges of wide-ranging commentary, and traces Jefferson's advance from the ashamed bitterness of the disillusioned idealist to an attitude of skeptical pragmatism" (243). The same entry states that Warren has created "a colloquial catechism" in which he tries to go "as far as he could go without imposing the methods of the novelist on the poet's habitual shorthand" (244).

On the other hand, the book may strike the reader as a play with a unified plot that moves from one scene to the other until it reaches the climax with the murder of the slave in the meat-house and ends tragically with the death of most of its characters. However, Warren, in the beginning of his book, warns the reader from dealing with the work as a play: "But even if the present version is a dialogue spoken by characters, it is definitely not a play, and must not be taken as such" (xv).

In addition, using blank and free verse and drawing from history make the text look like a historical document written in verse. Warren, nevertheless, makes a distinction between poetry and history in his "Forward" to *Brother to Dragons*, explaining how a poet should use history in his poetry. He concludes that "[h]istorical sense and poetic sense should not, in the end, be contradictory, for if poetry is the little myth we make, history is the big myth we live, and in our living, constantly remake" (xiii). Although this conclusion serves to emphasize the poetic form of the text, it does not deny the use of other forms more suitable for its historical content. In other words, it does not explain how the form used in the text would help the reader see clearly the lines that differentiate fact from fiction in the work.

Although the lack of a definite form for *Brother to Dragons* could suggest its richness and diversity, it also shows its inability to contain its message. R.P.W., the embodiment of Robert Penn Warren in *Brother to Dragons*, evidently illustrates the failure of form to convey the meaning of this story in his example of the ballad form. He says that he wants to write a ballad about the historical records he has found in the old Square House "but the form / Was not adequate: the facile imitation / Of folk simplicity would scarcely serve" (31). He also gives his reasons for the inadequacy of the form. The ballad's "folksiness / Is a pleasure of snobbish superiority or neurotic yearning" and its action would not be explained because it is not complex enough to meet "our / Complicities and our sad virtue" (31). Jefferson further emphasizes this point in his reply to R.P.W: "There is no form to hold / Reality and its insufferable intransigence. / I know, for I once thought to contrive / A form to hold the purity of man's hope. / But only dumped hot coals in that croker sack" (31–32).

Furthermore, the fact that the poem itself has undergone different versions until it reaches its final stages is a sign of the inadequacy of language. Hendricks considers the inadequacy of language the main reason behind the actual change the poem goes through:

> This yearning, this urgency to know and utter in a world where 'the question is the only answer,' is the poet's dilemma as well as the naturalist's and lies at the bottom of Warran's intense revisions. The textual history of *Brother to Dragons* provides clues for us here:

it nagged Warren from the time of its first publication in 1953 until the new version was published in 1979— really a new poem in significant ways. (86)[2]

The semantics of the text plays an important role in illustrating the inadequacy of language in *Brother to Dragons*. This role could be obviously detected in two important and recurrent elements in the text. These two elements are the characters' constant search for the appropriate words to express themselves and their constant search for a true definition for the meaning of good and evil and life and death in this story.

The characters in *Brother to Dragons* struggle to articulate their ideas and express their feelings. Hendricks shows how the characters are aware of their involvement in "a process of creating, even in a process of composition" and how they "often speak with a keen awareness that their words, to borrow Warren's own phrase, rise to the surface like bubbles and then burst, failing to contain their meanings" (136–37). Hendricks gives Jefferson's first speech as an example and contrasts the 1979 version of *Brother to Dragons* with the 1953 version to highlight the language's inadequacy to contain or deliver meaning:

> Jefferson announces the theme of the inadequacy of language in his opening speech in the 1979 version: "Language betrays. / There are no words to tell Truth" (7). The point is emphasized even more in the language of the 1953 version: "I had not meant to speak thus. Language betrays. / What I mean is, words are always the truth, and always the lie" (8). (136–7)

He also shows that Jefferson's speech "foreshadows the general tendency in the poem for characters to speak, retract, and respeak, to press language to the very edge of its usefulness and then try again" (137).

Another good example to illustrate how characters are aware of the inadequacy of their language is Charles Lewis's narration of his part of the story. In that part, he sounds lost for the appropriate words to express himself accurately. He tells the story in chopped sentences, trying to provide meaning and explanations for simple words: "I took / Myself and mine, / Mine being myself, / And fled" (11). The difficulty of expressing himself is most obvious from his statement "*Fled*—that's the word" (italics original 11). R.P.W. also exhibits a conscious effort to express himself: "But the word's not *know*. Guess will do better. / For even Lilburne couldn't *know*—" (71) He prefers to use the word "guess" to "know" because this is what he is and the other characters are doing while they are using the language. They guess the meanings and try to attach them to their realities. The attempts of Charles, R.P.W., and the other characters to choose the appropriate words to express themselves acquire a psychological dimension when they become internal struggles to find the truth about their world and discover their true identities. Hendricks states that:

> What we witness continually in the poem is more than voices countering other voices, thesis and antith-esis played out between the voices and within the struggling consciousness of single voices. We see in several of the characters' speeches a continuing inward struggle to frame the truth accurately in language that continually fails. There is thus no synthesis in the usual sense, yet the recognition of the failure of their lan-guage is part of the success finally. (138)

In other words, the characters of *Brother to Dragons* find the truth of their language through failure and that is what makes them succeed in finding their identities.

Although Robert Lowell thinks that *Brother to Dragons* is "slightly flawed by some fifty repetitions of the word 'definition,'" (qtd. in Strandberg 6), this word is actually a key to understanding how lan-guage has failed the characters in this book. Different characters ask in different parts of the poem about the definition of humanity and life and the importance of words to convey these meanings. Thomas Jeffer-son, at the very beginning of the poem, states his goal of coming back to life. He says he "might try / To defend my old definition of man" (5). R.P.W. also explains that Lilburne is trying to "defend civilization, define / The human mission, bring light to the dark place" (95) when he has defended the pitcher that symbolizes his love of his mother and the real value of his life.

However, Jefferson realizes later in the poem that "we were only men, / Defined in our errors and interests" (7) and that "there's no defense of the human definition" (71). For this reason, he realizes that the definition he has reached is useless and meaningless:

> If then I had known what I now know,
> I had thought it exquisitely better
> To seize the hot coals of the human definition
> In bare hands, and scream, and run what steps
> I could before I fell, and the white
> Articulation of hand-bones trellised through
> Fire-black flesh. (32)

The reduction of all the meaningful and expressive words of this definition to a scream followed by a physical escape and a fall shows the meaninglessness of the means with which it is defined. Jefferson's resort to run and fall, both non-verbal ways of communicating his despair, further proves the uselessness of the verbal ways of expression.

In fact, screams are one of the alternative ways used by the characters to try to express their emotions. In addition to Jefferson in the above-mentioned example, the scream of John, the murdered Negro, is heard everywhere so that "it came and filled the room" (36). Letitia hears it too and hears the whole world echoing it:

> the world
> Started screaming too, by itself, like I
> Had been waiting for years for it to start, and every
> Dead leaf in the woods just screamed like a tongue,
> Each little leaf weak, but all together
> One big scream filling
> My head,
> Like one big hollow echo, my poor head big enough
> To hold the world, and all the stars,
> The stars all screaming. (36)

The tongues the leaves possess are ironically used here to indicate that, as human organs used to produce words and speeches, they are useless because even when they are attached to other creatures, they fail to articulate words, and pain comes through as an endless universal scream shared by all the elements of the universe. This is to show that the inadequacy of language and the inability to express one's suffering is a universal thing shared by all creatures and is not limited only to human beings. R.W.P. connects the scream to the characters' ultimate reality of their goal and actions when he says in his defense of Lilburne:

> And unreality grew around him like a fog,
> And he must strike through the fog, strike hard to find
> Contact with something real,
> Something that will, perhaps, scream out its reality,
> And in that scream affirm, at last, poor Lilburne's own.
> For all we all ask in the end is that:
> Reality. (71)

Even the scream as a means of communication, however, becomes useless in this poem. Letitia explains her inability to scream in response to the scream she has heard at the night of the murder. She prefers to run and fall to end the anguish she has been feeling: "And the next I knew / I was out on the stairs, and was going / To fall. Then, of a sudden, / Was happy, for to fall / Might end whatever there'd been to scream about. / And so I fell" (36). Isham makes the case even worse when he actually cannot hear the scream of the Negro boy: "Yeah, the axe comes down, / But not a sound, and that nigger spreads his mouth, / And I strain and strive / To hear—oh, Lord, if only— / Then maybe something gets finished" (83). He even denies the reality of the scream because he cannot hear it: "Or maybe it's not real, since I can't hear—" (83). Jefferson, in the opening speech, asks the question "What was your silence then? / Before the scream?" This question even eliminates the importance of the scream and traces its origin back in history to silence. Silence here is much more preferred as a means of communication to screams and words because it takes human beings back to their original state of purity and to their original ability to communicate in an uncorrupted state and world.

The syntax of *Brother of Dragons* is also carefully used to show the inadequacy of language. From the opening lines of the poem, Jefferson drops the subjects from some of his sentences: "Cannot, though dead, set / My mouth to the dark stream that I may unknow / All my knowing. Cannot, for it, / Kneeling in that final thirst, I thrust / Down my face, I see come glimmering upward, / White, white out of the absolute dark of depth, / My face" (5). Dropping the subjects from the sentences in which he shows his inability to comprehend his current, corrupted, and dead state, and his inability to go back to a purer, more innocent condition and understanding of the world, comes in sharp contrast with the idealism and individuality that Jefferson represents as a leader of a nation taking the first baby steps in history. Instead of asserting this individuality, Jefferson's missing subjects show a loss of identity and an affirmation of one's own responsibility as a doer of actions and as a thinking, intellectual being capable of perceiving the meaning of one's life.

Lucy, Charles Lewis's wife, gives another example of a character dropping the subjects of her sentences. She drops the subject from her expression of love for her children when she realizes the inherent evil and darkness in her husband's face while he is asleep: "I loved my children. Love them. But know, too / The way my husband's face looked locked in sleep" (17). Dropping the subject in her case shows that even a woman's natural, motherly instinct to express her love for her children is lost in a world where darkness lurks in the background. Language here fails even the mother's instinct to assert her natural love for her children.

In other instances, Jefferson and the other characters leave their sentences dangling without a verb or a complement, shown in the text by dashes that mark silences, pauses, or interruptions in what is supposed to be a flowing dialogue between these characters. In quite a short dialogue between Jefferson and R.P.W., there are four dashes that show incomplete sentences. Jefferson, describing Louisiana, stops to comment on this land. R.P.W. then interrupts him to be interrupted by Jefferson, who in turn is interrupted by Charles Lewis:

> Jefferson: . . . Bold Louisiana,
> The landfall of my soul—
> Or then it seemed—
> R.P.W.: But—
> Jefferson: The house—
> Charles: I built it . . . (10)

These dashes show that carrying a conversation for a short period of time is a difficult task to undertake in a world where language has stopped to be an effective way of communicating.

These silences, pauses, and interruptions are sometimes followed by questions that urge the characters to finish their sentences and complete their meanings or force them to question their attitudes or interpretations of the situation. In a conversation between Isham and R.P.W., Isham leaves his sentences unfinished and is interrupted, therefore, by R.P.W. twice to ask him to finish his sentences:

> Isham: But then—
> R.P.W.: Then what?
> Isham: Just I don't understand. Like the last—
> R.P.W.: The last what? (73)

A good example that shows how questions are used to force the characters to think about their own attitude toward a particular issue is when Jefferson explains that he has thought that the monster in man is innocent. He is immediately interrupted by a question by R.P.W. that forces him to go back and check his attitude toward the evil nature of man. While Isham is describing how John is screaming while he is being murdered, he is interrupted by R.P.W.'s question: "Oh, what's one nigger more / In the economy of pain?" (83). This question forces the other characters to go back and see where this murder falls in the greater picture of crime and justice in history.

The incomplete sentences might also be followed by an interruption by another character to finish the sentence and complete the meaning or draw the attention of the readers to a particular point or in a different direction. In his narration of the murder, R.P.W. is interrupted by Isham, who finishes the sentence for R.P.W. and describes the rest of the murder: "R.P.W. . . . Lilburne said— / Isham: He turned from the fire . . . And said . . ." (88).

Most of these interruptions and questions are made by R.P.W., who functions as a facilitator for these conversations to make it easier for the other characters to express their ideas. Richard G. Law describes R.P.W's character "as a combined historian and detective, visiting the site, sifting through the old court records, and pondering the motives which led to the slaying" (195). The whole book, from

Joseph Blotner's perspective, is a "tale in verse and voices [that] moves complexly, interrupted by argument, commentary, and (in a familiar Warren strategy) two substantial digressions. They are the very personal narrative of R.P.W. reflecting upon the events and their echoes in his own life" (286–7). The entry on Robert Penn Warren in *American Writers* describes him as "a twentieth-century 'interlocutor' desperately involved in the problem of evil versus aspiration" (243). Richard Law thinks that he is the "cynical realist" who has "a dogged, nagging determination to test every conclusion, to measure every generalization of Jefferson's against all the facts at his disposal" (195). Law's analysis of his character proves that the questions he asks are his way to find definition and press for a meaning of life. He is actually the one who can give some of the characters the meanings of their names. He tells Letitia the meaning of her name and shows at the same time that she does not know it. He says, "Ah, poor Letitia! What a joke of a name / For her to be named Joy. / Even if likely she never knew what the name meant—" (35). He also tells Lucy the meaning of her name: "But I know your name means, etymologically, *light*" (18). Here we can notice again the connection the characters make between language and history. In order for them to find the meaning of their words, they go back to history and study the etymology of the word to try to find its present meaning.

However, R.P.W. himself is a good representative of the inadequacy of language because he does not use his full name in the text. Hendricks says that "[i]t is interesting how often Warren refers to himself in muted or abbreviated forms in his poems" (68). Using the letters to stand for his name instead of the full name shows that, just as the full words do not really convey their meanings, the full name does not convey the real personality of the author or his true message and reason behind writing. R.P.W. describes himself in the text as "[a] fellow of forty, a stranger, and a fool, / Red-headed, freckled, lean, a little stooped, / Who yearned to be understood, to make communication" (20). In this description, we realize that R.P.W. is aware of his need to communicate his feelings and ideas. This need springs from his understanding of the impossibility of the task because he knows that language will fall short of meeting his needs. In addition, Richard Law thinks that the questions and interruptions he is making actually "reflect a deep strain of anxiety as well as skepticism" (195). He adds that R.P.W.'s "compulsion to analyze indicates a tacit, not wholly conscious acceptance of 'naturalism,' a view of the world as meaningless mechanism" (195).

The whole idea behind the inadequacy of language in *Brother to Dragons* amounts to this nihilist and naturalist approach of life discussed in the texts. All the definitions Jefferson has been seeking have led to nothing, and he has changed his ideal view of life to a pessimistic one. For Jefferson, positive abstract concepts like dreams, hope, and reason turn into negative and empty ones that show life's meaninglessness, despair, and darkness. He says: "Reason? That's the word / I sought to live by—but, oh, / We have been lost in the dark, and I / Was lost who had dreamed there was a light" (119).

All the characters have felt nothing and have in reality expressed nothing for this reason. Letitia, during the aftermath of the night she has spent with Lilburne, knows that there is no "word now to say" (49). She goes on describing the epic she has to go through to express herself. When she is asked by Lilburne if she loves him, she admits that "[her] lips wouldn't move" (49). Even when he insists to know how she has felt toward him, "[her] words wouldn't come and [her] poor chest was a bigness / That hurt like something swelled there" (49). She actually admits that she cannot express her emotions and describes the action of pronouncing the word "Love" when it is pronounced by Lilburne as if he "spat it out from his mouth, / Like spit hawkd up and cold on your tongue and you spit it, / And [she] saw the word on the floor, / On the board like a glob to quiver and glimmer a gleam-like, / And the word—it was *love*" (51) For Letitia it is a struggle to pronounce words like love because she does not feel the word she is pronouncing. When she finally says it, she knows that the "words were over and done" (51).

The only solution of the inadequacy of language is suggested by R.P.W. at the end of the poem. He proposes that people should move to the world of action because it is more reliable and fruitful than the verbal world. He himself is "prepared / To go into the world of action and liability" because it is a world "[s]weeter than hope in that confirmation of late light" (132). Although the light is late, actions will actually bring out the desired results and extract the true meaning of hope from its concept, the notion and idea from its written form. *Brother to Dragons* proves that although language is limited, it can overcome its inadequacy when it evokes thoughts and ideas that transcend the abstractedness of life and go beyond its physical boundaries.

The relatively hopeful note with which *Brother to Dragons* ends and the relatively black humor that surrounds the world of *As I Lay Dying* pose the questions: Is there hope for language? Can language overcome its inadequacy? The answer is a paradox. Faulkner and Warren reveal language's true nature: its inadequacy and its potentials paradoxically and simultaneously. Through their thorough examination of how different aspects of language fail to fulfill its purpose to communicate meaning, and though their characters resort to non-verbal means of communication, they face language accusingly with its inadequacy. However, they also refer indirectly to language's potentials through their actual writings. Their writings not only reveal their brilliance as writers but also show hope in language. This hope of a transcendence of language comes from the very fact that both Faulkner and Warren are writers who have not given up on language and use it as the main tool of their craft with the full realization of its inadequacy.

Notes

1. Although *Brother to Dragons* is considered mainly a long narrative poem, I resorted to page numbers in all citations of the work because of Warren's use of features of other genres and the unnumbered lines in the poem.

2. All quotations cited in this paper from *Brother to Dragons* are based on the revised 1979 version, which is chosen here because it represents a paradoxically open-ended and relative resolution of Warren's struggle with the limited nature of language.

Works Cited

Blotner, Joseph. *Robert Penn Warren: A Biography*. New York: Random House, 1997. Print.

Faulkner, William. *As I Lay Dying: The Corrected Text*. New York: Vintage International, 1990. Print.

Hendricks, Randy. *Lonelier than God: Robert Penn Warren and the Southern Exile*. Athens: U of Georgia P 2000. Print.

Law, Richard G. "*Brother to Dragons*: The Fact of Violence vs. the Possibility of Love." *Critical Essays on Robert Penn Warren*. Ed. William Bedford Clark. Boston: G.K. Hall, 1981. 193–209. Print.

"Robert Penn Warren." *American Writers: A Collection of Literary Biographies*. Ed. Leonard Unger. New York: Charles Scribner's Sons, 1974. 243. Print.

Strandberg, Victor. *The Poetic Vision of Robert Penn Warren*. Lexington: U P of Kentucky, 1977. Print.

Walker, Marshall. *Robert Penn Warren: A Vision Earned*. New York: Barnes & Noble, 1979. Print.

Warren, Robert Penn. *Brother to Dragons: A Tale in Verse and Voice—A New Version*. Baton Rouge: Louisiana State University Press, 1996. Print.

Watkins, Floyd C. *The Flesh and the Word: Eliot, Hemingway, Faulkner*. Nashville: Vanderbilt U P, 1971. Print.

Notes on Contributors

Daniel Anderson teaches courses in American literature and composition at Dominican University in River Forest, Illinois, where he also serves as an Honors advisor and the director of the university's summer bridge program. Before taking his Ph.D. in English at the University of Minnesota, he earned his M.A. in English at Boston College and his B.S. in Journalism at Northwestern University.

Ted Atkinson is an associate professor of English at Mississippi State University and the editor of *Mississippi Quarterly*. He is the author of a book entitled *Faulkner and the Great Depression: Aesthetics, Ideology, and Cultural Politics*, as well as essays in *A Companion to William Faulkner*, *Faulkner and Formalism: Returns of the Text*, and *Faulkner and Morrison*. He has contributed essays to *Journal of American Studies*, *Southern Literary Journal*, and *Faulkner Journal*, among others.

Patricia L. Bradley is a professor of English at Middle Tennessee State University, where she teaches Southern literature, American literature, and English education. Her book *Robert Penn Warren's Circus Aesthetic and the Southern Renaissance* was published by the University of Tennessee Press in 2004, and she has published as well in such venues as *The Southern Literary Journal*, *Critique*, *Early American Literature*, *Mississippi Quarterly*, and *The South Carolina Review*.

Françoise Buisson is Associate Professor at the University of Pau (France) where she teaches translation and US history and literature. A member of AFEA (Association Française d'Etudes Américaines), she has written a Ph.D. dissertation on "Faulkner as a short story writer: tradition and modernity" and published critical essays on William Faulkner, Mark Twain, and contemporary writers such as Kaye Gibbons, TC Boyle, and Bret Easton Ellis.

Phillip Gordon wrote his dissertation at the University of Mississippi on homosexual elements in the works of William Faulkner. He is currently Assistant Professor of American Literature and LGBT Studies at the University of Wisconsin-Platteville.

Robert W. Hamblin is Professor Emeritus of English and the founding director of the Center for Faulkner Studies at Southeast Missouri State University. He has co-edited seventeen books on Faulkner and is the author of *"Myself and the World": A Biography of William Faulkner*, forthcoming from the University Press of Mississippi.

Andrew B. Leiter is Associate Professor of English at Lycoming College in Williamsport, Pennsylvania. He is author of *In the Shadow of the Black Beast: African American Masculinity in the Harlem and Southern Renaissances* (LSU Press, 2010) and editor of *Southerners on Film: Essays on Hollywood Portrayals Since the 1970s* (McFarland, 2011).

Shinya Matsuoka is Associate Professor of English at Ryukoku University in Japan. His recent publications include "Hunting for Cultural Hybridity in Faulkner and Morrison," published in *Faulkner and Morrison*.

Fadia Mereani is a Ph.D. candidate at Middle Tennessee State University and a lecturer at Umm Al-Qura University in Saudi Arabia. Currently, she is working on her dissertation, which focuses on food and drink imagery in T.S. Eliot's writings.

Dennis Negron is the Vice President for Student Services at Southern Adventist University. He was an associate professor of English at the same institution.

Conor Picken teaches English and Interdisciplinary Studies at Bellarmine University. His teaching, research, and publications focus on Southern literature, modernism, and social change.

Rebekah Taylor is a doctoral candidate and teaching fellow at Kent State University, focusing on literature and environment. Her dissertation argues for the ecological-ness of modernist literary form and considers literary modernism as symptomatic of the Anthropocene.

Benjamin J. Wilson is a Ph.D. student at the University of Kentucky, focusing on Southern literature in the context of global modernist studies. Originally from Louisville, Kentucky, he received his M.A. from Xavier University (Cincinnati), writing his thesis on Flannery O'Connor's pastoral stories.

Jason Zerbe holds a master's degree in English from the University of Mississippi, where he explored the relationship between mainstream American sports culture in the early to mid-twentieth century and the works of William Faulkner. He is primarily interested in Faulkner's engagement with the masculinization of tennis in the 1920s, the broad nationalization of college football in the late-1930s, and "Baseball's Great Experiment" with racial integration in 1947.